1–2 THESSALONIANS

WISDOM COMMENTARY

Volume 52

1 Thessalonians

Florence M. Gillman

Mary Ann Beavis
Volume Editor

2 Thessalonians

Mary Ann Beavis and HyeRan Kim-Cragg

Linda Maloney
Volume Editor

Barbara E. Reid, OP
General Editor

A Michael Glazier Book

LITURGICAL PRESS

Collegeville, Minnesota

www.litpress.org

A Michael Glazier Book published by Liturgical Press

Cover design by Ann Blattner. *Chapter Letter 'W'*, *Acts of the Apostles, Chapter 4*, Donald Jackson, Copyright 2002, *The Saint John's Bible*, Saint John's University, Collegeville, Minnesota USA. Used by permission. All rights reserved.

The map of the Via Egnatia crossing the south of the Balkans by Eric Gaba; Wikimedia Commons.

Scripture texts in this work are taken from the *New Revised Standard Version Bible*, © 1989, Division of Christian Education of the National Council of the Churches of Christ in the United States of America. Used by permission. All rights reserved.

1	2	3	4	5	6	7	8	9

Library of Congress Cataloging-in-Publication Data

Names: Gillman, Florence Morgan, author. 1 Thessalonians. | Beavis, Mary Ann, author. 2 Thessalonians.

Title: 1 Thessalonians / Florence M. Gillman ; Mary Ann Beavis, volume editor. 2 Thessalonians / Mary Ann Beavis and HyeRan Kim-Cragg ; Linda Maloney, volume editor ; Barbara E. Reid, OP, general editor.

Description: Collegeville, Minnesota : LITURGICAL PRESS, 2016. | Series: Wisdom commentary ; Volume 52 | "A Michael Glazier book." | Includes bibliographical references and index.

Identifiers: LCCN 2016009629 (print) | LCCN 2016015247 (ebook) | ISBN 9780814682012 | ISBN 9780814682265

Subjects: LCSH: Bible. Thessalonians—Commentaries.

Classification: LCC BS2725.53 .A15 2016 (print) | LCC BS2725.53 (ebook) | DDC 227/.8107—dc23

LC record available at https://lccn.loc.gov/2016009629

Contents

Abbreviations

The English text of quotations from the Bible is that of the New Revised Standard Version (NRSV) unless otherwise indicated.

1 QPHab	*Pesher Habakkuk*
AB	Anchor Bible
ABD	*Anchor Bible Dictionary*
AnBib	Analecta Biblica
BECNT	Baker Exegetical Commentary on the New Testament
BETL	Bibliotheca Ephemeridum Theologicarum Lovaniensium
BibInt	Biblical Interpretation
BJRL	*Bulletin of the John Rylands University Library of Manchester*
CBQ	*Catholic Biblical Quarterly*
ECL	Early Christianity and Its Literature
FCB	Feminist Companion to the Bible
Hermeneia	Hermeneia: A Critical and Historical Commentary on the Bible
HTR	*Harvard Theological Review*
HTS	Harvard Theological Studies
IBC	Interpretation Bible Commentary
IFT	Introductions in Feminist Theology
JBL	*Journal of Biblical Literature*

JECS	*Journal of Early Christian Studies*
JFSR	*Journal of Feminist Studies in Religion*
JSNTSup	Journal for the Study of the New Testament Supplement Series
JSOTSup	Journal for the Study of the Old Testament Supplement Series
KJV	King James Version
LIMC	*Lexicon Iconographicum Mythologiae Classicae*
LS	*Louvain Studies*
LSJ	*A Greek-English Lexicon* (Liddell, Scott, and Jones)
LXX	Septuagint
NAB	New American Bible
NABRE	New American Bible Revised Edition
NICNT	New International Commentary on the New Testament
NovT	*Novum Testamentum*
NRSV	New Revised Standard Version
NT	New Testament
NTS	*New Testament Studies*
OBT	Overtures to Biblical Theology
PRSt	*Perspectives in Religious Studies*
PsychoanalQ	*Psychoanalytic Quarterly*
RelEd	*Religious Education*
SBL	Society of Biblical Literature
SemeiaSt	Semeia Studies
SP	Sacra Pagina
SR	*Studies in Religion*
SymS	Symposium Series
TNIV	Today's New International Version
WUNT	Wissenschaftliche Untersuchungen zum Neuen Testament
ZECNT	Zondervan Exegetical Commentary Series: New Testament

Contributors

Regina A. Boisclair, PhD, is professor of religious studies and Cardinal Newman Chair of Catholic Theology at Alaska Pacific University in Anchorage, Alaska. Her major research interest concerns the hermeneutical features of the selections, collections, and calendrical assignments of biblical passages appointed to the lectionaries currently used in Western churches.

John Gillman received his PhD in religious studies, specializing in the Pauline letters, from the University of Louvain (KUL) in Belgium. For many years he has taught at San Diego State University. He is also a dually certified (ACPE and NACC) supervisor of Clinical Pastoral Education, who has directed CPE programs in community settings for the underserved, at major medical centers, and for a national hospice provider.

Maria Pascuzzi received her licentiate in Sacred Scripture (SSL) from the Pontifical Biblical Institute, Rome, and her doctorate in biblical theology (STD) from the Gregorian University, Rome. Her teaching, research, and publishing have focused on the letters of Saint Paul. She is currently a visiting scholar at Saint Joseph's College, New York City, where she is working on commentaries for 1 and 2 Corinthians.

Nancy Pia D. Sison received her MA in religious studies at Maryhill School of Theology. She teaches biblical courses at the Institute of Formation and Religious Studies and De La Salle University, where she is a PhD candidate in applied theology specializing in biblical studies.

Foreword

"Come Eat of My Bread . . . and Walk in the Ways of Wisdom"

Elisabeth Schüssler Fiorenza
Harvard University Divinity School

J ewish feminist writer Asphodel Long has likened the Bible to

> a magnificent garden of brilliant plants, some flowering, some fruiting,
> some in seed, some in bud, shaded by trees of age old, luxurious growth.
> Yet in the very soil which gives it life the poison has been inserted. . . .
> This poison is that of misogyny, the hatred of women, half the human
> race.[1]

To see Scripture as such a beautiful garden containing poisonous ivy
requires that one identify and name this poison and place on all biblical
texts the label "Caution! Could be dangerous to your health and survival!" As critical feminist interpretation for well-being this Wisdom
Commentary seeks to elaborate the beauty and fecundity of this

---

1. Asphodel Long, *In a Chariot Drawn by Lions: The Search for the Female in the Deity*
(London: Women's Press, 1992), 195.

Scripture-garden and at the same time points to the harm it can do when one submits to its world of vision. Thus, feminist biblical interpretation engages two seemingly contradictory insights: The Bible is written in kyriocentric (i.e., lord/master/father/husband-elite male) language, originated in the patri-kyriarchal cultures of antiquity, and has functioned to inculcate misogynist mind-sets and oppressive values. At the same time it also asserts that the Bible as Sacred Scripture has functioned to inspire and authorize wo/men[2] in our struggles against dehumanizing oppression. The hermeneutical lens of wisdom/Wisdom empowers the commentary writers to do so.

In biblical as well as in contemporary religious discourse the word *wisdom* has a double meaning: It can either refer to the quality of life and of people and/or it can refer to a figuration of the Divine. Wisdom in both senses of the word is not a prerogative of the biblical traditions but is found in the imagination and writings of all known religions. Wisdom is transcultural, international, and interreligious. Wisdom is practical knowledge gained through experience and daily living as well as through the study of creation and human nature. Both word meanings, that of capability (wisdom) and that of female personification (Wisdom), are crucial for this Wisdom Commentary series that seeks to enable biblical readers to become critical subjects of interpretation.

Wisdom is a state of the human mind and spirit characterized by deep understanding and profound insight. It is elaborated as a quality possessed by the sages but also treasured as folk wisdom and wit. Wisdom is the power of discernment, deeper understanding, and creativity; it is the ability to move and to dance, to make the connections, to savor life, and to learn from experience. Wisdom is intelligence shaped by experience and sharpened by critical analysis. It is the ability to make sound choices and incisive decisions. Its root meaning comes to the fore in its Latin form *sapientia*, which is derived from the verb *sapere*, to taste and to savor something. Hence, this series of commentaries invites readers to taste, to evaluate, and to imagine. In the figure of *Chokmah-Sophia-Sapientia-Wisdom*, ancient Jewish Scriptures seek to hold together belief in the "one" G*d[3] of Israel with both masculine and feminine language and metaphors of the Divine.

---

2. I use wo/man, s/he, fe/male and not the grammatical standard "man" as inclusive terms and make this visible by adding /.

3. I use the * asterisk in order to alert readers to a problem to explore and think about.

In distinction to traditional Scripture reading, which is often individu-alistic and privatized, the practice and space of Wisdom commentary is public. Wisdom's spiraling presence (*Shekhinah*) is global, embracing all creation. Her voice is a public, radical democratic voice rather than a "feminine," privatized one. To become one of Her justice-seeking friends, one needs to imagine the work of this feminist commentary series as the spiraling circle dance of wisdom/Wisdom,[4] as a Spirit/spiritual intel-lectual movement in the open space of wisdom/Wisdom who calls read-ers to critically analyze, debate, and reimagine biblical texts and their commentaries as wisdom/Wisdom texts inspired by visions of justice and well-being for everyone and everything. Wisdom-Sophia-imagination engenders a different understanding of Jesus and the movement around him. It understands him as the child and prophet of Divine Wisdom and as Wisdom herself instead of imagining him as ruling King and Lord who has only subalterns but not friends. To approach the N*T[5] and the whole Bible as Wisdom's invitation of cosmic dimensions means to acknowledge its multivalence and its openness to change. As bread—not stone.

In short, this commentary series is inspired by the feminist vision of the open cosmic house of Divine Wisdom-Sophia as it is found in biblical Wisdom literatures, which include the N*T:

Wisdom has built Her house
She has set up Her seven pillars . . .
She has mixed Her wine,
She also has set Her table.
She has sent out Her wo/men ministers
to call from the highest places in the town . . .
"Come eat of my bread
and drink of the wine I have mixed.
Leave immaturity, and live,
And walk in the way of Wisdom." (Prov 9:1-3, 5-6)

4. I have elaborated such a Wisdom dance in terms of biblical hermeneutics in my book *Wisdom Ways: Introducing Feminist Biblical Interpretation* (Maryknoll, NY: Orbis Books, 2001). Its seven steps are a hermeneutics of experience, of domination, of suspicion, of evaluation, of remembering or historical reconstruction, of imagination, and of transformation. However, such Wisdom strategies of meaning making are not restricted to the Bible. Rather, I have used them in workshops in Brazil and Ecuador to explore the workings of power, Condomblé, Christology, imagining a the*logical wo/men's center, or engaging the national icon of Mary.

5. See the discussion about nomenclature of the two testaments in the introduction, page xxxi.

Editor's Introduction to Wisdom Commentary

"She Is a Breath of the Power of God" (Wis 7:25)

Barbara E. Reid, OP
General Editor

Wisdom Commentary is the first series to offer detailed feminist interpretation of every book of the Bible. The fruit of collaborative work by an ecumenical and interreligious team of scholars, the volumes provide serious, scholarly engagement with the whole biblical text, not only those texts that explicitly mention women. The series is intended for clergy, teachers, ministers, and all serious students of the Bible. Designed to be both accessible and informed by the various approaches of biblical scholarship, it pays particular attention to the world in front of the text, that is, how the text is heard and appropriated. At the same time, this series aims to be faithful to the ancient text and its earliest audiences; thus the volumes also explicate the worlds behind the text and within it. While issues of gender are primary in this project, the volumes also address the intersecting issues of power, authority, ethnicity, race, class, and religious belief and practice. The fifty-eight volumes include the books regarded as canonical by Jews (i.e., the Tanakh); Protestants (the "Hebrew Bible" and the New Testament); and Roman Catholic, Anglican, and Eastern Orthodox Communions (i.e., Tobit, Judith, 1 and 2 Maccabees, Wisdom of Solomon, Sirach/Ecclesiasticus, Baruch, including the Letter of Jeremiah, the additions to Esther, and Susanna and Bel and the Dragon in Daniel).

A Symphony of Diverse Voices

Included in the Wisdom Commentary series are voices from scholars of many different religious traditions, of diverse ages, differing sexual identities, and varying cultural, racial, ethnic, and social contexts. Some have been pioneers in feminist biblical interpretation; others are newer contributors from a younger generation. A further distinctive feature of this series is that each volume incorporates voices other than that of the lead author(s). These voices appear alongside the commentary of the lead author(s), in the grayscale inserts. At times, a contributor may offer an alternative interpretation or a critique of the position taken by the lead author(s). At other times, she or he may offer a complementary interpretation from a different cultural context or subject position. Occasionally, portions of previously published material bring in other views. The diverse voices are not intended to be contestants in a debate or a cacophony of discordant notes. The multiple voices reflect that there is no single definitive feminist interpretation of a text. In addition, they show the importance of subject position in the process of interpretation. In this regard, the Wisdom Commentary series takes inspiration from the Talmud and from *The Torah: A Women's Commentary* (ed. Tamara Cohn Eskenazi and Andrea L. Weiss; New York: Women of Reform Judaism, Federation of Temple Sisterhood, 2008), in which many voices, even conflicting ones, are included and not harmonized.

Contributors include biblical scholars, theologians, and readers of Scripture from outside the scholarly and religious guilds. At times, their comments pertain to a particular text. In some instances they address a theme or topic that arises from the text.

Another feature that highlights the collaborative nature of feminist biblical interpretation is that a number of the volumes have two lead authors who have worked in tandem from the inception of the project and whose voices interweave throughout the commentary.

Woman Wisdom

The title, Wisdom Commentary, reflects both the importance to feminists of the figure of Woman Wisdom in the Scriptures and the distinct wisdom that feminist women and men bring to the interpretive process. In the Scriptures, Woman Wisdom appears as "a breath of the power of God, and a pure emanation of the glory of the Almighty" (Wis 7:25), who was present and active in fashioning all that exists (Prov 8:22-31; Wis 8:6). She is a spirit who pervades and penetrates all things (Wis 7:22-23), and she provides guidance and nourishment at her all-inclusive table (Prov 9:1-5). In both postexilic biblical and nonbiblical Jewish sources, Woman Wisdom is often equated with Torah, e.g., Sir 24:23-34; Bar 3:9–4:4; 38:2; 46:4-5; 2 Bar 48:33, 36; 4 Ezra 5:9-10; 13:55; 14:40; 1 Enoch 42.

The New Testament frequently portrays Jesus as Wisdom incarnate. He invites his followers, "take my yoke upon you and learn from me" (Matt 11:29), just as Ben Sira advises, "put your neck under her [Wisdom's] yoke and let your souls receive instruction" (Sir 51:26). Just as Wisdom experiences rejection (Prov 1:23-25; Sir 15:7-8; Wis 10:3; Bar 3:12), so too does Jesus (Mark 8:31; John 1:10-11). Only some accept his invitation to his all-inclusive banquet (Matt 22:1-14; Luke 14:15-24; compare Prov 1:20-21; 9:3-5). Yet, "wisdom is vindicated by her deeds" (Matt 11:19, speaking of Jesus and John the Baptist; in the Lucan parallel at 7:35 they are called "wisdom's children"). There are numerous parallels between what is said of Wisdom and of the *Logos* in the Prologue of the Fourth Gospel (John 1:1-18). These are only a few of many examples. This female embodiment of divine presence and power is an apt image to guide the work of this series.

Feminism

There are many different understandings of the term "feminism." The various meanings, aims, and methods have developed exponentially in recent decades. Feminism is a perspective and a movement that springs from a recognition of inequities toward women, and it advocates for changes in whatever structures prevent full human flourishing. Three waves of feminism in the United States are commonly recognized. The first, arising in the mid-nineteenth century and lasting into the early twentieth, was sparked by women's efforts to be involved in the public sphere and to win the right to vote. In the 1960s and 1970s, the second wave focused on civil rights and equality for women. With the third wave, from the 1980s forward, came global feminism and the emphasis on the contextual nature of interpretation. Now a fourth wave may be emerging, with a stronger emphasis on the intersectionality of women's concerns with those of other marginalized groups and the increased use of the internet as a platform for discussion and activism.[1] As feminism has matured, it has recognized that inequities based on gender are interwoven with power imbalances based on race, class, ethnicity, religion, sexual identity, physical ability, and a host of other social markers.

Feminist Women and Men

Men who choose to identify with and partner with feminist women in the work of deconstructing systems of domination and building structures of equality are rightly regarded as feminists. Some men readily identify with experiences of women who are discriminated against on the basis of sex/gender, having themselves had comparable experiences; others who may not have faced direct discrimination or stereotyping recognize that inequity and problematic characterization still occur, and they seek correction. This series is pleased to include feminist men both as lead authors and as contributing voices.

Feminist Biblical Interpretation

Women interpreting the Bible from the lenses of their own experience is nothing new. Throughout the ages women have recounted the biblical stories, teaching them to their children and others, all the while interpreting them afresh for their time and circumstances.[2] Following is a very brief sketch of select foremothers who laid the groundwork for contemporary feminist biblical interpretation.

One of the earliest known Christian women who challenged patriarchal interpretations of Scripture was a consecrated virgin named Helie, who lived in the second century CE. When she refused to marry, her

---

1. See Martha Rampton, "Four Waves of Feminism" (October 25, 2015), at http://www.pacificu.edu/about-us/news-events/four-waves-feminism; and Ealasaid Munro, "Feminism: A Fourth Wave?," https://www.psa.ac.uk/insight-plus/feminism-fourth-wave.

2. For fuller treatments of this history, see chap. 7, "One Thousand Years of Feminist Bible Criticism," in Gerda Lerner, *Creation of Feminist Consciousness: From the Middle Ages to Eighteen-Seventy* (New York: Oxford University Press, 1993), 138–66; Susanne Scholz, "From the 'Woman's Bible' to the 'Women's Bible,' The History of Feminist Approaches to the Hebrew Bible," in *Introducing the Women's Hebrew Bible*, IFT 13 (New York: T & T Clark, 2007), 12–32; Marion Ann Taylor and Agnes Choi, eds., *Handbook of Women Biblical Interpreters: A Historical and Biographical Guide* (Grand Rapids, MI: Baker Academic, 2012).

parents brought her before a judge, who quoted to her Paul's admonition, "It is better to marry than to be aflame with passion" (1 Cor 7:9). In response, Helie first acknowledges that this is what Scripture says, but then she retorts, "but not for everyone, that is, not for holy virgins."[3] She is one of the first to question the notion that a text has one meaning that is applicable in all situations.

A Jewish woman who also lived in the second century CE, Beruriah, is said to have had "profound knowledge of biblical exegesis and outstanding intelligence."[4] One story preserved in the Talmud (b. Berakot 10a) tells of how she challenged her husband, Rabbi Meir, when he prayed for the destruction of a sinner. Proffering an alternate interpretation, she argued that Psalm 104:35 advocated praying for the destruction of sin, not the sinner.

In medieval times the first written commentaries on Scripture from a critical feminist point of view emerge. While others may have been produced and passed on orally, they are for the most part lost to us now. Among the earliest preserved feminist writings are those of Hildegard of Bingen (1098–1179), German writer, mystic, and abbess of a Benedictine monastery. She reinterpreted the Genesis narratives in a way that presented women and men as complementary and interdependent. She frequently wrote about feminine aspects of the Divine.[5] Along with other women mystics of the time, such as Julian of Norwich (1342–ca. 1416), she spoke authoritatively from her personal experiences of God's revelation in prayer.

In this era, women were also among the scribes who copied biblical manuscripts. Notable among them is Paula Dei Mansi of Verona, from a distinguished family of Jewish scribes. In 1288, she translated from Hebrew into Italian a collection of Bible commentaries written by her father and added her own explanations.[6]

Another pioneer, Christine de Pizan (1365–ca. 1430), was a French court writer and prolific poet. She used allegory and common sense to

---

3. Madrid, Escorial MS, a II 9, f. 90 v., as cited in Lerner, *Feminist Consciousness*, 140.

4. See Judith R. Baskin, "Women and Post-Biblical Commentary," in *The Torah: A Women's Commentary*, ed. Tamara Cohn Eskenazi and Andrea L. Weiss (New York: Women of Reform Judaism, Federation of Temple Sisterhood, 2008), xlix–lv, at lii.

5. Hildegard of Bingen, *De Operatione Dei*, 1.4.100; PL 197:885bc, as cited in Lerner, *Feminist Consciousness*, 142–43. See also Barbara Newman, *Sister of Wisdom: St. Hildegard's Theology of the Feminine* (Berkeley: University of California Press, 1987).

6. Emily Taitz, Sondra Henry, Cheryl Tallan, eds., *JPS Guide to Jewish Women 600 B.C.E.–1900 C.E.* (Philadelphia: JPS, 2003), 110–11.

subvert misogynist readings of Scripture and celebrated the accomplishments of female biblical figures to argue for women's active roles in building society.[7]

By the seventeenth century, there were women who asserted that the biblical text needs to be understood and interpreted in its historical context. For example, Rachel Speght (1597–ca. 1630), a Calvinist English poet, elaborates on the historical situation in first-century Corinth that prompted Paul to say, "It is well for a man not to touch a woman" (1 Cor 7:1). Her aim was to show that the biblical texts should not be applied in a literal fashion to all times and circumstances. Similarly, Margaret Fell (1614–1702), one of the founders of the Religious Society of Friends (Quakers) in Britain, addressed the Pauline prohibitions against women speaking in church by insisting that they do not have universal validity. Rather, they need to be understood in their historical context, as addressed to a local church in particular time-bound circumstances.[8]

Along with analyzing the historical context of the biblical writings, women in the eighteenth and nineteenth centuries began to attend to misogynistic interpretations based on faulty translations. One of the first to do so was British feminist Mary Astell (1666–1731).[9] In the United States, the Grimké sisters, Sarah (1792–1873) and Angelina (1805–1879), Quaker women from a slaveholding family in South Carolina, learned biblical Greek and Hebrew so that they could interpret the Bible for themselves. They were prompted to do so after men sought to silence them from speaking out against slavery and for women's rights by claiming that the Bible (e.g., 1 Cor 14:34) prevented women from speaking in public.[10] Another prominent abolitionist, Sojourner Truth (ca. 1797–1883), a former slave, quoted the Bible liberally in her speeches[11] and in so doing challenged cultural assumptions and biblical interpretations that undergird gender inequities.

---

7. See further Taylor and Choi, *Handbook of Women Biblical Interpreters*, 127–32.

8. Her major work, *Women's Speaking Justified, Proved and Allowed by the Scriptures*, published in London in 1667, gave a systematic feminist reading of all biblical texts pertaining to women.

9. Mary Astell, *Some Reflections upon Marriage* (New York: Source Book Press, 1970, reprint of the 1730 edition; earliest edition of this work is 1700), 103–4.

10. See further, Sarah Grimké, *Letters on the Equality of the Sexes and the Condition of Woman* (Boston: Isaac Knapp, 1838).

11. See, for example, her most famous speech, "Ain't I a Woman?," delivered in 1851 at the Ohio Women's Rights Convention in Akron, OH; http://www.fordham.edu/halsall/mod/sojtruth-woman.asp.

Another monumental work that emerged in nineteenth-century England was that of Jewish theologian Grace Aguilar (1816–1847), *The Women of Israel*,[12] published in 1845. Aguilar's approach was to make connections between the biblical women and contemporary Jewish women's concerns. She aimed to counter the widespread notion that women were degraded in Jewish law and that only in Christianity were women's dignity and value upheld. Her intent was to help Jewish women find strength and encouragement by seeing the evidence of God's compassionate love in the history of every woman in the Bible. While not a full commentary on the Bible, Aguilar's work stands out for its comprehensive treatment of every female biblical character, including even the most obscure references.[13]

The first person to produce a full-blown feminist commentary on the Bible was Elizabeth Cady Stanton (1815–1902). A leading proponent in the United States for women's right to vote, she found that whenever women tried to make inroads into politics, education, or the work world, the Bible was quoted against them. Along with a team of like-minded women, she produced her own commentary on every text of the Bible that concerned women. Her pioneering two-volume project, *The Woman's Bible*, published in 1895 and 1898, urges women to recognize that texts that degrade women come from the men who wrote the texts, not from God, and to use their common sense to rethink what has been presented to them as sacred.

Nearly a century later, *The Women's Bible Commentary*, edited by Sharon Ringe and Carol Newsom (Louisville, KY: Westminster John Knox Press, 1992), appeared. This one-volume commentary features North American feminist scholarship on each book of the Protestant canon. Like Cady Stanton's commentary, it does not contain comments on every section of the biblical text but only on those passages deemed relevant to women. It was revised and expanded in 1998 to include the Apocrypha/Deuterocanonical books, and the contributors to this new volume reflect the global face of contemporary feminist scholarship. The revisions made in the third edition, which appeared in 2012, represent the profound advances in feminist biblical scholarship and include newer voices. In both the second and third editions, *The* has been dropped from the title.

---

12. The full title is *The Women of Israel or Characters and Sketches from the Holy Scriptures and Jewish History Illustrative of the Past History, Present Duty, and Future Destiny of the Hebrew Females, as Based on the Word of God.*

13. See further, Eskenazi and Weiss, *The Torah: A Women's Commentary*, xxxviii; Taylor and Choi, *Handbook of Women Biblical Interpreters*, 31–37.

Also appearing at the centennial of Cady Stanton's *The Woman's Bible* were two volumes edited by Elisabeth Schüssler Fiorenza with the assistance of Shelly Matthews. The first, *Searching the Scriptures: A Feminist Introduction* (New York: Crossroad, 1993), charts a comprehensive approach to feminist interpretation from ecumenical, interreligious, and multicultural perspectives. The second volume, published in 1994, provides critical feminist commentary on each book of the New Testament as well as on three books of Jewish Pseudepigrapha and eleven other early Christian writings.

In Europe, similar endeavors have been undertaken, such as the one-volume *Kompendium Feministische Bibelauslegung*, edited by Luise Schottroff and Marie-Theres Wacker (Gütersloh: Gütersloher Verlagshaus, 2007), featuring German feminist biblical interpretation of each book of the Bible, along with apocryphal books, and several extrabiblical writings. This work, now in its third edition, has recently been translated into English.[14] A multivolume project, *The Bible and Women: An Encylopaedia of Exegesis and Cultural History*, edited by Irmtraud Fischer, Adriana Valerio, Mercedes Navarro Puerto, and Christiana de Groot, is currently in production. This project presents a history of the reception of the Bible as embedded in Western cultural history and focuses particularly on gender-relevant biblical themes, biblical female characters, and women recipients of the Bible. The volumes are published in English, Spanish, Italian, and German.[15]

Another groundbreaking work is the collection The Feminist Companion to the Bible Series, edited by Athalya Brenner (Sheffield: Sheffield Academic Press, 1993–2015), which comprises twenty volumes of commentaries on the Old Testament. The parallel series, Feminist Companion

---

14. *Feminist Biblical Interpretation: A Compendium of Critical Commentary on the Books of the Bible and Related Literature*, trans. Lisa E. Dahill, Everett R. Kalin, Nancy Lukens, Linda M. Maloney, Barbara Rumscheidt, Martin Rumscheidt, and Tina Steiner (Grand Rapids, MI: Eerdmans, 2012). Another notable collection is the three volumes edited by Susanne Scholz, *Feminist Interpretation of the Hebrew Bible in Retrospect*, Recent Research in Biblical Studies 7, 8, 9 (Sheffield: Sheffield Phoenix Press, 2013, 2014, 2016).

15. The first volume, on the Torah, appeared in Spanish in 2009, in German and Italian in 2010, and in English in 2011 (Atlanta, GA: Society of Biblical Literature). Four more volumes are now available: *Feminist Biblical Studies in the Twentieth Century*, ed. Elisabeth Schüssler Fiorenza (2014); *The Writings and Later Wisdom Books*, ed. Christl M. Maier and Nuria Calduch-Benages (2014); *Gospels: Narrative and History*, ed. Mercedes Navarro Puerto and Marinella Perroni (2015); and *The High Middle Ages*, ed. Kari Elisabeth Børresen and Adriana Valerio (2015). For further information, see http://www.bibleandwomen.org.

to the New Testament and Early Christian Writings, edited by Amy-Jill Levine with Marianne Blickenstaff and Maria Mayo Robbins (Sheffield: Sheffield Academic Press, 2001–2009), contains thirteen volumes with one more planned. These two series are not full commentaries on the biblical books but comprise collected essays on discrete biblical texts.

Works by individual feminist biblical scholars in all parts of the world abound, and they are now too numerous to list in this introduction. Feminist biblical interpretation has reached a level of maturity that now makes possible a commentary series on every book of the Bible. In recent decades, women have had greater access to formal theological education, have been able to learn critical analytical tools, have put their own interpretations into writing, and have developed new methods of biblical interpretation. Until recent decades the work of feminist biblical interpreters was largely unknown, both to other women and to their brothers in the synagogue, church, and academy. Feminists now have taken their place in the professional world of biblical scholars, where they build on the work of their foremothers and connect with one another across the globe in ways not previously possible. In a few short decades, feminist biblical criticism has become an integral part of the academy.

Methodologies

Feminist biblical scholars use a variety of methods and often employ a number of them together.[16] In the Wisdom Commentary series, the authors will explain their understanding of feminism and the feminist reading strategies used in their commentary. Each volume treats the biblical text in blocks of material, not an analysis verse by verse. The entire text is considered, not only those passages that feature female characters or that speak specifically about women. When women are not apparent in the narrative, feminist lenses are used to analyze the dynamics in the text between male characters, the models of power, binary ways of thinking, and dynamics of imperialism. Attention is given to how the whole text functions and how it was and is heard, both in its original context and today. Issues of particular concern to women—e.g., poverty, food, health, the environment, water—come to the fore.

16. See the seventeen essays in Caroline Vander Stichele and Todd Penner, eds., *Her Master's Tools? Feminist and Postcolonial Engagements of Historical-Critical Discourse* (Atlanta, GA: SBL, 2005), which show the complementarity of various approaches.

One of the approaches used by early feminists and still popular today is to lift up the overlooked and forgotten stories of women in the Bible. Studies of women in each of the Testaments have been done, and there are also studies on women in particular biblical books.[17] Feminists recognize that the examples of biblical characters can be both empowering and problematic. The point of the feminist enterprise is not to serve as an apologetic for women; it is rather, in part, to recover women's history and literary roles in all their complexity and to learn from that recovery.

Retrieving the submerged history of biblical women is a crucial step for constructing the story of the past so as to lead to liberative possibilities for the present and future. There are, however, some pitfalls to this approach. Sometimes depictions of biblical women have been naïve and romantic. Some commentators exalt the virtues of both biblical and contemporary women and paint women as superior to men. Such reverse discrimination inhibits movement toward equality for all. In addition, some feminists challenge the idea that one can "pluck positive images out of an admittedly androcentric text, separating literary characterizations from the androcentric interests they were created to serve."[18] Still other feminists find these images to have enormous value.

One other danger with seeking the submerged history of women is the tendency for Christian feminists to paint Jesus and even Paul as liberators of women in a way that demonizes Judaism.[19] Wisdom Commentary aims

17. See, e.g., Alice Bach, ed., *Women in the Hebrew Bible: A Reader* (New York: Routledge, 1998); Tikva Frymer-Kensky, *Reading the Women of the Bible* (New York: Schocken, 2002); Carol Meyers, Toni Craven, and Ross S. Kraemer, *Women in Scripture* (Grand Rapids, MI: Eerdmans, 2000); Irene Nowell, *Women in the Old Testament* (Collegeville, MN: Liturgical Press, 1997); Katharine Doob Sakenfeld, *Just Wives? Stories of Power and Survival in the Old Testament and Today* (Louisville, KY: Westminster John Knox, 2003); Mary Ann Getty-Sullivan, *Women in the New Testament* (Collegeville, MN: Liturgical Press, 2001); Bonnie Thurston, *Women in the New Testament* (New York: Crossroad, 1998).

18. Cheryl Exum, "Second Thoughts about Secondary Characters: Women in Exodus 1.8–2.10," in *A Feminist Companion to Exodus to Deuteronomy*, FCB 6 (Sheffield: Sheffield Academic Press, 1994), 75–97, at 76.

19. See Judith Plaskow, "Anti-Judaism in Feminist Christian Interpretation," in *Searching the Scriptures: A Feminist Introduction* (New York: Crossroad, 1993), vol. 1, 117–29; Amy-Jill Levine, "The New Testament and Anti-Judaism," in *The Misunderstood Jew: The Church and the Scandal of the Jewish Jesus* (San Francisco: HarperSanFrancisco, 2006), 87–117.

to enhance understanding of Jesus as well as Paul as Jews of their day and to forge solidarity among Jewish and Christian feminists.

Feminist scholars who use historical-critical methods analyze the world behind the text; they seek to understand the historical context from which the text emerged and the circumstances of the communities to whom it was addressed. In bringing feminist lenses to this approach, the aim is not to impose modern expectations on ancient cultures but to unmask the ways that ideologically problematic mind-sets that produced the ancient texts are still promulgated through the text. Feminist biblical scholars aim not only to deconstruct but also to reclaim and reconstruct biblical history as women's history, in which women were central and active agents in creating religious heritage.[20] A further step is to construct meaning for contemporary women and men in a liberative movement toward transformation of social, political, economic, and religious structures.[21] In recent years, some feminists have embraced new historicism, which accents the creative role of the interpreter in any construction of history and exposes the power struggles to which the text witnesses.[22]

Literary critics analyze the world of the text: its form, language patterns, and rhetorical function.[23] They do not attempt to separate layers of tradition and redaction but focus on the text holistically, as it is in its present

---

20. See, for example, Phyllis A. Bird, *Missing Persons and Mistaken Identities: Women and Gender in Ancient Israel* (Minneapolis: Fortress Press, 1997); Elisabeth Schüssler Fiorenza, *In Memory of Her: A Feminist Theological Reconstruction of Christian Origins* (New York: Crossroad, 1984); Ross Shepard Kraemer and Mary Rose D'Angelo, eds., *Women and Christian Origins* (New York: Oxford University Press, 1999).

21. See, e.g., Sandra M. Schneiders, *The Revelatory Text: Interpreting the New Testament as Sacred Scripture*, rev. ed. (Collegeville, MN: Liturgical Press, 1999), whose aim is to engage in biblical interpretation not only for intellectual enlightenment but, even more important, for personal and communal transformation. Elisabeth Schüssler Fiorenza (*Wisdom Ways: Introducing Feminist Biblical Interpretation* [Maryknoll, NY: Orbis Books, 2001]) envisions the work of feminist biblical interpretation as a dance of Wisdom that consists of seven steps that interweave in spiral movements toward liberation, the final one being transformative action for change.

22. See Gina Hens Piazza, *The New Historicism*, Guides to Biblical Scholarship, Old Testament Series (Minneapolis: Fortress Press, 2002).

23. Phyllis Trible was among the first to employ this method with texts from Genesis and Ruth in her groundbreaking book *God and the Rhetoric of Sexuality*, OBT (Philadelphia: Fortress Press, 1978). Another pioneer in feminist literary criticism is Mieke Bal (*Lethal Love: Feminist Literary Readings of Biblical Love Stories* [Bloomington: Indiana University Press, 1987]). For surveys of recent developments in literary methods, see Terry Eagleton, *Literary Theory: An Introduction*, 3rd ed. (Minneapolis: University of Minnesota Press, 2008); Janice Capel Anderson and

form. They examine how meaning is created in the interaction between the text and its reader in multiple contexts. Within the arena of literary approaches are reader-oriented approaches, narrative, rhetorical, structuralist, post-structuralist, deconstructive, ideological, autobiographical, and performance criticism.[24] Narrative critics study the interrelation among author, text, and audience through investigation of settings, both spatial and temporal; characters; plot; and narrative techniques (e.g., irony, parody, intertextual allusions). Reader-response critics attend to the impact that the text has on the reader or hearer. They recognize that when a text is detrimental toward women there is the choice either to affirm the text or to read against the grain toward a liberative end. Rhetorical criticism analyzes the style of argumentation and attends to how the author is attempting to shape the thinking or actions of the hearer. Structuralist critics analyze the complex patterns of binary oppositions in the text to derive its meaning.[25] Post-structuralist approaches challenge the notion that there are fixed meanings to any biblical text or that there is one universal truth. They engage in close readings of the text and often engage in intertextual analysis.[26] Within this approach is deconstructionist criticism, which views the text as a site of conflict, with competing narratives. The interpreter aims to expose the fault lines and overturn and reconfigure binaries by elevating the underling of a pair and foregrounding it.[27] Feminists also use other postmodern approaches, such as ideological and autobiographical criticism. The former analyzes the system

Stephen D. Moore, eds., *Mark and Method: New Approaches in Biblical Studies*, 2nd ed. (Minneapolis: Fortress Press, 2008).

24. See, e.g., J. Cheryl Exum and David J. A. Clines, eds., *The New Literary Criticism and the Hebrew Bible* (Valley Forge, PA: Trinity Press International, 1993); Edgar V. McKnight and Elizabeth Struthers Malbon, eds., *The New Literary Criticism and the New Testament* (Valley Forge, PA: Trinity Press International, 1994).

25. See, e.g., David Jobling, *The Sense of Biblical Narrative: Three Structural Analyses in the Old Testament*, JSOTSup 7 (Sheffield: Sheffield University, 1978).

26. See, e.g., Stephen D. Moore, *Poststructuralism and the New Testament: Derrida and Foucault at the Foot of the Cross* (Minneapolis: Fortress Press, 1994); *The Bible in Theory: Critical and Postcritical Essays* (Atlanta, GA: Society of Biblical Literature, 2010); Yvonne Sherwood, *A Biblical Text and Its Afterlives: The Survival of Jonah in Western Culture* (Cambridge: Cambridge University Press, 2000).

27. David Penchansky, "Deconstruction," in *The Oxford Encyclopedia of Biblical Interpretation*, ed. Steven McKenzie (New York: Oxford University Press, 2013), 196–205. See, for example, Danna Nolan Fewell and David M. Gunn, *Gender, Power, and Promise: The Subject of the Bible's First Story* (Nashville, TN: Abingdon, 1993); David Rutledge, *Reading Marginally: Feminism, Deconstruction and the Bible*, BibInt 21 (Leiden: Brill, 1996).

of ideas that underlies the power and values concealed in the text as well as that of the interpreter.[28] The latter involves deliberate self-disclosure while reading the text as a critical exegete.[29] Performance criticism attends to how the text was passed on orally, usually in communal settings, and to the verbal and nonverbal interactions between the performer and the audience.[30]

From the beginning, feminists have understood that interpreting the Bible is an act of power. In recent decades, feminist biblical scholars have developed hermeneutical theories of the ethics and politics of biblical interpretation to challenge the claims to value neutrality of most academic biblical scholarship. Feminist biblical scholars have also turned their attention to how some biblical writings were shaped by the power of empire and how this still shapes readers' self-understandings today. They have developed hermeneutical approaches that reveal, critique, and evaluate the interactions depicted in the text against the context of empire, and they consider implications for contemporary contexts.[31] Feminists also analyze the dynamics of colonization and the mentalities of colonized peoples in the exercise of biblical interpretation. As Kwok Pui-lan explains, "A postcolonial feminist interpretation of the Bible needs to investigate the deployment of gender in the narration of identity, the negotiation of power differentials between the colonizers and the colonized, and the reinforcement of patriarchal control over spheres where these elites could exercise control."[32] Methods and models from sociology and cultural anthropology

---

28. See Tina Pippin, ed., *Ideological Criticism of Biblical Texts: Semeia* 59 (1992); Terry Eagleton, *Ideology: An Introduction* (London: Verso, 2007).

29. See, e.g., Ingrid Rose Kitzberger, ed., *Autobiographical Biblical Interpretation: Between Text and Self* (Leiden: Deo, 2002); P. J. W. Schutte, "When *They*, *We*, and the Passive Become *I*—Introducing Autobiographical Biblical Criticism," *HTS Teologiese Studies / Theological Studies* vol. 61 (2005): 401–16.

30. See, e.g., Holly Hearon and Philip Ruge-Jones, eds., *The Bible in Ancient and Modern Media: Story and Performance* (Eugene, OR: Cascade Books, 2009).

31. E.g., Gale Yee, ed., *Judges and Method: New Approaches in Biblical Studies* (Minneapolis: Fortress Press, 1995); Warren Carter, *The Gospel of Matthew in Its Roman Imperial Context* (London: T & T Clark, 2005); *The Roman Empire and the New Testament: An Essential Guide* (Nashville, TN: Abingdon, 2006); Elisabeth Schüssler Fiorenza, *The Power of the Word: Scripture and the Rhetoric of Empire* (Minneapolis: Fortress Press, 2007); Judith E. McKinlay, *Reframing Her: Biblical Women in Postcolonial Focus* (Sheffield: Sheffield Phoenix Press, 2004).

32. Kwok Pui-lan, *Postcolonial Imagination and Feminist Theology* (Louisville, KY: Westminster John Knox, 2005), 9. See also, Musa W. Dube, ed., *Postcolonial Feminist Interpretation of the Bible* (St. Louis, MO: Chalice Press, 2000); Cristl M. Maier and

are used by feminists to investigate women's everyday lives, their experiences of marriage, childrearing, labor, money, illness, etc.[33]

As feminists have examined the construction of gender from varying cultural perspectives, they have become ever more cognizant that the way gender roles are defined within differing cultures varies radically. As Mary Ann Tolbert observes, "Attempts to isolate some universal role that cross-culturally defines 'woman' have run into contradictory evidence at every turn."[34] Some women have coined new terms to highlight the particularities of their socio-cultural context. Many African American feminists, for example, call themselves *womanists* to draw attention to the double oppression of racism and sexism they experience.[35] Similarly, many US Hispanic feminists speak of themselves as *mujeristas* (*mujer* is Spanish for "woman").[36] Others prefer to be called "Latina feminists."[37] Both groups emphasize that the context for their theologizing is *mestizaje* and *mulatez* (racial and cultural mixture), done *en conjunto* (in community), with *lo cotidiano* (everyday lived experience) of Hispanic women as starting points for theological reflection and the encounter with the divine. Intercultural analysis has become an indispensable tool for working toward justice for women at the global level.[38]

Carolyn J. Sharp, *Prophecy and Power: Jeremiah in Feminist and Postcolonial Perspective* (London: Bloomsbury, 2013).

33. See, for example, Carol Meyers, *Discovering Eve: Ancient Israelite Women in Context* (New York: Oxford University Press, 1991); Luise Schottroff, *Lydia's Impatient Sisters: A Feminist Social History of Early Christianity*, trans. Barbara and Martin Rumscheidt (Louisville, KY: Westminster John Knox, 1995); Susan Niditch, *"My Brother Esau Is a Hairy Man": Hair and Identity in Ancient Israel* (Oxford: Oxford University Press, 2008).

34. Mary Ann Tolbert, "Social, Sociological, and Anthropological Methods," in *Searching the Scriptures*, 1:255–71, at 265.

35. Alice Walker coined the term (*In Search of Our Mothers' Gardens: Womanist Prose* [New York: Harcourt Brace Jovanovich, 1967, 1983]). See also Katie G. Cannon, "The Emergence of Black Feminist Consciousness," in *Feminist Interpretation of the Bible*, ed. Letty M. Russell (Philadelphia: Westminster, 1985), 30–40; Renita Weems, *Just a Sister Away: A Womanist Vision of Women's Relationships in the Bible* (San Diego: Lura Media, 1988); Nyasha Junior, *An Introduction to Womanist Biblical Interpretation* (Louisville, KY: Westminster John Knox, 2015).

36. Ada María Isasi-Díaz (*Mujerista Theology: A Theology for the Twenty-first Century* [Maryknoll, NY: Orbis Books, 1996]) is credited with coining the term.

37. E.g., María Pilar Aquino, Daisy L. Machado, and Jeanette Rodríguez, eds., *A Reader in Latina Feminist Theology* (Austin: University of Texas Press, 2002).

38. See, e.g., María Pilar Aquino and María José Rosado-Nunes, eds., *Feminist Intercultural Theology: Latina Explorations for a Just World*, Studies in Latino/a Catholicism (Maryknoll, NY: Orbis Books, 2007).

Some feminists are among those who have developed lesbian, gay, bisexual, and transgender (LGBT) interpretation. This approach focuses on issues of sexual identity and uses various reading strategies. Some point out the ways in which categories that emerged in recent centuries are applied anachronistically to biblical texts to make modern-day judgments. Others show how the Bible is silent on contemporary issues about sexual identity. Still others examine same-sex relationships in the Bible by figures such as Ruth and Naomi or David and Jonathan. In recent years, queer theory has emerged; it emphasizes the blurriness of boundaries not just of sexual identity but also of gender roles. Queer critics often focus on texts in which figures transgress what is traditionally considered proper gender behavior.[39]

Feminists also recognize that the struggle for women's equality and dignity is intimately connected with the struggle for respect for Earth and for the whole of the cosmos. Ecofeminists interpret Scripture in ways that highlight the link between human domination of nature and male subjugation of women. They show how anthropocentric ways of interpreting the Bible have overlooked or dismissed Earth and Earth community. They invite readers to identify not only with human characters in the biblical narrative but also with other Earth creatures and domains of nature, especially those that are the object of injustice. Some use creative imagination to retrieve the interests of Earth implicit in the narrative and enable Earth to speak.[40]

Biblical Authority

By the late nineteenth century, some feminists, such as Elizabeth Cady Stanton, began to question openly whether the Bible could continue to be regarded as authoritative for women. They viewed the Bible itself as the source of women's oppression, and some rejected its sacred origin

39. See, e.g., Bernadette J. Brooten, *Love between Women: Early Christian Responses to Female Homoeroticism* (Chicago and London: University of Chicago Press, 1996); Mary Rose D'Angelo, "Women Partners in the New Testament," *JFSR* 6 (1990): 65–86; Deirdre J. Good, "Reading Strategies for Biblical Passages on Same-Sex Relations," *Theology and Sexuality* 7 (1997): 70–82; Deryn Guest, *When Deborah Met Jael: Lesbian Feminist Hermeneutics* (London: SCM Press, 2011); Teresa Hornsby and Ken Stone, eds., *Bible Trouble: Queer Readings at the Boundaries of Biblical Scholarship* (Atlanta, GA: Society of Biblical Literature, 2011).

40. E.g., Norman C. Habel and Peter Trudinger, *Exploring Ecological Hermeneutics*, SymS 46 (Atlanta, GA: Society of Biblical Literature, 2008); Mary Judith Ress, *Ecofeminism in Latin America*, Women from the Margins (Maryknoll, NY: Orbis Books, 2006).

and saving claims. Some decided that the Bible and the religious traditions that enshrine it are too thoroughly saturated with androcentrism
and patriarchy to be redeemable.[41]

In the Wisdom Commentary series, questions such as these may be
raised, but the aim of this series is not to lead readers to reject the authority of the biblical text. Rather, the aim is to promote better understanding
of the contexts from which the text arose and of the rhetorical effects it
has on women and men in contemporary contexts. Such understanding
can lead to a deepening of faith, with the Bible serving as an aid to bring
flourishing of life.

Language for God

Because of the ways in which the term "God" has been used to sym-
bolize the divine in predominantly male, patriarchal, and monarchical
modes, feminists have designed new ways of speaking of the divine.
Some have called attention to the inadequacy of the term *God* by trying
to visually destabilize our ways of thinking and speaking of the divine.
Rosemary Radford Ruether proposed *God/ess*, as an unpronounceable
term pointing to the unnameable understanding of the divine that transcends patriarchal limitations.[42] Some have followed traditional Jewish
practice, writing *G-d*. Elisabeth Schüssler Fiorenza has adopted *G*d*.[43]
Others draw on the biblical tradition to mine female and non-gender-
specific metaphors and symbols.[44] In Wisdom Commentary, there is not
one standard way of expressing the divine; each author will use her or
his preferred ways. The one exception is that when the tetragrammaton,
YHWH, the name revealed to Moses in Exodus 3:14, is used, it will be
without vowels, respecting the Jewish custom of avoiding pronouncing
the divine name out of reverence.

41. E.g., Mary Daly, *Beyond God the Father: A Philosophy of Women's Liberation* (Boston: Beacon, 1973).

42. Rosemary Radford Ruether, *Sexism and God-Talk: Toward a Feminist Theology*
(Boston: Beacon, 1983).

43. Elisabeth Schüssler Fiorenza, *Jesus: Miriam's Child, Sophia's Prophet; Critical Issues
in Feminist Christology* (New York: Continuum, 1994), 191 n. 3.

44. E.g., Sallie McFague, *Models of God: Theology for an Ecological, Nuclear Age* (Philadelphia: Fortress Press, 1987); Catherine LaCugna, *God for Us: The Trinity and Christian Life* (San Francisco: Harper Collins, 1991); Elizabeth A. Johnson, *She Who Is: The
Mystery of God in Feminist Theological Discourse* (New York: Crossroad, 1992). See
further, Elizabeth A. Johnson, "God," in *Dictionary of Feminist Theologies*, 128–30.

Nomenclature for the Two Testaments

In recent decades, some biblical scholars have begun to call the two Testaments of the Bible by names other than the traditional nomenclature: Old and New Testament. Some regard "Old" as derogatory, implying that it is no longer relevant or that it has been superseded. Consequently, terms like Hebrew Bible, First Testament, and Jewish Scriptures and, correspondingly, Christian Scriptures or Second Testament have come into use. There are a number of difficulties with these designations. The term "Hebrew Bible" does not take into account that parts of the Old Testament are written not in Hebrew but in Aramaic.[45] Moreover, for Roman Catholics, Anglicans, and Eastern Orthodox believers, the Old Testament includes books written in Greek—the Deuterocanonical books, considered Apocrypha by Protestants. The term "Jewish Scriptures" is inadequate because these books are also sacred to Christians. Conversely, "Christian Scriptures" is not an accurate designation for the New Testament, since the Old Testament is also part of the Christian Scriptures. Using "First and Second Testament" also has difficulties, in that it can imply a hierarchy and a value judgment.[46] Jews generally use the term Tanakh, an acronym for Torah (Pentateuch), Nevi'im (Prophets), and Ketuvim (Writings).

In Wisdom Commentary, if authors choose to use a designation other than Tanakh, Old Testament, and New Testament, they will explain how they mean the term.

Translation

Modern feminist scholars recognize the complexities connected with biblical translation, as they have delved into questions about philosophy of language, how meanings are produced, and how they are culturally situated. Today it is evident that simply translating into gender-neutral formulations cannot address all the challenges presented by androcentric texts. Efforts at feminist translation must also deal with issues around authority and canonicity.[47]

---

45. Gen 31:47; Jer 10:11; Ezra 4:7–6:18; 7:12-26; Dan 2:4–7:28.
46. See Levine, *The Misunderstood Jew*, 193–99.
47. Elizabeth Castelli, "*Les Belles Infidèles*/Fidelity or Feminism? The Meanings of Feminist Biblical Translation," in *Searching the Scriptures*, 1:189–204, at 190.

Because of these complexities, the editors of Wisdom Commentary series have chosen to use an existing translation, the New Revised Standard Version (NRSV), which is provided for easy reference at the top of each page of commentary. The NRSV was produced by a team of ecumenical and interreligious scholars, is a fairly literal translation, and uses inclusive language for human beings. Brief discussions about problematic translations appear in the inserts labeled "Translation Matters." When more detailed discussions are available, these will be indicated in footnotes. In the commentary, wherever Hebrew or Greek words are used, English translation is provided. In cases where a wordplay is involved, transliteration is provided to enable understanding.

Art and Poetry

Artistic expression in poetry, music, sculpture, painting, and various other modes is very important to feminist interpretation. Where possible, art and poetry are included in the print volumes of the series. In a number of instances, these are original works created for this project. Regrettably, copyright and production costs prohibit the inclusion of color photographs and other artistic work. It is our hope that the web version will allow a greater collection of such resources.

Glossary

Because there are a number of excellent readily available resources that provide definitions and concise explanations of terms used in feminist theological and biblical studies, this series will not include a glossary. We refer you to works such as *Dictionary of Feminist Theologies*, edited by Letty M. Russell with J. Shannon Clarkson (Louisville, KY: Westminster John Knox, 1996), and volume 1 of *Searching the Scriptures*, edited by Elisabeth Schüssler Fiorenza with the assistance of Shelly Matthews (New York: Crossroad, 1992). Individual authors in the Wisdom Commentary series will define the way they are using terms that may be unfamiliar.

Bibliography

Because bibliographies are quickly outdated and because the space is limited, only a list of Works Cited is included in the print volumes. A comprehensive bibliography for each volume is posted on a dedicated website and is updated regularly. The link for this volume can be found at wisdomcommentary.org.

A Concluding Word

In just a few short decades, feminist biblical studies has grown exponentially, both in the methods that have been developed and in the number of scholars who have embraced it. We realize that this series is limited and will soon need to be revised and updated. It is our hope that Wisdom Commentary, by making the best of current feminist biblical scholarship available in an accessible format to ministers, preachers, teachers, scholars, and students, will aid all readers in their advancement toward God's vision of dignity, equality, and justice for all.

Acknowledgments

There are a great many people who have made this series possible: first, Peter Dwyer, director, and Hans Christoffersen, publisher of the academic market at Liturgical Press, who have believed in this project and have shepherded it since it was conceived in 2008. Editorial consultants Athalya Brenner-Idan and Elisabeth Schüssler Fiorenza have not only been an inspiration with their pioneering work but have encouraged us all along the way with their personal involvement. Volume editors Mary Ann Beavis, Carol J. Dempsey, Amy-Jill Levine, Linda M. Maloney, Ahida Pilarski, Sarah Tanzer, Lauress Wilkins Lawrence, and Seung Ai Yang have lent their extraordinary wisdom to the shaping of the series, have used their extensive networks of relationships to secure authors and contributors, and have worked tirelessly to guide their work to completion. Two others who contributed greatly to the shaping of the project at the outset were Linda M. Day and Mignon Jacobs, as well as Barbara E. Bowe of blessed memory (d. 2010). Editorial and research assistant Susan M. Hickman has provided invaluable support with administrative details and arrangements. I am grateful to Brian Eisenschenk and Christine Henderson who have assisted Susan Hickman with the Wiki. There are countless others at Liturgical Press whose daily work makes the production possible. I am especially thankful to Lauren L. Murphy, Andrea Humphrey, Lauress Wilkins Lawrence, and Justin Howell for their work in copyediting.

1 Thessalonians

Acknowledgments

During the course of preparing this commentary on 1 Thessalonians, I presented papers on various aspects of the material at the Catholic Biblical Association of America and at the Katholieke Universiteit te Leuven (KUL), Leuven, Belgium. I am grateful for the engaging dialogue with many scholars during those sessions. In particular I would like to thank my mentor, Prof. Dr. Jan Lambrecht, SJ, as well as my former teacher, Prof. Dr. Raymond Collins, for their ongoing inspiration in both research and teaching. To the University of San Diego I also express my appreciation for the sabbatical time I have been afforded and the various internal grants that enabled my research. And, to my editors, Dr. Mary Ann Beavis and Dr. Barbara Reid, I am much indebted. In the latter stages this manuscript was carefully commented upon by Dr. John Gillman, my husband, and Dr. Maria Pascuzzi. Their insightful reading has been invaluable.

Throughout the years of research, preparing conference papers, and completing my final manuscript, the steady encouragement and support that enabled me to finish the tasks at hand came from John and our daughter, Anne. This book is dedicated to them in gratitude for their unwavering love and support.

Florence Morgan Gillman
2016

Author's Introduction to 1 Thessalonians

Context and Musing about Women and Thessalonica

When Paul composed 1 Thessalonians ca. 50 CE, he had been preaching about the resurrection of Jesus for more than a decade. Paul's intellectual formation as a Pharisee (Phil 3:5) had prepared him to explain in depth the profound traditions of Judaism. Building on that theological bedrock, Paul's approach to Christian evangelization in the middle years of the first century CE would have been as a mature teacher who had come to understand his Jewish monotheism through the interpretive lens of the resurrected Jesus. His message must have been carefully crafted as he spoke to the Thessalonians during his short time with them, at most a few months, in the year 49 CE. By then Paul's approach in announcing the gospel news that had so jolted his own life would have been delivered to new listeners skillfully focused on what he deemed essential. Further, by 49 CE Paul was no longer a novice at adapting his message for a wide spectrum of people with cultural, geographic, ethnic, and religious differences. And, by mid-century, not only Paul's converts but also his co-workers included both Jewish and Gentile women and men. Just some months before the Thessalonian visit Paul had participated in the pivotal debate in Jerusalem about the question of mandating circumcision for Gentile converts (Gal 2:1-10; Acts 15), an event that affirmed Paul's missionary strategy to the Gentiles.

5

While 1 Thessalonians may not be the first letter Paul wrote to the early churches, it is the earliest extant Christian document.[1] It presents us with the first known written communication about the kerygma. But we should caution ourselves not to think we are hearing Christianity's very first formulation of its message. First Thessalonians is not the nascent voice of the preaching about Jesus that our historically demanding minds so wish we had; its wording reflects many years of Paul's thought[2] and evangelizing, following his life-changing event on the road to Damascus (Gal 1:15-16; Acts 9:3-9; 22:6-11). One therefore approaches this letter recognizing that we are reading the experienced Paul who had carefully formulated in preaching, and probably in writing,[3] for both Jewish and Gentile listeners, what he considered essential in his presentation of the gospel. As the oldest known document of the early Christians, 1 Thessalonians draws a reader closer than any other NT sources to the rippling effects emanating from the life, death, and resurrection of Jesus into the early Christian mission. To hear the voice of Paul in 1 Thessalonians in the year 50, over a decade after he himself had become a follower of Jesus, is to also learn about the status of the Christian movement as it was first being adopted and lived in the vibrant Greco-Roman city of Thessalonica.

Before turning to details about that city and its inhabitants, this introduction will cover some preliminary considerations. First, I will describe

1. This commentary proceeds on the widely held view that none of Paul's other authentic letters were written before 1 Thessalonians. Further, it considers 2 Thessalonians to be post-Pauline (see the commentary in this volume by Mary Ann Beavis and HyeRan Kim-Cragg). The term "Christian(s)" is anachronistically used throughout my text merely for convenience as one among numerous synonyms to refer to the members of Paul's churches; it is unlikely the Thessalonian believers would have used that designation for themselves (see Acts 11:26).

2. The weight of current scholarship generally expresses no compelling doubts about the integrity of this letter, although 1 Thess 2:14-16 has been assessed by some to be an interpolation. This commentary assumes the letter's integrity. On 2:14-16, see below, pp. 53–56.

3. See, in contrast, Beverly Roberts Gaventa, *Our Mother Saint Paul* (Louisville, KY: Westminster John Knox Press, 2007), 17, who considers 1 Thessalonians to be Paul's very first letter to a Christian group so that "we must keep the experimental character of the letter in the foreground as we read and interpret it." In contrast, I think Paul could have written earlier letters (which regrettably were not preserved). I therefore read 1 Thessalonians as reflective of well-honed Pauline teaching as of the point he wrote it, albeit containing comments formulated to dialogue specifically with the Thessalonian believers. On Paul's experience as a letter writer, see my comment below on 5:27, p. 94.

my feminist approach (1). Then, turning to Thessalonica, some information will be reviewed about the city and the famous Via Egnatia (2). That
is followed by two stories about women: one is a tale of a Macedonian
princess, which may have been told to Paul (3.a), and the other is a story
about a Roman woman whose poignant life trajectory is often chronicled
by feminists today (3.b). The story of the latter woman's links to Thessalonica is included here especially for "us," the feminist researchers for
whom her life is informative and fascinating. The recounting of those
narratives and the historical summaries they are threaded into will take
us chronologically through the Macedonian period of Thessalonica and
into the Roman era of Paul; that section ends with reference to the Roman
civil wars and the Macedonian politarchs (3.c). Finally, to round out
information about the background of 1 Thessalonians, I sketch the context of the letter within Paul's journeys and the structure of the letter (4).

1. A Feminist Commentary on 1 Thessalonians

The existence of many comprehensive commentaries on 1 Thessalonians[4] argues against writing another. The Wisdom Commentary series
within which this volume is included, however, has recognized the use-
fulness of a feminist treatment of the whole letter to add to those (usually
briefer) feminist studies of 1 Thessalonians already published.[5] The aim
of this study is therefore to dialogue with primarily those aspects of the

4. See, e.g., Earl J. Richard, *First and Second Thessalonians*, SP 11 (Collegeville, MN:
Liturgical Press, 1995); Beverly Roberts Gaventa, *First and Second Thessalonians*, IBC
(Louisville, KY: John Knox Press, 1998); Gordon D. Fee, *The First and Second Letters to
the Thessalonians*, NICNT (Grand Rapids, MI: Eerdmans, 2009); Abraham J. Malherbe,
The Letters to the Thessalonians: A New Translation with Introduction and Commentary,
AB 32B (New York: Doubleday, 2000); Gary Steven Shogren, *1 and 2 Thessalonians*,
ZECNT (Grand Rapids, MI: Zondervan, 2012); Jeffrey A. D. Weima, *1–2 Thessalonians*,
BECNT (Grand Rapids, MI: Baker Academic, 2014).

5. See, e.g., Pheme Perkins, "1 Thessalonians," in *The Women's Bible Commentary*, ed.
Carol. A. Newsom and Sharon H. Ringe (Louisville, KY: Westminster John Knox Press,
1992), 349–50; Lone Fatum, "1 Thessalonians," in *Searching the Scriptures*, vol. 2, *A
Feminist Commentary*, ed. Elisabeth Schüssler Fiorenza (New York: Crossroad, 1993),
250–62; Jutta Bickman, "1 Thessalonians: Opposing Death by Building Community,"
in *Feminist Biblical Interpretation: A Compendium of Critical Commentary on the Books of
the Bible and Related Literature*, ed. Luise Schottroff and Marie-Theres Wacker (Grand
Rapids, MI: Eerdmans, 2012), 810–20; Monya A. Stubbs, "1 Thessalonians," in *Women's
Bible Commentary*, ed. Carol A. Newsom, Sharon H. Ringe, and Jacqueline E. Lapsley,
3rd ed. (Louisville, KY: Westminster John Knox Press, 2012), 588–91.

text that touch upon the broad range of feminist concerns; as such, the material included here is intended to be complementary to, rather than repetitive of, the various commentaries already published.

Yet an obvious question arises: What is there to be discussed in 1 Thessalonians from the perspective of feminist interests since this epistle says almost nothing about women and, furthermore, is one which some think Paul wrote to an exclusively male congregation?[6] This "disinterested in females" surface impression of the letter prompted Lone Fatum to observe that "involving oneself as a feminist theologian in the interpretation of 1 Thessalonians is like forcing one's way into male company, uninvited and perhaps unwanted."[7] She forcefully defended the position that the letter is addressed only to men.[8] In concert with many feminist and other interpreters, however, I do not share Fatum's sense of exclusion, except regarding 1 Thess 4:3-8.[9] While the letter is undoubtedly androcentric, commenting on it from the perspective of the broad range of feminist interests, such as issues of gender, family concerns, power, social status, and imperialism, opens up many avenues of dialogue to consider regarding the women of the earliest church in Thessalonica.

In thinking of those women, it must be recalled that Paul's letters reflect that, throughout his travels, he lived and worked on "Main Street" and, as far as the evidence points, his churches generally met in the houses of his converts. Paul comes across in his own writings neither as a hermit nor as an aloof teacher but rather as a man socially embedded in the living spaces and daily life of his female and male contacts, including both adults and children. This reality shines through in 1 Thessalonians wherein Paul draws on a wide choice of gender-related metaphors taken from family relationships as well as everyday experiences.[10] For

---

6. See below pp. 31–33.

7. Fatum, "1 Thessalonians," 250.

8. Fatum comments: "We may conclude that although women were surely among the converts in Thessalonica, they were not among the brothers as members of the community. Because they were defined and qualified as women, they were not seen as Christians and their sociosexual presence among the brothers was virtually a nonpresence" (ibid., 262).

9. See below pp. 73–74.

10. On Paul's use of metaphor as a rhetorical strategy, see esp. Trevor J. Burke, *Family Matters: A Socio-Historical Study of Kinship Metaphors in 1 Thessalonians*, JSNTSup 247 (London and New York: T & T Clark International, 2003); Jennifer Houston McNeel, *Paul as Infant and Nursing Mother: Metaphor, Rhetoric, and Identity in 1 Thessalonians 2:5-8*, ECL 12 (Atlanta, GA: Society of Biblical Literature, 2015).

example, he uses domestic comparisons involving birth pangs and women nursing infants.[11] As Carolyn Osiek and Margaret MacDonald have observed:

> It is important to remember that house-churches were places of women giving birth. They were places of women's labor (including sometimes very difficult labor), delivery, deaths of infants and mothers in childbirth, nursing babies, and the precarious work of keeping a baby alive. . . . If the household *familia* included many slaves, labor and delivery could have been a frequent occurrence. On the basis of the frequency of births and the presence of children, house-church meetings must have been noisy and bustling places.[12]

In 1 Thessalonians Paul also refers to bad times in family households, especially happenings at night, such as when a thief breaks in or when drinkers are drunk.[13] Paul lived, and therefore wrote, as an ordinary, social person who interacted with people of all ages and both sexes.

My approach to feminist analysis, with reliance on the historical-critical method, is interested in the world of people behind the text of 1 Thessalonians, that is, the subject location underlying the biblical document. This includes learning primarily about the women, their experiences, and their concerns that have usually been overlooked, submerged, ignored, or even disvalued not only in ancient male writers' androcentric worldviews but also in later interpreters' explications of the text. This informs my broader aim, which is to contribute to a more detailed and gender-balanced narrative about Paul's texts and the history of early Christianity, and to enable contemporary readers to engage with those data. I will approach the text using a hermeneutics of suspicion, i.e., the supposition that the androcentric text conceals more than it reveals about women. This leads to attempts to search out how both the women and men in Paul's churches related to and were affected by his teaching and writing. I also raise questions about how Paul may have reacted to elements in the culture and lives of the believers with whom he interacted. This can be of great interest, and not merely historically, to those who read a text today, those who now "stand in front of the text." Certainly many feminist issues, for example, experiences of power relationships

11. For a major study concerning Paul's use of maternal imagery, see Gaventa, *Our Mother*.
12. Margaret Y. MacDonald, Carolyn Osiek, and Janet Tulloch, *A Woman's Place: House Churches in Earliest Christianity* (Minneapolis: Fortress Press, 2006), 66–67.
13. See below pp. 84–86, on 5:2, 7.

between the sexes and among various socio-economic groups, are types of dynamics felt across the centuries. I recognize, of course, that, as I work with the text of 1 Thessalonians, the feminist points of discussion I pursue to an extent correlate with my own social location. To summarize that for the reader: I write as a middle-class, white American female, married and a mother, educated in both the United States and Europe (Leuven, Belgium), and as a professor of biblical studies.

The contributing voices who have joined with me in this commentary, Regina Boisclair, John Gillman, and Maria Pascuzzi, likewise write from their individual perspectives. Each has offered a brief comment on her or his social location as well.

> Regina Boisclair: "I was born and raised in Massachusetts, traveled much of the world and never lost my Boston accent! My academic path followed the scenic route. While I am one of the few biblical scholars in Alaska, I also teach world religions, death and dying, ecumenics as well as biblical studies. My research interest in lectionaries unites what impacts worshiping assemblies as well as the academy of scholars."

> John Gillman: "A Hoosier at heart, I grew up in a small town in south-eastern Indiana, received my education in the United States and Europe, and have worked for many years in both academics and the pastoral care arena. Most recently I have served as a supervisor of Clinical Pastoral Education in a hospice setting, and before that in an urban-based CPE program whose mission was outreach to the marginalized. My ancestors are predominantly German. I am a white, middle-class male, married, and have one adult daughter."

> Maria Pascuzzi: "I write as a middle-class, white, bilingual American female. I grew up in Brooklyn, New York, enriched by the encounter with so many diverse peoples and ideas. I remain most at home in environments characterized by great diversity. I was educated in the United States, Europe (Rome, Italy), and the Middle East (Israel). I have taught biblical studies at the undergraduate and graduate level for over twenty-five years."

2. The Road to Thessalonica

By the time Paul, Silvanus, and Timothy entered Thessalonica in ca. 49, the city was a significant crossroads and port within the Roman Empire. As their travels in the region can be reconstructed from 1 Thessalonians and are generally corroborated by Acts (17:1-9), it seems that the trio headed for the city mainly because the famous Roman highway, the Via Egnatia, led there; they may have had specific people (suggested by their recent contacts in Philippi) to look up as well. The three travelers had only some months earlier sailed from Troas and disembarked in Macedonia; when they trekked inland, it appears they let the Egnatia plot their itinerary, much like a modern traveler might decide to drive a freeway and let the exits determine where to stop.

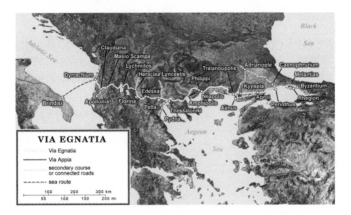

It is interesting to speculate about travel on that great highway, sections of which still exist. The mix of military, foreign, local, commercial, and adventuring characters on or near the road, including pilferers and panhandlers, must have been engaging, and at times dangerous, especially for strangers like Paul and his companions. They were colorful individuals themselves with a pressing message they wanted to proclaim, yet they seem to have been newcomers to Roman Macedonia. Even today on the various sections of the Egnatia that have survived and are gradually being developed into an international cross border hiking trail (with sections in Albania, Greece, and Turkey), interesting encounters abound.[14] One can only imagine the conversations Paul and his companions might have had and the situations in which they stayed. Their options included the infamous, colorful roadside inns,[15] as well as their own tents and the homes of locals like Lydia, who had given

14. For information on this route, see Louis Werner, "Via Egnatia: To Rome and Byzantium," *Aramco World* 66 (2015): 20–31.

15. One ancient source (dated 333 CE) that lists the stops along the Via Egnatia, e.g., *mansiones* (full-service-type inns) and *mutationes* (minimal facilities for travelers located at intervals between *mansiones*), is the travel account by the anonymous Bordeaux Pilgrim. That the writer was a female has been proposed by Laurie Douglass, "A New Look at the *Itinerarium Burdigalense*," *JECS* 4 (1996): 313–33, who argues that the Pilgrim's writing reveals "an idiosyncratic interest in women" (325). For a

accommodation to the missionaries in Philippi just prior to their time in Thessalonica (Acts 16:15).[16] Once they arrived in Thessalonica, Jason was their host (Acts 17:7).[17]

3. Famous Women Entwined with Thessalonica's Greco-Roman History

Newcomers to Thessalonica like Paul, Silvanus, and Timothy, if they had a penchant for learning history and especially if they were fascinated by being in the home region of Alexander the Great, were probably told captivating stories about his Argead dynasty as well as about the later Roman takeover of the area. If Alexander intrigued them, they would have learned not only tales about him and his generals but also lore about their female counterparts, the powerful Macedonian royal women. Explaining the name of the city to visitors would in itself have occasioned telling at least some details about the Argead princess it commemorated, Thessalonike. One might ask, however, if such narratives would have had an impact on Paul. While there is no way to assess that, if the stories were told with an androcentric emphasis, the Macedonian royal women may have been cast as dangerous manipulators. They were indeed dangerous, but they were also struggling to survive within a murderous environment. It is interesting to review Thessalonike's story as we set out to think about the era of Paul in her city.

a. Thessalonike Was Used to Legitimate Male Power

The city of Thessalonica, now modern Saloniki, has a feminine name that honors the princess Thessalonike. She was linked to three very powerful men: her father, Philip II; her half-brother, Alexander III (the

---

critical response, see Susan Weingarten, "Was the Pilgrim from Bordeaux a Woman? A Reply to Laurie Douglass," *JECS* 7 (1999): 291–97.

16. On Lydia, see, e.g., Florence Morgan Gillman, *Women Who Knew Paul* (Collegeville, MN: Liturgical Press, 1992), 29–38; Kate Cooper, *Band of Angels: The Forgotten World of Early Christian Women* (New York: The Overlook Press, 2013), 15–20; on the difficulty of assessing the historicity of Lydia, see Jason T. Lamoreaux, *Ritual, Women, and Philippi: Reimagining the Early Philippian Community*, Matrix: The Bible in Mediterranean Context Series (Eugene, OR: Cascade Books, 2013), 105–6. He concludes the evidence in Acts is insufficient to make a determination.

17. See Florence Morgan Gillman, "Jason of Thessalonica (Acts 17,5-9)," in *The Thessalonian Correspondence*, BETL 87, ed. Raymond F. Collins (Louvain: Leuven University Press, 1990), 39–49.

Great); and her husband, Cassander. The latter founded the city in 316 BCE and named it in her honor, although his obvious motive for doing so was to use her ancestry to legitimate his weak claim to rule. Thessalonike's story would have been kept alive for successive generations of Thessalonians and others in the wider region of Macedonia as a significant part of the history of the era of Alexander the Great and the Argead dynasty. Her life story, like that of many women in her circles, was one of a tumultuous existence lived within an ever-dangerous web of royal intrigues.[18]

Born about 352 BCE, Thessalonike was a daughter of Philip II and his Thessalian wife, Nikesipolis.[19] She was thus a half-sister of Alexander the Great, the son of Philip II by his wife Olympias. Because her birth occurred the day the Macedonians and the Thessalian league won a victory in Thessaly, the Battle of the Crocus Field, her father declared her name should be "victory [νίκη] in Thessaly." Thessalonike's mother died shortly after her birth, and Olympias took over her upbringing. The two, stepmother and stepdaughter, became very close throughout the ensuing decades until the death of Olympias resulted in Thessalonike being thrust literally into the arms of her stepmother's murderer.

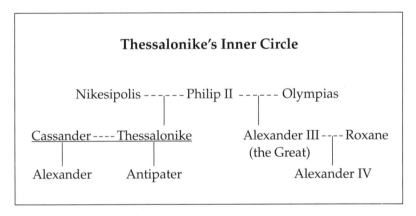

Thessalonike's Inner Circle

Nikesipolis ------- Philip II ------- Olympias

Cassander ---- Thessalonike   Alexander III ---- Roxane
                                      (the Great)

Alexander   Antipater   Alexander IV

Olympias had married the already polygamous Philip II in 357 BCE. She became the most dominant among his current and subsequent wives.

18. On Thessalonike's more immediate family within the dynasty, see esp. Olga Palagia, "The Grave Relief of Adea, Daughter of Cassander and Cynnana," in *Macedonian Legacies: Studies in Ancient Macedonian History and Culture in Honor of Eugene N. Borza*, ed. Timothy Howe and Jeanne Reames (Claremont, CA: Regina Press, 2008), 195–214.

19. Alternatively, her mother may also have been Philip's Thessalian wife Philina. See ibid., 207.

Their son, Alexander III (the Great), was born in 356. Over time Olympias became estranged from Philip, but she retained her powerful status among his wives. She was living in her home region of Epirus at the time of Philip's murder in 336. Olympias then returned to Macedonia to support Alexander's claims to the throne. In the decade following, during his lengthy and extensive eastern expedition (334– 323), she came to distrust and hence to intrigue against Alexander's regent, Antipater, who exercised that office during Alexander's absence and continued to do so following Alexander's sudden death in 323. So powerful was Antipater (grandfather of Thessalonike's son of the same name) that he even retained his authority during the successive joint rule of Alexander the Great's posthumously born son, Alexander IV, and Alexander's half-brother, Philip III Arrhidaeus.

Olympias was not successful in undermining Antipater. When he died in 319 she did, however, support his chosen successor, Polyperchon. But this thereby placed her in opposition to Antipater's son, Cassander, who was threatened by Polyperchon's power. In 317 Olympias murdered Alexander's half-brother Philip III Arrhidaeus and his wife Eurydice. That resulted in making her grandson, Alexander IV, the son of Alexander the Great and the Sogdian princess, Roxane, the sole king. Thessalonike, along with Olympias and other members of the royal family, had returned to Macedonia in 317. But in 316 Cassander successfully captured them as they held out in the fortress of Pydna. He then triggered the murder of Olympias by the avenging relatives of Philip III. With that loss of her allied stepmother, Thessalonike was taken by Cassander to become his wife. When Cassander gave his new wife's name to Thessalonica that same year he was relying on her bloodline to ensure his path to the throne.

The cycle of dynastic murders continued when Cassander in 309, to further strengthen his rule of Macedonia, and with Olympias no longer around as a protector, murdered Alexander IV and Roxane. From 305–297, in the absence of no living heir to the throne, Cassander finally called himself king, legitimizing his claim to the title because of his marriage to Thessalonike. Olga Palagia has noted that at their marriage in 316 Thessalonike and Cassander were middle-aged by ancient standards, and she observes that, since it would be inconceivable that two Macedonians of the highest nobility would have remained single until then, Thessalonike may have been a widow.[20] Cassander, like most of the Macedonian rulers of his era, appears to have been polygamous.

---

20. Ibid., 207.

Thessalonike became the mother of two sons, Antipater and Alexander. When Cassander died of sickness in 297 his older son Philip, probably the son of another mother, ruled for a short time until his own death. Antipater was expected to succeed him. However, Thessalonike favored Alexander. Antipater, jealous of his mother's preference for his younger brother, ordered her death in 295.[21]

In the subsequent history of the city of Thessalonica, the location Cassander had chosen for the new city remained advantageous. It was slightly to the northwest of an existing small settlement, Therme, and had a deep harbor with a drop off some thirty to fifty feet close to the coast. Effectively Cassander enlarged what had been some twenty-six small towns; he also moved various local populations into the new city. From that time forward Thessalonica, regarded as having the best of the Aegean seaports, became a crossroads for routes going north into central Europe, west to the Adriatic, and east to Byzantium. Macedonian dominance, however, eventually gave way to the Romans.

First-century CE visitors to Thessalonica such as Paul, Silvanus, and Timothy no doubt knew some Roman history. But more detailed stories would have been told in the local lore. The general thrust of tales of the Macedonians, following the demise of the Argead dynasty and their successors, was about loss and conquest. The Romans, under Aemilius Paullus, defeated the Macedonians in 168 BCE and then divided the region into four republics. In 146 it became a full Roman province with Thessalonica retaining its Greek name as the capital. Under the Romans the status of the city escalated; it became a major administrative nerve center. Already a hub, the Romans increased that importance when, using existing trade routes, they constructed the Via Egnatia between 146 and 120 BCE. Leading both east and west from Thessalonica, and passing outside the west fortification walls of the city, the sturdy road extended some seven hundred miles from Dyrrachium on the Adriatic Sea east to Byzantium. Long before the time Paul and his companions traversed its eastern Macedonian stretches, the route had become a significant avenue of movement and communication.

b. Our Friend Tullia Ciceronis

Along with lore about the days of the Argeads, no doubt vivid stories of the successive Roman period in Macedonia were also passed on to

---

21. On the current excavation of a magnificent royal tomb from this period, whose occupants are yet to be identified, see below p. 41.

newcomers. Maybe Paul and his companions were told that the famous
Roman orator, Cicero, had lived briefly in Macedonia. Exiled in Greece
from May 58 BCE until August 57 BCE, Cicero spent most of that time
in Thessalonica. An aspect of Cicero's story, however, that is unlikely to
have been included in local stories Paul heard concerns Cicero's daughter
Tullia. But we contemporary scholars interested in her might find it illuminating. While the course of her fragile yet tenacious female existence
is often cited today as an example of a Roman woman's life cycle, the
impact of her father's Thessalonian period upon her life may be lesser-
known data. That suggests a reason to recount it here. Tullia's story also
offers the current reader an encounter with an identified Roman woman.
An elite urbanite, she was probably analogous to some women of Thessalonica Paul may have encountered. Interestingly, Acts 17:12 reports
that "not a few" of the Thessalonian women of "high standing" had
become believers.

Tullia was the daughter of Cicero and his first wife, Terentia. The bi-
ographies of Terentia and particularly of Tullia are well known to those
fascinated with women's lives in the Roman world.[22] Tullia, also called
by the diminutive Tulliola, was probably born ca. 79 or 78 BCE.[23] Her
adult life included a first marriage at the age of sixteen, widowhood,
two more marriages, and two divorces, interspersed with two pregnan-
cies. She died a month after the second birth at the age of thirty. To
contextualize part of this scenario, however, with material usually not
mentioned in sketches of Tullia, it is worth noting that Cicero's Thessalonian sojourn from 58 to 57 BCE had an enormous impact on her life
as well as her mother's.[24]

Cicero had escaped his political enemies in Rome, primarily the tri-
bune Clodius, by going to Thessalonica just before a formal decree of
exile was passed. While there he suffered severe depression, with suicidal
tendencies. He had refused to allow Terentia to accompany him, insisting
she remain behind, although in great personal danger to herself. She was
to manage his chaotic financial affairs and protect Tullia and her younger
brother. The marriage of Cicero and Terentia might well have ended at

---

22. See esp. Susan Treggiari, *Terentia, Tullia and Publilia: The Women of Cicero's Family* (London and New York: Routledge, 2007).

23. Marjorie Lightman and Benjamin Lightman, *Biographical Dictionary of Ancient
Greek and Roman Women: Notable Women from Sappho to Helena* (New York: Checkmark
Books, 2000), 220–23; 230–32.

24. See Treggiari, *Terentia*, 56–70.

that point although it did not. Terentia *de facto* remained in charge of Cicero's finances and shouldered the responsibility for the financial security of Tullia and her brother. Although Tullia was already married to her first husband, Gaius Calpurnius Piso Frugi, her father was still making payments on her dowry. His self-exile, and the ensuing formal exile decree, which stated that all his property was to be confiscated, left his daughter in dire financial straits. Terentia managed to assist Tullia nevertheless, and both of them, with extraordinary fortitude, publically protested Cicero's exile. So dangerous was their situation that when Cicero's home on the Palatine was burned, Terentia took refuge with her half-sister, a Vestal Virgin.

The year 57 BCE brought many changes for Tullia and her mother. Tullia's first husband died. Then Cicero's decree of exile was lifted. Tullia traveled at great effort to meet him on his return. He had journeyed across the Via Egnatia from Thessalonica to Dyrrachium, then taken a ship to Brundisium, where she was waiting. Rather surprisingly, after his return, Cicero became dissatisfied with how Terentia had handled his financial affairs. He was "neither grateful nor even understanding of the difficulties with which she successfully coped."[25] His disenchantment eventually precipitated their divorce in 46, followed by his marriage to Publilia, whom he then also quickly divorced. Cicero's estrangement from Terentia did not, however, weaken his deep emotional attachment to Tullia. Her political influence on him remained significant as well. Cicero was close to Tullia until she died shortly after giving birth in 45.[26] Cicero's own death followed two years later. As for the intrepid Terentia, she too remained bonded to Tullia throughout their lives. And

25. Lightman and Lightman, *Biographical Dictionary*, 222.
26. There is a sentimental legend about a tomb found in Rome in the fifteenth century that was supposedly Tullia's. As the story goes, the body seemed to have been buried the day it was found and there was a glowing lamp inside, assumed to have been burning for fifteen centuries. Later the poet John Donne further romanticized this in the eleventh stanza of his Eclogue of December 26, 1613. In a section titled "The Good Night," an *epithalamium* (a poem written for a bride on the way to her marital bed) honoring the marriage of the Earl of Somerset and Frances Howard (see http://www.luminarium.org/sevenlit/donne/eclogue.php; accessed June 11, 2015) Donne wrote:
Now, as in Tullia's tomb, one lamp burnt clear,
   Unchanged for fifteen hundred year
   May these love-lamps we here enshrine
In warmth, light, lasting, equal the divine.

Terentia, having moved on in spite of her husband's ingratitude for all she had done during his Thessalonian self-exile, amazingly for her era, lived to be 103.

The lives of Tullia and her mother Terentia offer a glimpse of both advantages and forms of stress—personal, political, and economic—with which upper-class Roman females might have to cope. There were certainly such women in the vibrant Roman administrative nerve center of Thessalonica, and Acts, as noted above, reports that Paul converted some of them as well as men of the same class. One wonders how Paul would have framed his message to people like Tullia and Terentia. What does seem evident is that if such women decided to join Paul they would not have lacked determination to exercise some control over their own lives. They might also be especially competent as persons who, used to dealing with officials on many levels, could serve as leaders within or negotiators on behalf of Paul's community. Furthermore, wealthy women who joined Paul's churches would have expected to act as his patrons, as they customarily did with groups they belonged to and usually hosted and supported.[27]

c. The Romans and the Politarchs

As the Roman Empire's civil wars progressed throughout the 40s and 30s BCE, Thessalonica sometimes backed the losing side. The city nevertheless emerged following Octavian's triumph in 31 as a privileged "free city." This meant Thessalonica had the right to produce its own coins; it also was allowed some tax immunity and a degree of administrative and juridical freedom. With its prosperity ensured and its prime location, the population of the city is estimated to have grown to between 65,000 and 100,000 by Paul's era.

Thessalonica was allowed by the Romans to govern according to its local civic structures, which consisted of three levels. These were, from

---

27. See Elisabeth Schüssler Fiorenza, *In Memory of Her: A Feminist Theological Reconstruction of Christian Origins* (New York: Crossroad, 1983), 181: "The rich convert to Christianity . . . probably understood herself/himself as entering a club, and expected to exercise the influence of the patron on this club. Without question the house church, as a voluntary organization, was structured according to this patron-client relationship." On female patrons, see esp. Katherine Bain, *Women's Socioeconomic Status and Religious Leadership in Asia Minor in the First Two Centuries C.E.* (Minneapolis: Fortress Press, 2014), 97–135.

lowest to highest: a citizen assembly, a council, and the politarchs. The latter figures, essentially city officials, have drawn attention because they are referred to twice in Acts (17:6, 8).[28] As late as the early twentieth century, until the finding of inscriptional evidence verifying their presence in Thessalonica, Acts' use of the term "politarchs" had been seen as not historical.[29] It is now understood that the politarchs functioned "as a bridge between the Roman authorities and the local population"[30] and more recently it has been suggested that it is "highly probable that the politarchs had also some kind of judicial role. Some unpublished epigraphic material from the area seems to point in this direction."[31]

With this introductory material, a stage has been set for a feminist discussion of some aspects of 1 Thessalonians in the following five chapters. Before that, however, it is necessary to review the context in which Paul composed his document and set up a general outline of how he organized it.

4. The Context of Paul's Letter

In 1 Thess 3:6, Paul explains to the Thessalonians that "Timothy has just now come to us from you, and has brought us the good news of your faith and love. He has told us also that you always remember us kindly and long to see us—just as we long to see you." Paul's decision to write to the group suggests that he and Silvanus, who was presumably with him, had been awaiting news about them. Paul's quick turnaround in replying implies that while the report was largely positive, pressing issues had also emerged in Timothy's update that Paul needed to address. Timothy may also have relayed a letter to Paul from the Thessalonians. Some have thought the main evidence for that would be Paul's use of the formulaic περὶ δέ ("concerning") in 4:9 and 5:1, which could suggest he was responding to something written. However, that suggestion

---

28. Concerning the political situation in Thessalonica with which the Christians were in conflict as reflected in Acts 17:1-9, see Christopher Kavin Rowe, *World Upside Down: Reading Acts in the Graeco-Roman Age* (New York and Oxford: Oxford University Press, 2011), 91–137.

29. See Weima, *1–2 Thessalonians*, 8–9.

30. Ekaterini G. Tsalampouni, "The Jews and the Agoraioi of Thessaloniki (Acts 17:5)," *The Bible and Interpretation* (2012): 5, http://www.bibleinterp.com/articles/tsa368022.shtml.

31. Ibid.

cannot be conclusive since the phrase is more likely just a cliché used in letter writing to introduce a set of comments.[32]

Paul does not say where he was when he wrote 1 Thessalonians. He does indicate in 3:1-2 that, while he had been in Athens and when he could bear his separation from the Thessalonians no longer, "we [he and Silvanus] decided to be left alone . . . and [so] we sent Timothy . . . to strengthen and encourage you for the sake of your faith." Paul's way of referring to Athens intimates that he and Silvanus were no longer there as he was writing, but he fails to mention his current location. Acts, however, may offer some insight. Regarding Paul's time in Athens, the Lukan account states that Paul had been "deeply distressed to see that the city was full of idols" (Acts 17:16). Then Acts reports Paul's Areopagus event and says that Paul moved on to Corinth, giving no indication that Silas (as Silvanus is called in Acts) was with him. Instead, that source notes that Silas later came from Macedonia to Corinth along with Timothy.

The combined data from 1 Thessalonians and Acts has caused scholars to conclude that Paul wrote 1 Thessalonians from Corinth soon after receiving Timothy's report. As for Silvanus, it seems likely that he had been with Paul and had not returned to Thessalonica with Timothy. And, since Paul's sojourn in Corinth can be quite accurately dated to 49–51 CE,[33] we can conclude that these are the approximate dates for the reunion of Timothy with Paul and Silvanus; hence the letter's composition would be toward the beginning of that time frame, thus about 50.

From this supposition about Paul's location at Corinth and the dating of 50 CE for 1 Thessalonians, the broader context within his previous travels can be reconstructed. In 1 Thess 2:2, Paul points out that his preaching in Thessalonica came after the three missionaries had been "shamefully mistreated at Philippi." This accords with the data in Acts, which situated Paul's time in Thessalonica, then Athens and Corinth, during what has been conventionally called Paul's second journey. While Acts must be relied on with caution, it says in Acts 15:40–16:10 that earlier on this journey Paul had left Antioch with Silas and visited Derbe and Lystra,

32. Margaret M. Mitchell, "Concerning Peri De in 1 Corinthians," *NovT* 31 (1989): 229–56, at 253–54. See also Raymond F. Collins, *The Birth of the New Testament: The Origin and Development of the First Christian Generation* (New York: Crossroad, 1993), 115–16.

33. The dating is dependent on Paul's appearance in Corinth before Gallio and the so-called Gallio inscription that enables the close estimation of Gallio's period in that city; see Acts 18:12.

where he had asked Timothy to join them. The trio then passed through Phrygia and Galatia to Troas before sailing to Samothrace and passing through Neapolis. From there Paul and his companions reached Philippi (16:11-12). Following difficulties in Philippi, they then proceeded (apparently along the Via Egnatia, since the text says he passed through Amphipolis and Appollonia) to Thessalonica (17:1). The data from Acts parallels Paul's comments in 1 Thess 2:2 where he reports that he had gone from Philippi to Thessalonica after having been "shamefully mistreated at Philippi." And it also corresponds to Paul's indication that both Silvanus and Timothy had been with him in Thessalonica. Acts, however, tells a fuller story than Paul alludes to in 1 Thessalonians about his activities in both Philippi and Thessalonica, just as it does regarding his period in Corinth. Acts reports that while in Thessalonica Paul evangelized in the synagogue on three sabbaths. As a result, not only some Jews but also "a great many of the devout Greeks and not a few of the leading women" had been persuaded to join Paul and Silas (Acts 17:4). Other Jews who had become jealous, joined by some ruffians from the marketplaces, formed a mob. The mob attacked the house of a man named Jason, with whom Paul and Silas had been staying, dragging Jason and some believers before city authorities, accusing them all of "acting contrary to the decrees of the emperor, saying that there is another king named Jesus" (17:5-7). They were let go once Jason and others posted bail. "That very night the believers sent Paul and Silas off to Beroea" (17:10). In that small city, the two went to a synagogue where the Jews were "more receptive than those in Thessalonica" (17:11) so that many believed, "including not a few Greek women and men of high standing" (17:12). It was when the Jews of Thessalonica heard of Paul's preaching in Beroea and followed him there that the Beroean believers sent Paul off to the coast headed for Athens (presumably by ship). Interestingly, however, Silas and Timothy remained with the Beroeans, although Paul instructed them to "join him as soon as possible" (17:14-15).

As is obvious from this summary, the problem of correlating the data of 1 Thessalonians with that of Acts 17:1-15 is a thorny one. More recent scholarly solutions range from some few treating the Acts passage as generally accurate[34] to many other assessments expressing a degree of some or even extreme skepticism about Luke's report. In the end it seems

---

34. A recent contribution reflecting this approach is Murray J. Smith, "The Thessalonian Correspondence," in *All Things to All Cultures: Paul among Jews, Greeks, and Romans*, ed. Mark Harding and Alanna Nobbs (Grand Rapids, MI: Eerdmans, 2013).

best, as will be done in this commentary, to weigh each point of comparison as the issues are raised.

With respect to structure, 1 Thessalonians has two major parts: a lengthy section of thanksgivings followed by exhortations. In chapters 1–3, Paul expresses gratitude for the believers' conversions and then reminisces about the time he and his companions spent with them followed by their painful separation. In chapters 4–5, Paul offers exhortation and instructions.

Following the format of letter writing of the period, 1 Thessalonians opens with a salutation that identifies the senders and recipients and includes a greeting (1:1). The salutation leads into the senders' expression of gratitude concerning the recipients. This is followed by three successive thanksgivings (1:2-10; 2:13-16; and 3:9-10),[35] an unusual feature in Paul's letters. The thanksgivings constitute a major part of the letter's first section, so much so that some conclude they are actually part of the body of the document. What follows then in 4:1–5:24 could be considered the "rest" of the body. The material in 4:1–5:22 may be divided into sections that are paraenetic (4:1-12 and 5:12-22) and eschatological (4:13–5:11).[36] Paul then rounds out his missive with a final prayer (5:23-24), some last recommendations (5:25-28), including a solemn order about reading the letter to all the believers (5:27), and a concluding salutation (5:28).

35. See Jan Lambrecht, "Thanksgivings in 1 Thessalonians 1–3," in *Thessalonian Correspondence*, ed. Raymond F. Collins, BETL 87 (Louvain: Leuven University Press, 1990), 201: "Present, past and future, as well as the double focus of addressees and writer in their relation to God and Jesus Christ, appear to have been the structuring factors of Paul's thought in 1 Thes 1–3. Of course, over and against the first thanksgiving in 1,2-5, the thanksgiving of 2,13 is repetitive and, just as the first, rather static ('always, constantly'). The third of 3,9-10 refers to a more advanced point in history, a recent, peculiar event and Paul's joy at the return of Timothy."

36. Jan Lambrecht, "A Structural Analysis of 1 Thessalonians 4–5," in *Collected Studies on Pauline Literature and on the Book of Revelation*, ed. Jan Lambrecht, AnBib 147 (Rome: Editrice Pontificio Istituto Biblico, 2001), 282–87.

1 Thessalonians 1

The Women and Men Who "Turned to God from Idols" (1:9)

Paul's greeting in 1 Thess 1:1 indicates that the letter is not only from him but also from Silvanus and Timothy. This signals Paul's high regard for his two co-workers and the important roles they had in the evangelization of the Thessalonians. It is not evident (nor is it in the Acts portrayal of this same period) whether others, such as the wives of Silvanus and Timothy, were accompanying the trio. Nevertheless, since it would have been quite typical for the time to not mention women in such a group, Silvanus and Timothy, if married, may have had spouses with them. That Paul did not is confirmed by 1 Cor 9:5 where he states that he (along with Barnabas) had been exceptional in not exercising his right to be accompanied by a believing wife, at least up until the writing of 1 Corinthians (about 55–56 CE). In looking at this first extant letter of Paul and assessing his age as being in the early thirties or more when he wrote 1 Thessalonians in 50 CE, one might wonder about his own marital status prior to that point. While in his later writing (1 Cor 7:8) Paul indicates he then had no wife, it remains doubtful that he had not married earlier, particularly since as a deeply committed Pharisee he was dedicated to observance of the Law to the fullest.[1] This correlates with the judgment of numerous scholars that Paul was a widower.[2]

---

1. See especially Raymond F. Collins, *Accompanied by a Believing Wife: Ministry and Celibacy in the Earliest Christian Communities* (Collegeville, MN: Liturgical Press, 2013), 125–32.
2. See ibid., 132, n. 81.

1 Thess 1:1-10

¹·¹Paul, Silvanus, and Timothy,
To the church of the Thessalonians in God the Father and the Lord Jesus Christ:
Grace to you and peace.

²We always give thanks to God for all of you and mention you in our prayers, constantly ³remembering be-fore our God and Father your work of faith and labor of love and steadfastness of hope in our Lord Jesus Christ. ⁴For we know, brothers and sisters beloved by God, that he has chosen you, ⁵because our message of the gospel came to you not in word only, but also in power and in the Holy Spirit and with full conviction; just as you know

Paul's respect for Silvanus and Timothy is apparent throughout the letter,[3] notably in 1 Thess 2:7, where he describes them as being apostles along with himself.[4] Silvanus (Silas is a shortened Greek form) is generally held to be the Silas referred to in Acts. A leading member of the Jerusalem church, he was an early Jewish Christian (Acts 15:22), a prophet, a church emissary (15:32), and possibly a Roman citizen (16:37). Silas had begun to travel with Paul (15:40) following Paul's falling out with Barnabas. Paul's choice to be accompanied by Silas was "certainly astute, since it had the diplomatic advantage of placing the Pauline mission under the auspices of Jerusalem."[5] In naming Silvanus first in 1 Thess 1:1, Paul likely reflects that they had known and collaborated with each other much longer than had he and Timothy and perhaps that Silvanus was the older of these two co-workers.

When 1 Thessalonians was written, Timothy, who was later to become one of Paul's most often mentioned and dependable of co-workers, had been with Paul only for those months since Paul and Silas had preached first in Derbe and then in Lystra (Acts 16:2), Timothy's town. Timothy was the son of a Jewish mother, Eunice. She and her mother, Lois,[6] had become Christians, probably when Paul and Barnabas initially evangelized in their region. Their names are known from 2 Tim 1:5.

---

3. For a discussion on male bonding between Paul and his male co-workers, especially Timothy, see David J. A. Clines, "Paul, the Invisible Man," in *New Testament Masculinities*, ed. Stephen D. Moore and Janice Capel Anderson, SemeiaSt 45 (Atlanta, GA: Society of Biblical Literature, 2003), 188–89.

4. See below, p. 42.

5. John Gillman, "Silas," *ABD* 6 (1992): 22–23.

6. See Florence Morgan Gillman, *Women Who Knew Paul* (Collegeville, MN: Liturgical Press, 1992), 22–24.

what kind of persons we proved to be among you for your sake. ⁶And you became imitators of us and of the Lord, for in spite of persecution you received the word with joy inspired by the Holy Spirit, ⁷so that you became an example to all the believers in Macedonia and in Achaia. ⁸For the word of the Lord has sounded forth from you not only in Macedonia and Achaia, but in every place your faith in God has become known, so that we have no need to speak about it. ⁹For the people of those regions report about us what kind of welcome we had among you, and how you turned to God from idols, to serve a living and true God, ¹⁰and to wait for his Son from heaven, whom he raised from the dead—Jesus, who rescues us from the wrath that is coming.

According to Acts, Timothy was uncircumcised, a situation Paul determined he needed to rectify in order for Timothy to preach with him, that is, "because of the Jews who were in those places, for they all knew his father was a Greek" (16:3). Little can be speculated about Timothy's Gentile father,⁷ although it may be assumed Timothy would have grown up with the issues of a child raised in a family with one monotheistic (but rather nonobservant?) parent and one polytheistic parent.⁸ While Paul may have envisioned that Timothy's circumcision would increase his credibility with the Jews, he may also have discerned that Timothy's life experience within a "mixed marriage" would have been advantageous as a missionary to Gentiles. This may have been a major factor in Timothy's positive rapport with the Thessalonians to which the letter abundantly testifies.

The impact upon children raised like Timothy in mixed religious contexts could have had both positive and negative repercussions. While perhaps gaining insight into the religion of both parents and their

7. It is reasonable to posit that Timothy's father (if alive) and his mother had remained together since, if they had divorced, the father would have retained *potestas* (control) over any children, precluding Timothy's evangelization by his mother and grandmother. But the question can also be raised of whether Timothy's father was aware of his wife's Christian conversion. See Margaret Y. MacDonald, "Early Christian Women Married to Unbelievers," *SR* 19 (1990): 229–56, at 227, who observes about women married to unbelievers: "The thought of losing a child to a pagan father and stepmother must have inspired some mothers to keep their religious affiliations carefully hidden from unbelieving husbands."

8. On issues concerning children in families with only one believing Christian parent, see Cornelia B. Horn and John W. Martens, *"Let the Little Children Come to Me": Childhood and Children in Early Christianity* (Washington, DC: Catholic University of America Press, 2009), 101–6.

extended families, such children might have experienced bewilderment. Cornelia Horn and John Martens support the position that "children in the first centuries of the Christian movement perceived the new religion as socially dislocating."[9] Their exposure to the conversion of their elders is likely to have been "confusing and disorienting for them as it disturbed familial and kinship structures."[10] Whatever Timothy's familial religious dynamics had been like, he must have been prepared to evangelize a wide spectrum of people. Paul's dependence on him to act as emissary to the Thessalonian church when Paul himself could not (1 Thess 3:2) reflects the trust Paul had in Timothy as a minister.

As Paul expands the salutation in 1 Thess 1:1, he identifies the church (ἐκκλησία) of the Thessalonians as being "in God the Father and the Lord Jesus Christ." Paul's use of patriarchal language for God was typical for the Judaism of his time. The salutation also reflects his rootedness in his lifelong Jewish monotheism. Paul's understanding of Jesus' role within that religious context is clear throughout the letter. As Earl J. Richard has observed: "From the start Paul insists on the theological and Christological character of the community's being called together, namely, the community's monotheistic and loving relationship to the deity . . . and its commitment to God's messianic agent."[11] This salutation also has further suggestive overtones. In identifying Jesus with the titles "Lord" (κύριος) and "Christ" (χριστός), Paul employed a title for God's anointed in Israel (χριστός), his designation of Jesus as a king, while "Lord" (κύριος) was an honorific used for an emperor. In view of this, Maria Pascuzzi has observed: "By applying the emperor's public titles to Jesus, Paul suggests one of two things: Jesus and the emperor were equals or the emperor was neither Lord nor King, because Jesus was. Either way, this was dangerous if not outright treasonous."[12] Using these titles for Jesus is the first of many indications in this letter, some of which will be commented upon in later chapters, that Paul's perspective is critically anti-imperial.

A further point to be noted regarding Paul's indication in the salutation that 1 Thessalonians is from himself, Silvanus, and Timothy is that while Paul uses the first-person plural frequently throughout the text,

---

9. Ibid., 113.

10. Ibid.

11. Earl J. Richard, *First and Second Thessalonians*, SP 11 (Collegeville, MN: Liturgical Press, 1995), 38.

12. Maria Pascuzzi, *Paul: Windows on His Thought and His World* (Winona, MN: Anselm Academic, 2014), 253.

God the Father

In 1 Thessalonians, Paul, Silvanus, and Timothy name God once as "the Father" (1:1) and three times as "our God and Father" (1:3; 3:11, 13). With the addition of the first-person plural possessive pronoun, the co-authors include not only themselves but also the community of believers united under the same God. In the seven letters accepted as authentically Pauline, just over half of the instances where Paul uses "Father" as a designation for God (eleven out of twenty instances) with reference to the community of believers occur in the greeting (Rom 1:7; 1 Cor 1:3; 2 Cor 1:2, 3; Gal 1:1, 3, 4; Phil 1:2; Phlm 1; 1 Thess 1:1, 3). Hence, we can understand this common feature as part of the formulaic nature of the greeting. Paul's usage may be influenced by his understanding of God as the Father of our Lord Jesus Christ, so named in two other letters (Rom 15:6; 2 Cor 1:3; 11:31), although not in 1 Thessalonians. This undoubtedly goes back to the Jesus tradition known to Paul, for twice he refers to believers, who, empowered by the Spirit, cry out "Abba! Father!" (Gal 4:6; Rom 8:15; see also Mark 14:36), thus bearing witness that they are children of God (Rom 8:16).

How dominant is Paul's use of patriarchal language in naming the Divine? Considering that Paul uses "God" thirty-four times in 1 Thessalonians, the descriptor "Father" appears in 8.9% of the occurrences. This percentage decreases significantly in his three longest letters, Romans (1.8%), 1 Corinthians (2.8%), and 2 Corinthians (2.7%); it is the same in Philippians (8.9%) and increases in Galatians (12.1%). While it is difficult to draw hard conclusions, one wonders what factors may have influenced the notable reduction in patriarchal language in his lengthier letters, yet with an increase in Galatians, his most tendentious letter?

Regarding 1 Thessalonians, the reader is presented with a fuller picture of the Divine that transcends the limitations of patriarchal imagery. Entrusted with the "Gospel of God" (2:2, 8, 9), Paul places his courage in God (2:2), gives thanks to God (2:13; 3:9) and feels joyful before "our God" (3:9). In his closing exhortation he addresses the God of peace (5:23). In a most remarkable expression found only in this letter, Paul applies to all believers, both Jews and Gentiles, what had been originally reserved to Israel, namely, that they are "beloved by God" (ἠγαπημένοι ὑπὸ θεοῦ, 1:4). Paul perceives that God's love is now extended to the church, whose fledgling members have been taught by God "to love one another" (4:9), which they have already taken to heart as demonstrated by their love for all the faithful throughout Macedonia (4:10). So, God, called Father a few times in the letter, is the one who has destined those called "not for wrath" (5:9) but to embrace the abundant love God extended to the renewed Israel.

John Gillman

his vacillation into the first-person singular (2:18; 3:5; and 5:27) suggests he himself was the actual author.[13] For simplicity's sake I will generally refer to Paul as the writer of 1 Thessalonians, although realizing his authorship *de facto* may have included input from Silvanus and Timothy. We must also envision that Paul dictated what he composed to an amanuensis, a scribe, as was the widespread practice at the time. That person also may have had an impact on the formulation of the text.

In comparison with other Greco-Roman letters known from the same period, 1 Thessalonians is relatively long. Who might his scribe have been if Paul was located in Corinth? During Paul's later period there, when he wrote the epistle to the Romans (ca. 56), the scribe who worked with Paul was Tertius, a male with a Roman name (Rom 16:22). He appears to have been a believer since he sent his own greetings to the letter's recipients. In 50, however, when Paul composed 1 Thessalonians, what scribe might he have enlisted? While professional scribes were easy to retain, Paul is likely to have preferrred one who was a believer, a person who understood his conceptual language.

During Paul's first visit to Corinth, Acts 18:2 indicates that his closest contacts were Priscilla and Aquila, believers who had recently been forced out of Rome. A reasonable guess is that someone already in their circle of Christians, or even Aquila or Priscilla, was the scribe of 1 Thessalonians. Although Acts 18:3 describes the couple as tentmakers, making it unlikely either was literate, the thought that one of them was Paul's scribe should not be too quickly dismissed.

From various Greco-Roman inscriptions and literary references it is known that particularly in urban areas there were female scribes, although it appears that far fewer women than men had such training. Interestingly, the extant inscriptional evidence for female scribes suggests

---

13. See Gordon D. Fee, *The First and Second Letters to the Thessalonians*, NICNT (Grand Rapids, MI: Eerdmans, 2009), 4.

that some were slaves or freedwomen who functioned in urban contexts as employees whose literacy was at the service of upper-class women.[14] Given her social status as both Gentile and possibly of a higher class than her artisan Jewish husband, or as having formerly been a slave in an upper-class family, Priscilla may have been literate.[15] She quite possibly was the scribe of 1 Thessalonians.[16] In later years, when Paul wrote Romans from Corinth and Tertius was his scribe,[17] Priscilla and Aquila were by then in Rome; they were the first he singled out in his greetings to the Roman believers. Notably, he commented that "all the churches of the Gentiles" (Rom 16:4) owed them gratitude. While it is known that subsequent to their period in Corinth they had gone on to evangelize in Ephesus and then Rome, what is the meaning of this gratitude owed by *all* the Gentile churches? While interpreters have asked what this expansive claim meant,[18] it could be that Priscilla and Aquila had themselves carried on written communication with many groups, which underscores the possibility of the literacy of at least one of them. In fact, a possible reference is found in 1:8-9 to suggest that correspondence between them and the wider regions of Macedonia and Achaia may have been going on already in 50 as Paul wrote 1 Thessalonians. There Paul indicates that he had become aware (by letters received in Corinth? from visitors?) of how the Thessalonians were widely known as exemplars to other believers. Who was spreading this word, and how?

As with all of Paul's correspondence, the original papyrus of 1 Thessalonians is lost.[19] History is indebted for the letter's preservation to early

14. Kim Haines-Eitzen, "'Girls Trained in Beautiful Writing': Female Scribes in Roman Antiquity and Early Christianity," *JECS* 6 (1998): 629–46, at 635–37. See also Kim Haines-Eitzen, *Guardians of Letters: Literacy, Power, and the Transmitters of Early Christian Literature* (Oxford: Oxford University Press, 2000), 44.

15. See Gillman, *Women*, 49–57.

16. Priscilla has likewise been considered literate and was suggested as the author of Hebrews by Adolf von Harnack, "The Authorship of the Epistle to the Hebrews," *Lutheran Church Review* 19 (1900): 448–71; his theory was further developed by Ruth Hoppin, *Priscilla's Letter: Finding the Author of the Epistle to the Hebrews* (Fort Bragg, CA: Lost Coast Press, 2000).

17. Tertius's name is Latin for "third," a type of name often given to slaves. On his function as a scribe, see Robert Jewett, *Romans: A Commentary*, Hermeneia: A Critical and Historical Comentary on the Bible (Minneapolis: Fortress Press, 2007), 978–80.

18. See the suggestions summarized by ibid., 958.

19. For the manuscript history of 1 Thessalonians, see Raymond F. Collins, *The Birth of the New Testament: The Origin and Development of the First Christian Generation* (New York: Crossroad, 1993), 1–5.

copyists, most likely Christians who recognized an enduring value in Paul's writings.[20] Would that suggest these were unpaid copyists and therefore, even more than professional scribes needing to earn a living, likely to be females?

By addressing the greetings to the whole church (1 Thess 1:1), Paul ascertained that his communication was intended for all. He reiterates that as well at the close of the letter where he commands "by the Lord" that the letter be publically read (5:27), signaling his concern for the non-literate, probably the majority. In this earliest of his known epistles, one observes that Paul did not deal with the group via status or hierarchical distinctions; he did not write exclusively to their leaders on their behalf or as a channel to them. In his closing words too, while he certainly urges respect and esteem for the leaders who had "charge" of them (5:12), Paul does not suggest any members were more important than any others.

In 1 Thess 1:4 the translation of ἀδελφοί ("brothers and sisters"), the first of its frequent uses in this letter, has been closely scrutinized. It is the first instance of believers so referring to the members of their ecclesial group. Gordon Fee explains that "it reflects the imagery of the church as God's household, where Christ is the householder and all who are his are family related to one another as 'brothers and sisters.'"[21] Fee traces this metaphor for the believing community to Exod 2:11, where Moses visits his brothers and sees one being beaten by an Egyptian. He observes that early Christians would have additionally received a family-oriented

---

20. With respect to the characteristics of scribes in the later manuscript transmission of Christian documents, see Kim Haines-Eitzen, "Engendering Palimpsests: Reading the Textual Tradition of the Acts of Paul and Thecla," in *The Early Christian Book*, ed. William E. Klingshirn and Linda Safran (Washington, DC: The Catholic University of America Press, 2007), 177–93, at 183: "The earliest Christian papyri contain clues as to their copyists. The use of such stylistic features as the *nomina sacra*, the appearance of harmonistic tendencies—such features suggest that during the second and third centuries, early scribes worked privately and individually to reproduce early Christian texts. While some of the scribes may have been professionals, many of them—in contrast to the scribes who copied Greco-Roman literature more generally—seem to have been nonprofessionals who had a vested interest in the texts they were copying. Herein lies the significance of exploring the identities of early Christian scribes. They were not mindless copyists, the ancient equivalent of photocopy machines. Rather, they often took the 'care' to change, to manipulate, and (to their minds) to correct the text they were copying to make it say what they thought it meant. It is no coincidence that in the earliest Christian texts we find the most fluidity and variety of readings."

21. Fee, *Letters*, 30.

sense for the body of believers from Jesus himself in his references to God's family as being constituted by those who do God's will (see, e.g., Mark 3:34).[22]

While this letter is for the whole Thessalonian church (1 Thess 5:27), we can wonder who was explicitly denoted by the masculine plural ἀδελφοί. It is widely understood inclusively by translators (as in the NRSV) and therefore rendered "brothers and sisters." Nevertheless, when read in light of what has been described as the "unrelenting androcentrism of the text,"[23] some have suggested the term is exclusively male. Indeed, due to the absence of women's names in the letter and the lack of advice concerning women themselves, there is a sense of female invisibility in 1 Thessalonians. This contrasts with the other six authentically Pauline letters, all of which make references to women. The issue is compounded by the admonitory passage in 4:3-8 that is probably addressed only to men.[24]

Richard Ascough, in the course of his work on Macedonian associations, cautiously adopts the position that, in 1 Thessalonians, ἀδελφοί denotes only males.[25] He holds that Paul elsewhere does use the term inclusively. Ascough's conclusion about 1 Thessalonians is based on his assessment that the social structure underlying the nascent Thessalonian church was that of a voluntary association of perhaps tentmakers or leather workers. He suggests that Paul had collectively persuaded an existing professional group "to switch their allegiance from their patron deity or deities 'to serve a living and true God.' "[26] Ascough asserts that "while it is true that the text does not indicate the turning of an entire group to the veneration of Jesus, neither does it indicate what is assumed by most: individual conversions."[27] He concludes that 1 Thessalonians is addressed only to males on the assumption that female artisans would not belong to a group in a trade normally carried on by men. Noting that

22. Ibid., 31.
23. Melanie Johnson-DeBaufre, " 'Gazing Upon the Invisible': Archaeology, Historiography, and the Elusive Wo/men of 1 Thessalonians," in *From Roman to Early Christian Thessalonikē: Studies in Religion and Archeology*, ed. Laura S. Nasrallah, Charalambos Bakirtzēs, and Steven J. Friesen (Cambridge, MA: Harvard University Press, 2010), 73–108, at 75.
24. See below, p. 74.
25. Richard S. Ascough, *Paul's Macedonian Associations: The Social Context of Philippians and 1 Thessalonians*, WUNT 161 (Tübingen: Mohr Siebeck, 2003), 186–90.
26. Ibid., 185.
27. Ibid., 186.

1 Thessalonians contains no indication of women in the church, nor does it contain advice for women or families, he thinks that Paul offers advice germane only to males. He also finds support for this position in the statement in 4:4 "that each one of you know how to control your own body in holiness and honor." Ascough understands this reference, as have others, to being an admonition strictly to males to control their genitalia. That position can be held, however, without assuming that in all the rest of the letter Paul gave no thought in what he wrote to the women in the group. Furthermore, Ascough seems to mitigate against the strength of his own suggestion concerning the male-only interpretation of ἀδελφοί by noting that if the Thessalonian Christian group was male, then that church was atypical among Paul's communities, as known, e.g., from Corinth, Philippi, and Rome.[28]

Regarding Ascough's males-only interpretation, some additional concerns must be raised. First, would any one trade association have commanded Paul's total and restricted attention in the city? Also, were his converts not immediate stepping stones to their family and friends?[29] Additionally, while Ascough's work demonstrates the importance of Macedonian associations in the social context, and documents well the possibility that Paul did evangelize within such a structure, why consider only the associations of trades generally followed by men? Since the evangelization of the Thessalonians followed closely upon Paul's period in Philippi, where Lydia the purple cloth seller had been a key member and apparently the leader of the Philippian church (Acts 16:14-15, 40), she may have supplied contacts for Paul to engage with in Thessalonica. Since Ascough's presentation of inscriptional data itself includes a reference to an association of purple dyers in Thessalonica,[30] there is a likelihood that Paul connected with a group linked to the purple trade, e.g., dyers and sellers, a business known to have been carried on by women.

The supposition that ἀδελφοί in 1 Thessalonians is an exclusively male referent has been critiqued at length by Melanie Johnson-DeBaufre who argues that the invisibility of women in the text nevertheless offers no evidence that women were not members of the church. "While it is clear

28. Ibid., 186–90.
29. See Lone Fatum, "1 Thessalonians," in *Searching the Scriptures*, vol. 2, *A Feminist Commentary*, ed. Elisabeth Schüssler Fiorenza (New York: Crossroad, 1993), 250–62, who has taken the position that while women were certainly among the converts in Thessalonica, because according to patriarchal logic their lives were embedded in men's, they are not addressed in themselves in 1 Thessalonians.
30. Ascough, *Paul's Macedonian Associations*, 22.

that there were homosocial membership groups in the Greco-Roman world, there is no indication the Christ groups were among them."[31] Pointing to the tension often experienced between the androcentrism of many a written document when compared with the material reality of the archaeological record, she repeatedly underscores a basic principle of feminist historians: *"Wo/men were there."*[32] In essence, affirming the presence of women in the group of Thessalonian believers is not a form of feminist wishful thinking. The issue of 1 Thessalonians being addressed to women as well as men is not resolved by simply concluding women were there, however. The problem remains that even interpreters who do acknowledge women's presence in the group often proceed to make them invisible by overlooking them in their commentaries.

As Paul's remarks move forward in chapter 1 he reveals an interesting aspect of his thought concerning imitation. Paul characterizes the Thessalonians as persons of faith, love, and hope (1 Thess 1:3) and further as "imitators of us and of the Lord" (1:6). They in turn, as imitators, then became exemplars for other believers in Macedonia and Achaia (1:7-8). One strand of feminist commentary views Paul here exercising a discourse of power which is effectively "a demand for the erasure of difference."[33] Elizabeth Castelli's perception is that Paul's phrasing concerning imitation in 1:6 and 2:14 is a use of rhetoric "to rationalize and shore up a particular set of social relations or power relations within the early Christian movement."[34] Jeffrey Weima has responded to this by classifying Castelli's position as a misunderstanding of Paul's imitative or mimetic theme, one that "stems from reading too heavily the apostle's statement through the eyes of our contemporary cultural attitudes and concerns."[35] He states that current issues regarding patriarchalism and hierarchical relationships "can quickly create the conviction that any person urging others to imitate him is guilty of arrogance and an abuse of powers."[36]

31. Johnson-DeBaufre, "Gazing," 93.
32. Ibid., 73, 92. Her italics.
33. See Elizabeth A. Castelli, *Imitating Paul: A Discourse of Power*, Literary Currents in Biblical Interpretation (Louisville, KY: Westminster John Knox Press, 1991), 17.
34. Ibid., 116.
35. Jeffrey A. D. Weima, *1–2 Thessalonians*, BECNT (Grand Rapids, MI: Baker Academic, 2014), 98.
36. Ibid.; see also Trevor J. Burke, *Family Matters: A Socio-Historical Study of Kinship Metaphors in 1 Thessalonians*, JSNTSup 247 (London and New York: T & T Clark International, 2003), 146, where his assessment is that Castelli fails to understand Paul as a servant of the Lord and that imitating Paul "is only to follow the example of 'the Lord' (1:6; cf. 1 Cor. 11.1)."

Joseph Marchal, while applauding Castelli's efforts to "explicate the power dynamics of such argumentation,"[37] nevertheless critiques her work for what he perceives as an overwhelming emphasis on the dominating or repressive effects of mimetic persuasion. In his view, because power is also productive and produces reactions that cannot be constrained by the exerciser, Paul's call to imitation might also have elicited a "whole series of effects that are multiple, diffuse and ambiguous,"[38] particularly by women. Marchal urges future Pauline scholarship on mimesis to "continue to investigate and formulate the full range of complicated roles women likely played in these [Pauline] communities."[39]

Paul links the imitation of the three missionaries and the Lord with the persecution the Thessalonians had been experiencing (1 Thess 1:6). The reasons for the persecution that Paul refers to numerous times in the letter remain uncertain. Many assume, persuasively so in my view, that the social problems that rejection of polytheistic practices would have occasioned for the believers underlie the persecution.[40] This receives confirmation in 1:9, where Paul indicates that the conversion of the Thessalonians had been a turning away from idols and toward God in order to serve "a living and true God." In this phrase one can hear what Paul must have set before the believers: hitherto they had honored dead and false gods.

While serving the living and true God, they were simultaneously awaiting with steadfast hope the return of Jesus and their rescue by him from the wrath to come (1 Thess 1:10). The rejection of idols by the Thessalonians suggests the group was predominantly Gentile. This contrasts with Acts 17:1-4, which indicates that some of Paul's converts in Thessalonica were members of the synagogue, although the Acts tradition does allow the assumption that those Jewish converts were a small number and probably lived under pressure from the synagogue to leave Paul's group (see Acts 17:5, 11).

The subject of the earliest Christians' disentanglement from the worship of their former deities is intriguing. In 1 Thess 1:9, Paul could be implying that their abandonment of idols was complete. That is hard to imagine, however, and one wonders how quickly Paul expected his

---

37. Joseph A. Marchal, *The Politics of Heaven: Women, Gender, and Empire in the Study of Paul* (Minneappolis: Fortress Press, 2008), 66.

38. Ibid.

39. Ibid., 114.

40. See further on 2:14-16, p. 58.

Gentile converts to solidify such a radical break. It is more probable that Paul's statement that the Thessalonians had turned away from their idols is prescriptive and that the rejection was an ongoing process.

Turning from idols for this presumably small group of the very first Gentile Christian believers in their city must have been increasingly traumatic. On the difficulty of leaving behind the worship of their deities, Weima states in his recent commentary that "in a society where cultic activities were intimately connected with political, economic, and social interests, it is to be expected that there would be significant opposition to both Paul and his Thessalonian converts."[41] This observation refers to the resentment the believers would have felt from their non-Christian neighbors. They are presumed to have elicited anger and to have been perceived as arrogant and antisocial and as disloyal citizens, even to the point of becoming persecuted as Paul indicates throughout the letter, notably in 1 Thess 2:14-16. Another aspect of this distressing social situation would have been the inner difficulties in the thoughts and feelings of the believers as they left behind practices and beliefs they had hitherto taken seriously. Jennifer Houston McNeel has summarized the situation this way:

> After Paul left town, the Thessalonian believers faced the challenges of living in a countercultural manner, specifically the social ostracism that would have resulted from their withdrawal from pagan rituals honoring the gods and the Roman emperor. Given the very group-oriented Mediterranean culture, pressure and persecution from neighbors, severed family ties, and the collapse of business relations had led to a crisis of identity for the Thessalonians.[42]

These aspects of conversion, that is, the personal difficulties for and within the new believer in leaving behind the past, are especially interesting when gender is factored into the considerations. For example, what might be said about how the rejection of idols may on some levels have been a different experience for each gender? Further, one can wonder what Paul's guidance was like as he led the Thessalonians' transition from polytheism to monotheism. How existentially did he understand what he was asking of them? For Paul himself, his own radical transition

41. Weima, *1–2 Thessalonians*, 22.
42. Jennifer Houston McNeel, *Paul as Infant and Nursing Mother: Metaphor, Rhetoric, and Identity in 1 Thessalonians 2:5-8*, ECL 12 (Atlanta, GA: Society of Biblical Literature, 2015), 123.

in belief had been wholly within his lifelong Jewish monotheism; he had moved from his rejection of Jesus as resurrected to his belief that indeed God had raised Jesus, and then of course to adopting the theological implications that came with what he understood the resurrection of Jesus revealed. But to what extent was the intra-monotheistic transition Paul experienced analogous to what his Gentile converts underwent in their radical move from polytheism to monotheism?

Before proceeding on the assumption that Paul's Thessalonian converts were casting aside a web of beliefs in idols and the attendant social practices, however, the consideration could be made that, prior to meeting Paul, they may have already been tending toward monotheism. For example, were the Thessalonians godfearers (converts gradually moving into Judaism) before Paul met them? Acts 17:4 suggests this possibility with its reference to "a great many of the devout Greeks," i.e., presumably godfearers who, having heard Paul and Silas, joined with them. Yet nothing Paul says in 1 Thessalonians suggests that any of the Thessalonian believers already knew much about either Judaism or the Jewish Scriptures.

Still another explanation one could advance is that the Thessalonian converts were disaffected from the pagan religious milieu around them, and therefore were eager for a message such as Paul's. If so, they might easily have become countercultural. Again, nothing in 1 Thessalonians validates any supposition that alienation had been their prior stance. Assuming, therefore, that the group to whom Paul wrote 1 Thessalonians was predominantly Gentile and new to disengaging from polytheistic practices, the task here is to read the text with that in mind, although allowing as well that the Acts 17:4 reference to some few godfearers in the congregation might have some validity.

To explain a rapid, total move from the worship of idols to Christian beliefs it could be surmised that the apocalypticism of Paul's message set forth expectations so imminent and urgent that the conversion the Thessalonians were led into *had* to be completed immediately. Probably they had no realization that their converted status would go on for years, even decades, since they expected the imminent return of the Lord. One could guess they had therefore not thought through the social implications of abandoning their idols for a long future ahead, nor of how they risked local ostracism to the point of persecution. If indeed they had entered into what they envisioned as a short waiting period for the Lord they were still, some months later as Paul wrote, apparently generally maintaining their distance from their cultic past. At the same time, some of Paul's comments, especially as I will note regarding 1 Thess 4:3-8, suggest difficulties they may have continued to face in letting go of past involvements and practices. I will also make suggestions throughout the commentary of possible cultic related practices that may have drawn Christian women in particular into recidivism.

Paul states his own explanation of the Thessalonians' ability to reject their idols in 1 Thess 1:5, noting that the gospel had been communicated "not in word only, but also in power and in the Holy Spirit and with full conviction." For Paul it was "power and . . . the Holy Spirit" that had enabled the believers to become imitators of the three preachers and also to resist the persecution that ensued (1:5-6).

The issue of the Thessalonians' rejection of idols must be pursued further. It is most likely that new converts, who it appears had not debated long over their conversions, would need to be repeatedly reproselytized regarding the former religious practices that had pervaded their social context. As time went on and the Parousia of Jesus (1 Thess 4:13–5:8) had not materialized, and as the social difficulties of their new identities took hold, is not a certain amount of relapse to have been expected?

One could consider as a plausible example whether women would not have had great difficulties remaining withdrawn from cultic ways that had been deeply woven into their female, and in that era fragile, existences, especially practices surrounding childbirth. To assess how hard it may have been for ancient women to give up their prior customs, however, it would help to know what those were. This raises the subject of the cults of Thessalonica, about which information mainly comes from archaeological evidence.

The idols Paul refers to in the city would have ranged across a wide spectrum of deities related to the Greek pantheon, as well as various Egyptian and Roman gods, Roman emperor worship, and the God of the Jews.[43] The paucity of evidence from the ancient city, however, hampers detailed analysis of the cults as well as the levels of popularity and dominance among them. That scarcity is due to the continuous location of the city on the same land occupied by the ancient city[44] and the resulting

---

43. See esp. the survey in Katerina Tzanavari, "The Worship of Gods and Heroes in Thessaloniki," in *Roman Thessaloniki*, ed. D. V. Grammenos (Thessaloniki: Thessaloniki Archaeological Museum, 2003), 177–262.

44. See Laura S. Nasrallah, "Empire and Apocalypse in Thessaloniki: Interpreting the Early Christian Rotunda," *JECS* 13 (2005): 465–508, at 471, who suggests the engaging metaphor that "the cityscape of [modern] Thessaloniki is a palimpsest, where the ancient city underlies and at times emerges into modern Thessaloniki."

destruction of earlier buildings in order to build successive structures.[45] Another decisive factor in the view of Katerina Tzanavari was "the [later] popularity of Christianity, which while incorporating several elements of the earlier, so-called pagan religions, at the same time destroyed their sanctuaries."[46] While the minimal extant material related to the cults of Thessalonica has been scrutinized,[47] it remains uncertain if that mirrors for us which were the major or only cults thriving.[48]

Regardless of which deities they may have been attracted to, the earliest women who converted to Christianity, given their tiny numbers and lack of a wide system of ecclesial support, may have found it very difficult to abandon cultic practices regarding childbirth. Can we put ourselves in their place? As a woman's labor pangs set in and the possibility of difficulties and death confronted her,[49] would she have been able to resist traditional cultic customs? If practices involving amulets, possession of votive figurines, incantations, etc., had "helped" a birthing woman's mother, aunts, sisters, and friends, and were being pressed upon her by them and her midwife during her labor, would it not have seemed risky to resist their accumulated "wisdom" and women's standard practices?[50] Kathy Gaca summarizes what some of the traditions surrounding a birth would have been:

> Eileithyia, Artemis and Hera facilitated pregnant women's risky act of giving birth. At the liminal time of delivery, the midwife and other women assisting in a successful birth cried out a celebratory *ololygê*

---

45. Tzanavari, "The Worship of Gods," 178.

46. Ibid.

47. See, e.g., Karl P. Donfried, *Paul, Thessalonica, and Early Christianity* (Grand Rapids, MI: Eerdmans, 2002), 21–47; Laura S. Nasrallah, Charalambos Bakirtzēs, and Steven J. Friesen, eds., *From Roman to Early Christian Thessalonikē: Studies in Religion and Archaeology*, HTS 64 (Cambridge, MA: Harvard University Press, 2010), xv.

48. There is some hope for additional new archaeological data due to the building of Thessalonica's new subway (to be completed in 2018). As the largest excavation in its history, the underground construction of the six subway stations follows the route of the ancient Via Egnatia. In 2008 workers found more than one thousand graves. The study of information from the graves may be especially helpful regarding women because tomb inscriptions and contents are a major archaeological source for the lives of ancient women, especially the non-elite.

49. See below concerning 5:1-11, pp. 89–91.

50. On the authority accorded to midwives, see Margaret Y. MacDonald, Carolyn Osiek, and Janet Tulloch, *A Woman's Place: House Churches in Earliest Christianity* (Minneapolis: Fortress Press, 2006), 55.

[ὀλολυγή, "ululation"][51] to the goddesses. The critical period of labor, when the one pregnant woman became two viable human beings, or one, or none, was an especially heightened time of the goddesses' perceived presence.[52]

Additionally, midwives dedicated to Lucina (an epithet for Juno), the Roman goddess of childbirth, were known to wrap ribbons around the womb of a mother in labor and to set a place at table to give thanks to Lucina.[53] Beryl Rawson, commenting on data from Roman Italy, has observed that regarding the various divinities and spirits associated with birth and newborns "the origin of much of the ritual and superstition is difficult to establish, but the general thrust seems to be propitiation of superhuman forces, protection of the infant at a time of great danger, and cleansing of pollution."[54]

The transitioning from such "time-tested" practices must have been both daunting and gradual for the very earliest Thessalonian female Christians. It is logical to envision recidivism occurred. Would Paul have been surprised? For their later sisters and daughters it no doubt became easier as the group's numbers increased, social support became more widespread and females grew up within the already believing community. Paul's statement in 1 Thess 1:9 about turning from idols can be read both as hopefully prescriptive but also perhaps as reflecting his admiration for those of his Thessalonian converts who really had fully confirmed their leap into monotheism, including perhaps some courageous females who, as they gave birth, called on only the "living and true God" (1:9).

51. Ululation (from Latin *ululare*, "to howl") involved loud, high-pitched trilling; it was a very emotional wailing, usually invoking a god, and was performed by women at both times of joy and times of sorrow. This form of wailing is still practiced in many cultures. On Paul and ululation, see below, pp. 79–80, regarding 4:13.

52. Kathy L. Gaca, "Early Christian Antipathy toward the Greek 'Women Gods,'" in *Finding Persephone: Women's Rituals in the Ancient Mediterranean*, ed. Maryline G. Parca and Angeliki Tzanetou (Bloomington: Indiana University Press, 2007), 280.

53. Ibid., 285.

54. Beryl Rawson, *Children and Childhood in Roman Italy* (Oxford and New York: Oxford University Press, 2003), 109.

1 Thessalonians 2

Your Abandoned Nursing Goddess Has Been Replaced

Having expressed abundant thanksgivings for the faith of the Thessalonians, Paul next reflects on what his behavior and that of Silvanus and Timothy had been like during that initial evangelization. He indicates that it took courage for the three missionaries to preach to the Thessalonians after the mistreatment they had endured in Philippi (1 Thess 2:2). Does this suggest that in their travels between Philippi and Thessalonica they had undertaken no other proselytizing? That would accord with Acts 17:1, which states they had merely passed through Amphipolis[1] and Appollonia on the way to Thessalonica. It could also imply not only

---

1. It is often pointed out that a famous landmark statue along the journey to Thessalonica, which Paul and his companions would have seen, was the Lion of Amphipolis. Some have argued the Lion was the crowning point of the nearby Kasta Hill, a huge burial mound, although that continues to be debated. In 2014 Greek archaeologists excavating at Kasta Hill opened an extraordinary burial structure, now referred to as the Amphipolis Tomb; it has been dated to the last quarter of the fourth century BCE. That period correlates with the era of Thessalonike and Cassander. See above, pp. 12–15. While the remains of the five people found in the tomb are still undergoing analysis, it was assumed they were members of the Macedonian nobility. See, e.g., *The Amphipolis Tomb: Photos, news and map of the great Tomb in Amphipolis, Greece*; www.theamphipolistomb.com.

41

1 Thess 2:1-20

²:¹You yourselves know, brothers and sisters, that our coming to you was not in vain, ²but though we had already suffered and been shamefully mistreated at Philippi, as you know, we had courage in our God to declare to you the gospel of God in spite of great opposition. ³For our appeal does not spring from deceit or impure motives or trickery, ⁴but just as we have been approved by God to be entrusted with the message of the gospel, even so we speak, not to please mortals, but to please God who tests our hearts. ⁵As you know and as God is our witness, we never came with words of flattery or with a pretext for greed; ⁶nor did we seek praise from mortals, whether from you or from others, ⁷though we might have made demands as apostles of Christ. But we were gentle among you, like a nurse tenderly caring for her own children. ⁸So deeply do we care for you that we are determined to share with you not only the gospel of God but also our own selves, because you have become very dear to us.

⁹You remember our labor and toil, brothers and sisters; we worked night and day, so that we might not burden any of you while we proclaimed to you the gospel of God. ¹⁰You are witnesses, and God also, how pure, upright, and blameless our conduct was toward you believers. ¹¹As you know, we dealt with each one of you like a father with his

that the three left Philippi as fugitives from danger,² hurrying anywhere westward the Via Egnatia might lead them, but rather that they knew they were headed to Thessalonica. Was that because they had anticipated contacts to look up there, perhaps Lydia's network as suggested above?³

In drawing an apparent contrast with other itinerant preachers who aimed to influence their audiences, Paul says his purpose in preaching the gospel is to please God (1 Thess 2:2-4). He denies acting out of impure motives, or using deceit, trickery, and flattery (2:5-6). Rather, he, Silvanus, and Timothy actually had to summon the courage to speak the gospel with such faithfulness that God would witness with approval. One is surprised to notice that Paul then says they might have made demands as "apostles of Christ," not as "apostles of God." The genitive "of Christ" here is best understood as objective, i.e., they were apostles,⁴ teachers commissioned by God, to teach *about* Christ. Paul thus defines the content

2. Paul's mention of their difficulties in Philippi also agrees generally with Acts 16:16-39, although in 1 Thessalonians he does not describe actual incidents as Acts does.

3. See p. 32.

4. See Raymond F. Collins, *Accompanied by a Believing Wife: Ministry and Celibacy in the Earliest Christian Communities* (Collegeville, MN: Liturgical Press, 2013), 94, who notes that for Paul "apostle" was a title and a function: "It applies to early Christian

children, ¹²urging and encouraging you and pleading that you lead a life worthy of God, who calls you into his own kingdom and glory.

¹³We also constantly give thanks to God for this, that when you received the word of God that you heard from us, you accepted it not as a human word but as what it really is, God's word, which is also at work in you believers. ¹⁴For you, brothers and sisters, became imitators of the churches of God in Christ Jesus that are in Judea, for you suffered the same things from your own compatriots as they did from the Jews, ¹⁵who killed both the Lord Jesus and the prophets, and drove us out; they displease God and oppose everyone ¹⁶by hindering us from speaking to the Gentiles so that they may be saved. Thus they have constantly been filling up the measure of their sins; but God's wrath has overtaken them at last.

¹⁷As for us, brothers and sisters, when, for a short time, we were made orphans by being separated from you—in person, not in heart—we longed with great eagerness to see you face to face. ¹⁸For we wanted to come to you—certainly I, Paul, wanted to again and again—but Satan blocked our way. ¹⁹For what is our hope or joy or crown of boasting before our Lord Jesus at his coming? Is it not you? ²⁰Yes, you are our glory and joy!

of the gospel of God as Christ himself. A bit further in the text Paul commends the Thessalonians because, on their part, they accepted the gospel of Christ, that is, the word of God, "not as a human word but as . . . God's word" (2:13). Concerning this human/divine dynamic, Jan Lambrecht has observed: "Of course, human response and acceptance are needed. Yet, God's initiative possesses, as it were, an irresistible dynamic. . . . The powerful, effective word of God . . . is at work and remains compellingly active in the believers and, through them, in the world."⁵

From having mentioned various negative dimensions that could have characterized his initial encounter with the Thessalonians, Paul turns to what their interaction was actually like. In expressing the emotions he himself had felt (1 Thess 2:7-8), he draws on the feminine image of a nursing mother, applying it to himself, Silvanus, and Timothy. Strangely, this metaphor (technically a simile) suggests a female role for three men since τροφός ("wet nurse" or "nurse") is a feminine noun, a term Paul never uses elsewhere. Also puzzling is that the image used for three men

---

missionaries who were sent out to preach the Gospel in Jesus' name and in that way lay the foundation for a church, a gathering of believers."

5. Jan Lambrecht, "Thanksgivings in 1 Thessalonians 1–3," in *Thessalonian Correspondence*, ed. Raymond F. Collins, BETL 87 (Louvain: Leuven University Press, 1990), 205.

is of a single nurse, even though Paul in the same sentence had been using the nominative plural. Why did he not write "we were like nurses caring for our own children"? Even had he done that, however, we would still wonder about the choice of a feminine image.

In the immediate context, Paul expresses his intention in 1 Thess 2:6 and 9 that he would not be a burden to anyone. Did the image of a wet nurse perhaps fit that concern? Is the wet nurse an example of someone who worked "night and day" (2:9) as did Paul and his companions? And, did Paul, as a male, default to using a feminine image in order to express gentleness? It may additionally be noted that in 1 Thessalonians the strong personal tone of Paul's writing and the interrelationship between Paul, Silvanus, and Timothy with the Thessalonians receives some highlighting due to the use of ἑαυτοῦ. As Raymond Collins has pointed out, this reflexive pronoun appears many times in Paul's description of his visit to Thessalonica, precisely in passages "where Paul uses warm language to describe the intensity of affect that bound him and his companions to the Thessalonians" (see 2:7, 8, 11, 12).[6] This includes the nurse with her children metaphor in 2:7 where he modifies children, τέκνα, with the reflexive, i.e., "her own children."

Yet another observation is that Paul's use of feminine imagery in 1 Thess 2:7 is subsequently paralleled in the next few verses with a masculine image. Paul compares his and his companions' relationship to the believers with a father (again in the singular) relating to his children: "As you know, we dealt with each one of you like a father with his children" (2:11).[7] Yet, if the τροφός Paul envisions is a hired or slave wet nurse, these parallel female and male familial images may be asymmetrical.[8] A wet nurse would be of a lower social class than the metaphorical father, in this case the three missionaries, since the implication is that he has power over the family.[9]

---

6. Raymond F. Collins, *The Birth of the New Testament: The Origin and Development of the First Christian Generation* (New York: Crossroad, 1993), 18.

7. See Beverly Roberts Gaventa, *Our Mother Saint Paul* (Louisville, KY: Westminster John Knox, 2007), 6–7, for a comparison between Paul's use of maternal and paternal imagery throughout his letters.

8. For Paul to cast himself as a wet nurse would be effectively to identify with a female slave or a very low-paid free woman. See Jennifer Houston McNeel, *Paul as Infant and Nursing Mother: Metaphor, Rhetoric, and Identity in 1 Thessalonians 2:5-8*, ECL 12 (Atlanta, GA: Society of Biblical Literature, 2015), 138, who comments that for Paul to associate himself with such a figure "is not insignificant to understanding his character and his theology."

9. On Paul's use of paternal imagery, see esp. Trevor J. Burke, *Family Matters: A Socio-Historical Study of Kinship Metaphors in 1 Thessalonians*, JSNTSup 247 (London and New York: T & T Clark International, 2003), 148–51.

Regarding the image itself, τροφός comes from the verb τρέφω, meaning "to nurse, to feed." When taken with the phrase τὰ ἑαυτῆς τέκνα, it has been argued that the feeding is of the nurse's own children, with the implication that a mother nursing her own child has a greater depth of feeling for the infant than would a wet nurse merely performing her duty. But it has been countered that the reflexive ἑαυτῆς no longer had such an emphatic meaning and simply meant "her." It has also been argued that the use of θάλπω, meaning "to comfort, to cherish" adds a hint of affection so that the ἑαυτῆς should be understood precisely to mean "that Paul and colleagues act more like a nurse [i.e., a mother] towards her own children, than a nanny toward those under her charge."[10]

On the other hand, if the image in Paul's mind was of a wet nurse,[11] we can consider some illuminating comments about wet nurses from a medical manual titled *Gynecology*, written by Soranus, a Greek physician from Ephesus who practiced in Alexandria and Rome.[12] Writing in the latter half of the first century CE, he presented a vast amount of information about pregnancy, birth, and new infant care, including instructions about choosing wet nurses:

> One should choose a wet nurse not younger than twenty nor older than forty years, who has already given birth twice or thrice, who is healthy, of good habitus, of large frame, and of good color. . . . She should be self-controlled, sympathetic and not ill-tempered, a Greek, and tidy. . . . She should be in her prime because younger women are ignorant in the rearing of children and their minds are still somewhat careless and childish . . . for everything else being equal, milk from large bodies is more nourishing.[13]

10. Earl J. Richard, *First and Second Thessalonians*, SP 11 (Collegeville, MN: Liturgical Press, 1995), 83.

11. For comments on wet nursing, see Margaret Y. MacDonald, Carolyn Osiek, and Janet Tulloch, *A Woman's Place: House Churches in Earliest Christianity* (Minneapolis: Fortress Press, 2006), 65; Beryl Rawson, *Children and Childhood in Roman Italy* (Oxford and New York: Oxford University Press, 2003), 120–25.

12. Soranus, *Soranus' Gynecology*, trans. Owsei Temkin (Baltimore, MD: Johns Hopkins University Press, 1956; repr., 1991).

13. Ibid., 90–91. Soranus's concerns about choosing a wet nurse may be compared with a critique of education by Tacitus (written ca. 100 CE). See Cornelius Tacitus, "Dialogue on Oratory," in *The Complete Works of Tacitus*, ed. Moses Hadas, trans. Alfred John Church and William Jackson Brodribb (New York: Modern Library, 1942), 29: "In our day we entrust the infant to a little Greek servant-girl who is attended by one or two, commonly the worst of all the slaves, creatures utterly unfit for any important work. Their stories and their prejudices from the very first fill the child's

Soranus's advice may represent an ideal, however, since most practices regarding birth and newborn care remained in the hands of midwives for whom, like most of their contemporaries, "superstition, magic and religion continued to play a large part in general thinking about health."[14]

Before speculating about *why* Paul chose the imagery, a complicating text-critical issue in 1 Thess 2:7 must be noted. Within the phrase the NRSV renders as "we were gentle [ἤπιοι] among you, like a nurse tenderly caring for her own children," some manuscripts have the variant noun νήπιοι ("children" or "infants"), leading to wording that could be rendered as "we were infants among you, like a nurse tenderly caring for her own children." Without plunging into the detailed arguments over this *crux interpretem*, suffice it to say that exegetes generally agree that νήπιοι, especially on the basis of manuscript history, must have been the original reading. But, particularly on the basis of internal coherence,[15] the reading ἤπιοι is the text underlying most modern English translations. This preference overcomes the problem of a mixed metaphor within one sentence and is consistent with Paul's image of a nurse caring for her children. The reading ἤπιοι also intensifies the sense of maternal care that Paul's τροφός image communicates. As Collins observes, it is likewise "consistent with the moralist's description of the ideal philosopher with which Paul's autobiographical confession in 2:1-12 has so many similarities."[16] Yet, reflecting the obvious persuasiveness of both sides in this debate, he further points out that an original reading of νήπιοι remains defendable, possibly if taken as a vocative, but also when explained as Paul shifting his metaphors, which would not be unusual for him.

Approaching the Greek text from a different syntactical angle, Gordon Fee favors the reading νήπιοι, commenting that the evidence for ἤπιοι is so much weaker than it is for νήπιοι with the result that "under ordinary circumstances no living scholar would accept the former reading [ἤπιοι] as original."[17] For Fee, however, that difficulty of fitting the mixed metaphor of infants and nurse/nursing mother in the same sentence is over-

---

tender and uninstructed mind. No one in the whole house cares what he says or does before his infant master."

14. Rawson, *Children*, 98.

15. See, e.g., Joel Delobel, "One Letter Too Many in Paul's First Letter? A Study of (N)Epioi in 1 Thess 2:7," *LS* 20 (1995): 131, who judges on the level of intrinsic probability that νήπιοι in the end is a *lectio impossibilis*.

16. Collins, *The Birth*, 27.

17. Gordon D. Fee, *The First and Second Letters to the Thessalonians*, NICNT (Grand Rapids, MI: Eerdmans, 2009), 70.

come by his punctuation of the Greek text differently from, for example, the NRSV. While the phrases of 1 Thess 2:7b and 2:7c constitute a sentence in the NRSV, Fee prefers to see 2:7b as the end of the sentence containing 2:7a; he then takes 2:7c as beginning another sentence. He therefore favors reading 2:7 (as in the TNIV): "even though as apostles of Christ we could have asserted our prerogatives. But we were like young children among you. Just as a nursing mother cares for her children."[18] Other scholars favor a similar approach,[19] namely, that Paul uses νήπιοι as his image of comparison to end one thought and then indeed switches to another metaphor using the wet nurse/nursing mother language. Paul would thus be indicating, in contrast with negative charges sometimes made against, for example, wandering philosophers, that the identity of the three missionaries as "apostles of Christ" (2:7) was metaphorically as infants. "They were innocent characters, lacking the guile and deceit of a charlatan."[20]

Perhaps the most intriguing issue regarding Paul's τροφός metaphor is to ask *why* he chose the comparison. A recently expressed rationale comes from Jennifer Houston McNeel.

> Paul's infant [she favors the reading νήπιοι] and nurse metaphors in 2:7 serve his overall rhetorical goals in the letter by presenting Paul to the Thessalonians as an innocent infant and an affectionate and trustworthy mother, and presenting the Thessalonians to one another as a kinship group. . . . The metaphors serve to strengthen the community in the midst of persecution and social hostility.[21]

In prior decades, however, a theory promoted by Abraham Malherbe has been widely regarded as persuasive. In a 1970 publication,[22] Malherbe demonstrated similarities between Paul's description of his ministry in 1 Thess 2:1-12 and the picture sketched, for example, by the Cynic philosopher Dio Chrysostom (40–120 CE?) of himself and his work in his *Discourses (Orationes)*. Malherbe concluded that different types of Cynics

18. Ibid., 54, 72.
19. See the especially detailed studies of Beverly Roberts Gaventa, *Our Mother Saint Paul* (Louisville, KY: Westminster John Knox, 2007), 17–28; McNeel, *Paul as Infant*, 35–47; Jeffrey A. D. Weima, *1–2 Thessalonians*, BECNT (Grand Rapids, MI: Baker Academic, 2014), 180–87.
20. Gaventa, *Our Mother*, 26.
21. McNeel, *Paul as Infant*, 173.
22. Abraham J. Malherbe, " 'Gentle as a Nurse': The Cynic Background to I Thess 2," *NovT* 12 (1970): 203–17.

wandering about constituted "the context within which Paul describes his activity in Thessalonica."[23] Malherbe wrote: "Dio emphasizes that the philosopher, in spite of personal danger, seeks to benefit his hearers by adapting his message to their situation, and being kinder to them individually than even a father. He represents the view that the philosopher should not consistently be harsh . . . but should on occasion be gentle . . . as a nurse."[24] In his later commentary, Malherbe reiterated this same approach regarding Paul's language throughout 2:1-12: "In this self-description he makes use of language he borrowed from the popular philosophers of his day and adapts it according to his own self-understanding and the needs of his readers."[25] As to why Paul drew on the image, Malherbe states that "the comparison with a nurse is thus made in the first place to describe the deliberate decision to deal with the Thessalonians in a certain manner,"[26] namely, with much gentleness.

Malherbe's explanation has been widely adopted to illuminate Paul's use of the strange feminine metaphor for himself, Silvanus, and Timothy. For example, Pheme Perkins has observed regarding 1 Thess 2:1-12: "Paul depicts himself as the true philosopher guide, concerned for the welfare of his charges. . . . As examples from other male philosophers demonstrate, this image refers to the type of teacher who tries to adapt his words to the circumstances of his hearers."[27] From a feminist perspective Perkins also makes the additional observation (moving beyond the consideration of philosophers alone): "Evidence from later periods shows that males often identify with female saints or feminine characteristics when a religious conversion leads them to abandon honors or distinctions they might have gained by competing with other males in larger societies."[28]

Malherbe's suggestion that Paul stylized himself as a nurse under the influence of the self-presentation of various philosophers has been critiqued by Beverly Roberts Gaventa. She states that in a number of texts Malherbe cites the nurse is actually viewed negatively. What seems significant to me, an issue I will return to below, is that Gaventa also

23. Ibid., 217.
24. Ibid.
25. Abraham J. Malherbe, The *Letters to the Thessalonians: A New Translation with Introduction and Commentary*, AB 32B (New York: Doubleday, 2000), 134.
26. Ibid., 146.
27. Pheme Perkins, "1 Thessalonians," in *The Women's Bible Commentary*, ed. Carol A. Newsom and Sharon H. Ringe (Louisville, KY: Westminster John Knox, 1992), 440.
28. Ibid.

notes that the word τροφός, "nurse," was not used in the texts to which
Malherbe points. "Uniformly these texts employ the term τιθή ('wet
nurse') for the individual described."[29]

Gaventa's assessment is that while Malherbe has identified a *topos*,
contrasting ideal philosophers with charlatans, it is not evident that a
nurse's behavior had a consistently fixed place in the *topos*. She suggests
that a more helpful approach for understanding Paul's image is to examine how the nurse was perceived in the social context. Her conclusion,
based on the examination of a range of relevant literary texts, is that Paul's
metaphor would recall for his audience a beloved person, "a well-known
figure in the ancient world, one identified not only with the nurture of
infants but also with continued affection for her charges well into
adulthood."[30] Gaventa also points out, as have numerous other
interpreters,[31] that Num 11:12 may also have influenced Paul's choice of
the nurse metaphor.[32] In that text Moses complains to the Lord: "Did I
conceive all this people? Did I give birth to them, that you should say to
me, 'Carry them in your bosom, as a nurse carries a sucking child,' to the
land that you promised on oath to our ancestors?" However, that literary
link is weak considering that in 1 Thessalonians Paul does not appear to
cast himself in a role comparable to that of Moses. Also to be noted is that
the LXX term for the nurse in Num 11:12 is τιθηνός, not τροφός.

I would suggest that there is additional material to bring into this
discussion of why Paul seized upon the imagery of a nursing mother for
himself and his two companions, namely, the subject of nursing goddesses. This proposal needs to be prefaced by reiterating that Paul had
observed in 1 Thess 1:9 that the Thessalonians had turned from idols.
There is no doubt that would have been an enormous shift for them and
was likely an ongoing subject of daily conversation for Paul when evangelizing among the Gentiles, even to the point of inciting local controversy.[33] Certainly an element of Paul's catechesis of the Thessalonians

29. Gaventa, *Our Mother*, 22.
30. Ibid., 24–25.
31. See, e.g., McNeel, *Paul as Infant*, 108–10.
32. Gaventa, *Our Mother*, 24.
33. With respect to creating tumult regarding deities, see Acts 19:23-41. To the extent
that narrative may validly reflect the social troubles Paul's missionizing could create,
it describes a development in Ephesus according to which Paul was accused of saying that "gods made with hands are not gods" (19:26), i.e., Paul was preaching against
there being any power in "silver shrines" of Artemis (19:24). Since Acts describes
there having been "no little business" (19:24) for the artisans from whom Paul had

was a denial of the reality of their former gods and goddesses, including denying any power ascribed to or represented by the votive figurines or amulets of those deities. In light of that, one must also consider that Paul and his companions would have simultaneously employed a strategy of replacement, with attempts to suggest new slants on old concepts and substitutions for what was being discarded. As has been widely observed, Paul argued against imperial propaganda with concepts that not only denied its slogans but adopted and reinterpreted them. Presumably a similar teaching process took place as he attempted to explain away the Thessalonians' former deities. For example, in preaching to the Thessalonians that goddesses do not exist, much less nurture humans, Paul may have stressed that humans are actually nurtured by the gospel of God, and that he, a mere human, was God's vehicle, a τροφός, to bring the true gospel sustenance to them. Regarding Paul's self-perception as a nurturer, we might also note that later in 1 Cor 3:2 he wrote, "I fed you with milk [γάλα], not solid food, for you were not ready for solid food." Paul uses γάλα as a metaphor for the spiritual food his kerygma provided for the Corinthians. Therefore, it is quite possible that Paul used the image of a nurse for himself in order to reinterpret or co-opt the roles and terminology connected with goddesses who were patrons of nursing mothers. This suspicion is strengthened by recalling that archaeologists have unearthed troves of ancient votive figurines and amulets, many of which were small nursing mother statuettes known as κουροτρόφοι.[34]

The verb κουροτροφέω means "to raise children." Κοῦρος, a variant of the term κόρος, "boy," and τροφεύω, "to nurse," means "to raise children, to be child nourishing"; the compound noun thus effectively denotes a nursing mother. *Kourotrophos*, pl. *kourotrophoi*, as the terms are used in English, was also an epithet for certain female goddesses, viewed either as mothers themselves or as virgins raising youths. In Latin the equivalent of *kourotrophos* is *nutrix*, pl. *nutrices*, designating a woman's breast or a wet nurse. The numerous goddesses considered to be *kourotrophoi* or *nutrices* (the Latin term is used in English) were represented holding or nursing an infant, e.g., often in the form of small statuettes. The *kou-*

---

persuaded away "a considerable number of people" (19:26), the silver shrines against which Paul railed must have been small objects produced in volume, perhaps votive figurines or amulets.

34. See esp. Theodora Hadzisteliou Price, *Kourotrophos: Cults and Representations of the Greek Nursing Deities*, Studies of the Dutch Archaeological and Historical Society (Leiden: Brill, 1978).

rotrophos or *nutrix* is also sometimes portrayed as a wife-goddess along with the god with whom she has procreated and their infant. Many *kourotrophoi* statuettes are also representations of mortal women carrying their infants to the goddess. These latter statuettes of mortal *kourotrophoi* "were often votive offerings in sanctuaries of nursing deities."[35] Cults developed to such specific protective mother goddesses. Those cults are often reflected in dedications on reliefs and in terra-cotta statuettes of nursing goddesses, which women may have possessed as amulets or used in cultic situations.

From Thessalonica itself in a 1998 excavation in Ano Poli (as the steep north area of the city is known today) at least two *kourotrophoi* and perhaps fragments of more can be recognized among the more than 1,500 terra-cotta fragments of female figurines from the late Hellenistic and early Roman periods unearthed there.[36] The two large dumps of fragments have been assessed to be "remains of votives offered in a nearby sanctuary."[37] Georgios Mallios's analysis of the fragments has led him to conclude that, because of the presence of the *kourotrophoi*, the sanctuary where they were found may well have been "connected with the practicing of a kourotrophic cult."[38] Maillios was unable to be conclusive about which female deity was worshiped at the sanctuary from the first half of the third century BCE until the end of the first century CE, although he outlines many compelling reasons that it may have been a Nymphaion.[39]

Because the dating of a large number of fragments suggests the popularity of the cult both before and during Paul's time in Thessalonica, it may be surmised Paul had to argue regularly against female believers participating there. It is quite possible that Paul's use of the nursing mother metaphor, and specifically his unusual use of the term τροφός itself, hints at something about his preaching against Christian women's kourotrophic participation at the popular shrine upon the hill of Ano Poli.

Related to this discussion of *kourotrophoi*, I suggest there is further evidence that is possibly enlightening concerning Paul's reference to a nursing mother. This data comes from a region of the eastern Roman Empire to the north of Thessalonica. It was found in and near Roman

35. Ibid., x.
36. See Georgios K. Mallios, "A Hellenistic Sanctuary at Ano Poli, Thessalonica: The Terra Cotta Figurines," *Egnatia* 8 (2004): 239–66.
37. Ibid., 240.
38. Ibid., 243.
39. Ibid., 262–64.

Poetovio in the area of ancient Illyricum known as Pannonia, now in Slovenia, in a section of the city of Ptuj, now called Zgornji Breg. There, a local Celtic cult of the Nutrices Augustae, "the august nurses," was practiced.[40] The evidence analyzed from Poetovio reveals that the *nutrices* in some of the iconography were venerated in a plural form, most often portrayed as three women, although only one of them, the goddess, holds and breast-feeds the baby; the two others may be servants, or Nymphs.[41] These nursing goddesses probably reflect influence from Celtic *Matres* and *Matronae* traditions (which frequently represented motherhood with triads of figures), a development from when Celtic tribes settled there. Yet, others have proposed that the cult of the *nutrices* reflects instead influence coming from Greek kourotrophic practices.[42]

In considering the possible impact of *kourotrophoi* and *nutrices* when surmising why Paul referred to himself and his two companions as a nursing mother, it must be underscored that Paul would have argued regularly against the goddess cults. His battles against certain idols, particularly when women were in fear as they faced childbirth and as parents were desperate to nourish weak and dying children, must have been very uphill (maybe literally, thinking of Ano Poli). Paul had to co-opt the significance, the roles, the power, and even the terminology of the *kourotrophoi*. He needed to displace the nursing goddess to whom mothers turned by becoming her.

Further, it is also quite possible that within Macedonia itself cultic influences coming from Illyria had taken hold, perhaps imported into the area by the Roman army and their entourages.[43] If, by such an avenue, worship of the *nutrices* and the iconography of three females representing one goddess and two helpers had been introduced into Thessalonica, this might suggest why Paul used the singular form of τροφός to speak of himself, Silvanus, and Timothy. The subtext of Paul's τροφός metaphor could be that three men needed to supplant a popular *nutrice*.

---

40. See esp. the chapter "Nutrices Augustae Deae" with extensive photographs in Marjeta Šašel Kos, *Pre-Roman Divinities of the Eastern Alps and Adriatic, Dissertationes Musei Nationalis Sloveniae* (Ljubljana: Narodni Muzej Slovenije, 1999), 153–92.

41. Ibid., 180. See further 180–84 for a complete survey of the variations in the iconography. Also see esp. *LIMC* 6.2 (Zürich: Artemis, 1981–), plates 620–21, which show seven examples of votive reliefs of *nutrices*.

42. See the full discussion of influences in Šašel Kos, *Pre-Roman Divinities*, 187–88.

43. Roman Poetovio, a vibrant military base and flourishing city throughout the Roman Principate, is known to have been very cosmopolitan. See ibid., 153.

As Paul continues in 1 Thess 2:8-11 to describe what the missionaries were like among the Thessalonians, he reflects that the integrity of the minister is to be verified by witnesses on two levels: the community of people served and God (2:10). It is striking that Paul in his own context stressed how pure, upright, and blameless he, Silvanus, and Timothy were. That Paul found it necessary to do this indicates he was aware that it was not unheard of for newcomers in a place, as he had already alluded to in previous comments, to use their skills of flattery, motivated by deceit, impure motives, or the intent to trick their listeners, to their own advantage. Paul underscores how the qualities of being "pure, upright, and blameless" were lived out by elaborating in his next statement (2:11) that he and his co-workers had dealt with the believers "like a father with his children." He qualifies his image of a father with the ideas of urging, encouraging, and pleading (2:12).

In 1 Thess 2:14-16 Paul abruptly shifts from kinship imagery, such as a nursing mother or wet nurse, a father, and children, to a puzzling set of thoughts about persecution. Before commenting on 2:14-16, it may be noted that in 2:17 Paul returns to a final familial image when he compares how separation from the believers in Thessalonica had made him and his co-workers feel like orphans. Commentators debate the translation of the participle ἀπορφανισθέντες (from the verb ἀπορφανίζω, found only here in the NT). Since the literal meaning of the term is "to make an orphan of someone," Paul implies that the trio "had been made orphans." This same Greek term, however, can also refer to a parent separated from his or her children. Given Paul's other metaphors in this chapter, both translations, as a bereft parent or as an abandoned child, have been defended as resonating with the other familial imagery.[44]

With the use of the orphan or bereft parent image, Paul rounds out the range of familial comparisons employed in this chapter. It appears he drew on this metaphor cluster as a deliberate move in the face of the community's struggle with persecution and shaken social identity. Was it the thought of strain on his converts' kinship relations and the ensuing tensions that caused Paul to insert comments about the local persecution in 2:13-16? Those verses fit so awkwardly within his expressions of familial ties that some have regarded them as a post-Pauline interpolation. The seeming anti-Jewishness of 2:14-16 has also been cited as an indication the words cannot have been from Paul.

---

44. See the discussion summarized in McNeel, *Paul as Infant*, 38–42.

Without repeating the detailed arguments here,[45] a few salient points may be noted. First, in the manuscript history of 1 Thessalonians these verses are always found. Also, in spite of the disjointed sense a reader initially experiences *vis à vis* 2:13-16, the text can be related to Paul's thought at that point, as will be explained below. Further, assertions that Paul would not have written a text expressing anti-Judaism have also been countered by noting that 2:13-16 are not about all Jews but rather about certain Jews who persecuted other Jews in Judea.

Sunday Readings from 1 Thessalonians

Roman Missal Lectionary for Mass		Revised Common Lectionary	
1 Thess 1:1-5b	29th Sunday A	1 Thess 1:1-10	Proper 24 (29) A
1 Thess 1:5c-10	30th Sunday A	1 Thess 2:1-8	Proper 25 (30) A
1 Thess 2:7b-9, 13	31st Sunday A	1 Thess 2:9-13	Proper 26 (31) A
1 Thess 3:12-4:2	1st Advent C	1 Thess 3: 9-13	1st Advent C
1 Thess 4:13-18	32nd Sunday A	1 Thess 4:13-18	Proper 27 (32) A
1 Thess 5:1-6	33rd Sunday A	1 Thess 5:1-11	Proper 28 (33) A
1 Thess 5:16-24	3rd Advent B	1 Thess 5:16-24	3rd Advent B

Lectionaries establish a canon within the canon and determine what churchgoing Christians hear when they worship. The Roman Missal Lectionary and Revised Common Lectionary are three-year tables for Catholic and many mainline Protestant and Anglican churches. These tables appoint nearly identical passages from 1 Thessalonians. With one exception, they assign essentially the same lesson for the same occasion, although often the Revised Common Lectionary provides more comprehensive selections.

Concerns about the three-year lectionaries focus on two issues:

Some passages convey negative understandings of Jews and Judaism while many biblical women and female images are omitted. This sidebar centers on what is included, excluded, or of interest pertaining to these concerns in the Sunday readings from 1 Thessalonians.

The NABRE translates *adelphoi* as brothers (1:2; 2:1, 14, 17; 3:2, 7; 4:1, 6, 10, 13; 5:1, 4, 14, 25, 26). Many sense this reinforces the idea that 1 Thessalonians was addressed exclusively to men. However, Catholic pulpit lectionaries print all selections with ἀδελφοί as "brothers and sisters" so that proclamations are

---

45. See the recent detailed survey of scholarship on this issue in Weima, *1–2 Thessalonians*, 41–46.

heard inclusively. Churches that use the Revised Common Lectionary tend to use the New Revised Standard Version or the Common English Bible that already render ἀδελφοί as brothers and sisters. It is heartwarming that these lectionaries include the passage where Paul describes his care of the Thessalonians as a nursing mother (1 Thess 2:7) to illuminate the depth of his devotion to his converts with a female image.

While many consider 1 Thess 2:14-15 an addition to Paul's letter, these verses are part of the canonical text. It is fortuitous that this passage was omitted from the lectionaries because it accuses the Jews of killing Jesus. (Although some Jewish religious authorities brought Jesus to the

attention of the Romans, the Romans, not the Jews, executed Jesus.) Also, the passage declares Jews "do not please God and are opposed to everyone" and has the potential to convey negative understandings of Jews and Judaism today.

Paul's paraenesis includes a concern about sexual immorality (1 Thess 4:3-8) that would make no sense unless he believed this was a problem among the men in Thessalonica. The passage is not among the Sunday readings although this teaching would speak to the present promiscuity of contemporary western societies. These verses are included in the weekday reading(s) of both lectionaries.

Regina Boisclair

First Thessalonians 2:13-16 issue from Paul's thought in the midst of the cluster of kinship metaphors previously discussed. As Paul asserts the new bonds he and his converts share, he could not help but think of the flip side of what their conversions had entailed: fractured familial and other social and cultural bonds causing untold problems for the believers, even persecution. It is not surprising, then, that his thought shifts, albeit abruptly, even disjointedly, to comparing events he was aware of in Judea with what had happened to the Thessalonians in their city.

Some commentators hold that Paul's thought in 1 Thess 2:13-16 may be illuminated through a postcolonial interpretation.[46] From that perspective Paul is understood to have been aware that he was spreading a subversive movement that was "an alternative to the Roman imperial order,"[47] which, as he saw it, was subject to God's negative judgment.

46. See above regarding 1:1, p. 26, and below regarding 5:1-11, pp. 86–88. On the intersection of feminist and postcolonial analyses, see, e.g., Marchal, *Politics*, 4–10.

47. Abraham Smith, "'Unmasking the Powers': Toward a Post-Colonial Analysis of 1 Thessalonians," in *Paul and the Roman Imperial Order*, ed. Richard A. Horsley (Harrisburg, PA: Trinity Press International, 2004), 47–66, at 47–48.

Paul's critique is seen as lodged against the pro-Roman elite in Thessalonica who had successfully sought Roman favor. Abraham Smith points out that "there is ample literary, numismatic, epigraphic, and statuary evidence for a rich history of honor given to the Romans by the city of Thessalonica and particular figures of wealth and power."[48] Those data make it clear that imperial ideology, including various forms of emperor cults, would have been rampant in Thessalonica. From this perspective Paul draws an analogy in 2:13-16 in which he is probably critiquing the oppression caused by the pro-Roman powerful in Thessalonica by comparing them with the negative impact of the pro-Roman elite in Judea.[49]

As of the year 50, when Paul was writing 1 Thessalonians, he had no doubt remained informed about political events in Judea; Acts 15, if accurate, suggests he would have recently been updated during his presence in Jerusalem for the circumcision debate there. Prior to that, Paul's own firsthand experience of the Judean elite would have been during the mid-30s at the time of Stephen's death, and during whatever years he may have studied in Jerusalem (again if the information coming from Acts is reliable). It is unknown where Paul was when John the Baptist was executed and Jesus was killed. In his comments in 2:14-16, did he have recent events closer to 50 in mind as well? Certainly decades of reports and gossip about the actions and lifestyles of the powerful Roman-enamored ruling clients, the Herodian elite[50] of the province of Judea and the broader region, would have fueled any anti-imperialistic tendencies Paul had. But to delve into that here is too long a story.

48. Ibid., 57.
49. Ibid., 60.
50. On the death of the Baptist and the Herodian upper class from the perspective of the Herodian women, see, e.g., Florence Morgan Gillman, *Herodias: At Home in That Fox's Den* (Collegeville, MN: Liturgical Press, 2003).

1 Thessalonians 3

Forget Demeter and Isis—Even If Most Women Rely on Them

In 1 Thessalonians 3, Paul recalls how he decided in Athens to send Timothy back to Thessalonica and how Timothy had just then caught up with him in Corinth. Paul describes Timothy's report as good news, and then again (as in 1:6; 2:2, 14-16) he returns to the issue of persecution (1 Thess 3:3). He comments on what he himself had experienced and the difficulties the Thessalonians had been enduring. Earlier in 2:18 Paul had mentioned being blocked from returning to the believers by "the Satan" (ὁ σατανᾶς) who in 3:5 he calls "the Tempter" (ὁ πειράζων), that is, the one capable of luring the Thessalonians into apostasy. In theologically relating the persecutions of both the Thessalonians and himself to the same evil power, Paul encourages the believers to see their suffering as "a small manifestation of the larger conflict . . . taking place between the kingdom of God and the kingdom of evil."[1]

Paul manages his frustration in not foreseeing a return to his converts by continuous prayer with the hope that he would somehow eventually see them face-to-face (1 Thess 3:10). In 3:11-13 Paul expresses this, also

---

1. Jeffrey A. D. Weima, *1–2 Thessalonians*, BECNT (Grand Rapids, MI: Baker Academic, 2014), 217.

1 Thess 3:1-13

3:1Therefore when we could bear it no longer, we decided to be left alone in Athens; 2and we sent Timothy, our brother and co-worker for God in proclaiming the gospel of Christ, to strengthen and encourage you for the sake of your faith, 3so that no one would be shaken by these persecutions. Indeed, you yourselves know that this is what we are destined for. 4In fact, when we were with you, we told you beforehand that we were to suffer persecution; so it turned out, as you know. 5For this reason, when I could bear it no longer, I sent to find out about your faith; I was afraid that somehow the tempter had tempted you and that our labor had been in vain.

6But Timothy has just now come to us from you, and has brought us the good news of your faith and love. He has told us also that you always remember us kindly and long to see us— just as we long to see you. 7For this reason, brothers and sisters, during all

revealing what he considers lacking in their faith (3:10), that is, a need to increase their love for one another and to strengthen their hearts in holiness. As such, Paul's words transition into the exhortative and eschatological comments he was proceeding toward in chapters 4–5. Intriguingly, in 3:13 Paul envisions that Jesus would return "with all his saints." The identity of those holy beings or people has occasioned debate concerning whether Paul pictured them as angels or human believers. The vision of Jesus' coming that he later unfolds in 4:13-18 suggests that it is the believers he has in mind; the emphasis here should be on the qualifier "all," namely, as Paul will go on to say, the dead as well as the living.

While Paul had profound concern for the persecution the Thessalonians had endured from their own compatriots (1 Thess 2:14-16), and mentions that suffering again in 3:3, he still offers no specifics about the local issues. Nevertheless, undoubtedly great tension existed between the believers and their polytheistic neighbors over the converts' espousal of monotheism and consequent rejection of many cultic customs, observances, and feasts.

To suggest a more concrete picture, especially with respect to women, I would like to discuss some aspects of their involvement in two cults, two possible case studies. The rejection of prior participation in these cults by the earliest female believers in Thessalonica may have elicited very conflicted feelings about and within those women. I will also include an occasional comment about where these cultic experiences could have influenced some of their expectations about belonging to a Christian group. The two cults are those of the goddesses Demeter and Isis.

our distress and persecution we have been encouraged about you through your faith. [8]For we now live, if you continue to stand firm in the Lord. [9]How can we thank God enough for you in return for all the joy that we feel before our God because of you? [10]Night and day we pray most earnestly that we may see you face to face and restore whatever is lacking in your faith.

[11]Now may our God and Father himself and our Lord Jesus direct our way to you. [12]And may the Lord make you increase and abound in love for one another and for all, just as we abound in love for you. [13]And may he so strengthen your hearts in holiness that you may be blameless before our God and Father at the coming of our Lord Jesus with all his saints.

1. Demeter, Persephone, and the Cycle of Mothers and Daughters

The annual Thesmophoria[2] celebrations honoring the goddess Demeter must have been occasions of great difficulty for the earliest Christian married women in Thessalonica and perhaps were also a time of temptation to return to cultic involvement. While as of yet there is no significant archaeological data for the Demeter cult in the city itself, because worship of this goddess was widespread in other Greco-Roman cities, it is safe to assume that the same was true in Thessalonica.

The worship of Demeter, along with her daughter Persephone, respectively, Roman Ceres and Proserpina (also called Korē),[3] is founded on a classical mother-daughter myth,[4] a tale with regional variants. The story recounts that Demeter, goddess of the harvest, was a mother plunged into sorrow because Persephone had been raped by and then married to Hades, the god of the underworld. Demeter's anguished search for Persephone caused her to neglect the earth. The crops became so poor that Zeus intervened to prevent the world from becoming barren. He restored Persephone to Demeter at Eleusis and from then on allowed her to spend eight months every year with her mother. She had to live the other four in the underworld, and according to the myth, that is why

2. On the Thesmophoria, see esp. Nancy H. Demand, *Birth, Death, and Motherhood in Classical Greece* (Baltimore, MD: Johns Hopkins University Press, 1994), 114–20.

3. On Ceres and Proserpina in Rome, see, e.g., Nicola Denzey, *The Bone Gatherers: The Lost Worlds of Early Christian Women* (Boston: Beacon Press, 2007), 43–52.

4. Demand, *Birth*, 115, considers that the most accessible form of this story is found in the Homeric *Hymn to Demeter*, possibly dating to the seventh century BCE.

the earth lies fallow for four months. Actually, Hades would have allowed Persephone to return permanently to Demeter, but because she had already eaten some food in his realm, a mere four pomegranate seeds, she could not. For each seed she had to annually spend a month with Hades.

The goddess Demeter represented for women the mother of a daughter, Persephone, who became a maiden, was abducted and raped by Hades, and then became his wife. She was thus lost to her mother. Demeter's grief about the separation from her daughter and her fears for Persephone's future with Hades resonated with many women's feelings. Angeliki Tzanetou has commented:

> Few myths afforded mortal women the occasion to identify with the experiences of a divinity as closely and as powerfully as that of Persephone. For its ancient audience, the myth of Persephone's abduction by Hades and her mother's extreme grief represented the vulnerability of the young woman during her perilous journey to womanhood, which girls were expected to make through marriage.[5]

Persephone's life with Hades also symbolized the constraints and dangers of marriage, such as the risks of very early childbirth, known better to Demeter than to the young daughter who was abducted. The two great festivals in Demeter's honor were the Haloa and the Thesmophoria. These occasions were celebrated throughout Greek cities (with regional adaptations) and thus, as presumed here, also at Thessalonica. Because Demeter was at Eleusis (about twelve miles northwest of Athens) when her daughter was restored to her, the mysteries of her cult and especially the annual Thesmophoria (meaning "bringer of treasures") were most prominently held there. The popular mysteries of Demeter's cult and the Thesmophoria were the most heavily attended of all Greek religious festivals.

Only married women took part in the Thesmophoria. Leaving their homes and setting up temporary shelters, they effectively created "a 'polis of women' that was outside the framework of the normal male polis and, in a sense, temporarily supplanted it."[6] Men had to pay the costs but were not allowed to spy on the proceedings. Ironically, although a goal of the ceremony was to increase fertility, women prepared for the

5. Angeliki Tzanetou, "Ritual and Gender: Critical Perspectives," in *Finding Persephone: Women's Rituals in the Ancient Mediterranean*, ed. Maryline G. Parca and Angeliki Tzanetou (Bloomington: Indiana University Press, 2007), 3–26, at 3.
6. Demand, *Birth*, 116.

Thesmophoria by observing sexual abstinence. Among the celebratory customs, the women ate pomegranates on one of the days, perhaps signifying their recommitment to marriage—even though the fruit was regarded as a female contraceptive. The absence of men allowed women full freedom of speech, which enabled them to engage in obscene jokes and insults, a characteristic of many fertility rites.[7]

In raising the question of the real meaning of the Thesmophoria, Nancy Demand notes that from a male viewpoint it was seen as important for the fertility of the crops and of the women. From the female perspective, however, she thinks another dynamic was at play. Given the comparatively insignificant male contribution to reproduction (from ancient women's perspective) in contrast with their nine months of pregnancy, dangers of childbirth, and difficulties raising children, she thinks a different attitude prevailed: "The laughter of the participants in the Thesmophoria was aimed at least in part at the absurdity of the situation the male culture imposed upon them: little reward for great value given."[8] But she also thinks the laughter was directed at the futility of the female predicament. The Thesmophoria gave Greek women a chance to vent their frustration and thus "enable them to return to that situation, irrational as it was from their point of view."[9] The ritual enactment of Demeter's loss of Persephone, her anger, and eventual reconciliation also helped women deal with the complicated separation of mothers and daughters necessitated by marriage. They knew themselves to have been daughters who became mothers and soon had marrying daughters, an endless repetition. "The message of the Thesmophoria to women as mothers and daughters was clear: if Demeter and Persephone endured the suffering and separation entailed by marriage, so can you."[10]

Regarding Paul's female converts in Thessalonica, we can assume Christian married women were advised not to take part in the Thesmophoria. That restriction may have been difficult to accept. Recall here that I am envisioning the very first, most likely small number of, converts within the city, thus a group with no existing Christian support beyond themselves for the social problems occasioned by their conversions. As a minority of women in the city, their nonparticipation must have amounted to a great loss of camaraderie, self-exclusion from a typical

7. Ibid.
8. Ibid., 117.
9. Ibid., 118.
10. Ibid., 120.

experience of women sharing wit and wisdom. It may also have suggested to the wider population that the Christian women were no longer good citizens since they had rejected what others valued and enjoyed. Although scholarship rarely assumes that women's withdrawal from a prominent female cult could have contributed to the hostility against the Thessalonian Christians, it is a strong possibility that cannot be dismissed, given the importance of the cult of Demeter.

This consideration also raises the question of how Paul's preaching persuaded women to reject goddesses such as Demeter and Persephone. An answer to that is evident in his stressing that he preached the gospel of the *living* God; no doubt he simultaneously pronounced all other deities dead. But what was it like for a woman to shift in her thinking from having once thought of Demeter and Persephone as divinities to then being taught as Christians to regard them as dead, and perhaps at best as characters in a novel? Would Paul have allowed women's participation if they acknowledged Demeter and Persephone were "merely" mythic? Would Paul not have feared women relating to Demeter and Persephone even as fictional female archetypes?[11]

Kathy Gaca has touched on what Paul might have tolerated in her discussion of early Christian antipathy directed at Greek female deities.[12] As she points out, there is plenty of material in the Pentateuch and the Prophets with which Paul would have been imbued that concerned the danger of idol worship and syncretistic worship and along with it the prohibition of mixed marriages. Thus he most likely would have found problematic even any mythic, supposedly "fictional," inspiration coming from (to him) nonexistent female goddesses whose influence might insidiously permeate the sexual experience and life cycles of Greek women. It is doubtful Paul had any tolerance for Christian women's presence at the Thesmophoria, including being "just observers."

For the very earliest married women who converted to Christianity, however, it must have seemed strange to have spent years immersed in the camaraderie and inspiration of the Thesmophoria only to opt out of it. What was it like to lose Demeter as a divine life guide? And, what if the adult women in a family did not agree about abandoning her wor-

---

11. For a contemporary, poignant poem reflecting inspiration from Demeter in a legendary sense, see "The Pomegranate" by Eavan Boland, *In a Time of Violence* (New York: Norton, 1994), 26–27.

12. Kathy L. Gaca, "Early Christian Antipathy toward the Greek 'Women Gods,'" in Parca and Tzanetou, *Finding Persephone*, 278–87.

ship? What if, for example, a pagan mother continued her cult involvement with Demeter and a Christian daughter eschewed the goddess?

There is a fascinating parallel to this hypothetical situation in catacomb art of the late fourth century according to a detailed analysis by Nicola Denzey.[13] The series of images to be discussed was created long after the founding of Paul's Thessalonian community, and from a time when Christian women who abandoned Demeter would have had far more social support—and whoever still worshiped her would by then have been a rapidly dwindling number within the Christian Empire. Nevertheless, the emotion one can read in this catacomb ornamentation touches on the situation of families where some women did and some did not abandon Demeter. Denzey's study is of a section of the Via Latina Catacomb, also called the Catacomb of the Via Dino Compagni. She interprets the iconographic program in two of the cubicula within what was a private burial complex as follows: A Roman Ceres (Demeter) worshiping matron, who had outlived both her pagan husband and her Christian daughter, directed the preparation and adornment for their tombs. Respecting the daughter's Christianity, the mother had her tomb decorated with biblical scenes. Turning a corner to the tomb area of the mother and father, however, one sees only pagan scenes. Most interesting, for a prominent place on the wall transition between their tombs the mother had ordered a large portrayal of Ceres (Demeter). The overall situation in the two cubicula suggests the mother and daughter had been closely bonded, even though they did not agree religiously. For the surviving mother, who had the final word about the tomb art, her selection of an image linking their graves was a painting of Ceres. While it is not unusual to find Ceres in Roman funerary art, in which she is usually driving her chariot down to the underworld in search of Proserpina (Persephone), the unusual pose of Ceres in this tomb has her gazing upon the Christian daughter's grave.

The mother's choice of art speaks of her own belief and emotion. Ceres, who may have represented just a character in an old wives' tale to the Christian daughter, appears to have been an inspirational image to the pagan mother in her final years.[14] That she would have visited repeatedly and gazed upon the imagery she had commissioned is assumed. As Denzey observes:

13. Denzey, *The Bone Gatherers*, 25–57.
14. A virtual tour of the catacomb is possible via Google Maps by searching for Ipogeo di via Dino Compagni.

A Roman hypogeum was not a vault to be sealed up and forgotten. It was a sort of memory theater, a space set on the margins between ordinary life and another realm, a place where one could meet the dead halfway. The powerful combination of portraits, likenesses, and scriptural and mythological scenes enlivened by the soft light of flickering oil lamps not only rekindled a longing for one's beloveds, it confirmed their place in sacred history.[15]

2. The Cult of Isis in Thessalonica

To consider further what Christian women may have experienced as they shunned the idols they had once worshiped, some information about the cult of Isis can be illuminating. For this cult, unlike that of Demeter, there is archaeological material from Thessalonica, including inscriptions evidencing involvement by women.

Isis was the Egyptian goddess famous for searching for the body parts of her murdered husband Osiris (he was assimilated to the god Sarapis in Greece). Isis and Osiris were the parents of Horus (whose Roman name was Harpocrates). The cult of Isis was an export brought to Greece by Egyptian expatriates around 333 BCE.[16] This mystery religion, in which Isis also became assimilated with Demeter and was celebrated at the Thesmophoria,[17] was widely popular throughout the Greco-Roman world, eventually gaining the enthusiasm of some Roman emperors in the first century CE.

---

15. Denzey, *The Bone Gatherers*, 34. Denzey also sketches a probable scenario: "Once each year on the anniversary of her daughter's death, as was the custom for pagans and Christians alike, the woman would enter the dark stillness of the hypogeum in memory of her daughter and stand before her grave. She passed by her husband's grave too—he would be remembered on his own death anniversary, and in a different way—and the space prepared for her own body someday. As she passed through the narrow archway between their cubiculum and their daughter's, her torchlight danced off the wall, revealing Ceres standing with her own torch, lighting the way into the underworld, revealing to her the way to lost daughters" (55–56).

16. Helmut Koester, "Egyptian Religion in Thessalonikē: Regulation for the Cult," in *From Roman to Early Christian Thessalonikē*, ed. Laura S. Nasrallah, Charalambos Bakirtzēs, and Steven J. Friesen (Cambridge, MA: Harvard University Press, 2010), 133–50, at 134; Birgitte Bøgh, "The Greco-Roman Cult of Isis," in *The Handbook of Religions in Ancient Europe*, ed. Lisbeth Bredholt Christensen, Olav Hammer, and David A. Warburton (Durham, UK, and Bristol, CT: Acumen Pub. Ltd., 2013), 228–41.

17. On the ability of Isis to assimilate to other goddesses, see, e.g., Bøgh, "The Greco-Roman Cult of Isis," 229.

Following a large fire in Thessalonica in 1917, a temple was found in what is now the southwestern part of the city, the area known today as Dioiketerion. The original construction of this temple has been dated to the late third century BCE.[18] In 1939 a later and smaller Roman-era temple was discovered very near the precinct of the earlier discovery; beneath its narthex was a sealed subterranean crypt.[19] Of the thirty-six inscriptions found in this location, most refer to Isis and Sarapis, one of which was a small fragmentary inscription known as the "Hymn of Isis." It is uncertain to which of the two deities the temple, now called a Sarapeum, was dedicated.[20] Recently the Sarapeum has been assessed to have been even larger than previously thought,[21] although the size of the temple does not necessarily prove it was the dominant group among the cults of Thessalonica. Following its excavation the temple was reburied.[22]

By the early first century CE, the cult of Isis was widespread in the Roman Empire, especially in Mediterranean ports like Thessalonica. The Romans, given their emphasis on patriarchal control of women, had for a long time been opposed to the cult. This was due to the female empowerment it conveyed, but also because the worship of Isis had become associated with Cleopatra VII. For many, Cleopatra (69–30 BCE) was the living embodiment of Isis, but the Romans had feared and disliked her immensely due to her influence on Julius Caesar and Mark Antony. The conflation of Cleopatra with Isis may have been of some interest to Paul since it was in his home city of Tarsus in 41 BCE that Cleopatra, having styled herself as Isis, famously first encountered Antony.[23] The two became lovers and, of course, the rest, ending with their defeat at Actium in 31 BCE and subsequent suicides, is well-known history.

18. Charles Edson, "Cults of Thessalonica (Macedonia III)," *HTR* 41 (1948): 153–204, at 181.

19. Karl P. Donfried, *Paul, Thessalonica, and Early Christianity* (Grand Rapids, MI: Eerdmans, 2002), 123.

20. Koester, "Egyptian Religion," 135.

21. Ekaterini G. Tsalampouni, "The Cult of Theos Hypsistos in Roman Thessalonica and the First Christian Community of the City" (2011), https://www.academia.edu/1462334/The_Cult_of_Theos_Hypsistos_in_Roman_Thessalonica_in_English.

22. There is a model of it in the Archaeological Museum of Thessalonica.

23. Reginald E. Witt, *Isis in the Graeco-Roman World* (Ithaca, NY: Cornell University Press, 1971), 257, comments: "Cleopatra, whose Egyptian-style barge and Isis-like person, in the words of Shakespeare, 'beggared all description,' would have been for long a thrilling topic of conversation in the city on the Cydnus where the little Jewish boy Saul spent his childhood."

The Isis cult, in spite of Roman fears, gradually flourished even in imperial circles. For example, only about a decade before Paul wrote to the Thessalonians, the emperor Caligula (ruled 39–41) had built (or re-built) a large temple to Isis, the Isis Campense, in Rome's Campus Martius. Even closer to the time when Paul was writing 1 Thessalonians the emperor Claudius (ruled 41–54) was also adopting the religion of Isis. A cartouche of Claudius was inlaid on the Mensa Isiaca, a bronze altar top dedicated to Isis and also called the Bambine Table of Isis. His imperial enthusiasm for the goddess, occurring just a decade or two before Paul's writing of 1 Thessalonians, suggests that her worship was most likely quite vibrant in a major Roman port like Thessalonica.

As a goddess who mourned the death of Osiris with excessive and dramatic wailing, Isis sought to find and reassemble the fourteen parts of his mutilated body into a mummy, yet she found all but his phallus. While she could not bring Osiris back to life, and he remained a king in the other world, Isis was able to conceive his child, Horus. Isis thus became a goddess of fertility and marriage. She was considered kind and loving to her adherents and portrayed as a loving mother, nursing Horus (a *kourotrophos*).[24] She was often represented carrying a sistrum (rattle) and a ritual water bucket filled with Nile water, objects also used in her worship. The ritual elements of the cult of Isis included an initiation and a baptism; a promise of future salvation was also given the initiate.

Karl Donfried has summarized the inscriptional evidence of Isis in Thessalonica, observing that as far as can be determined her cult "was particularly anxious to extend her catholic claims of salvation and eternal life. Humility, confession of sin and repentance were urged prior to nocturnal initiation."[25] Numerous concepts in both the cult of Isis and Paul's preaching have some degree of comparability, for example, regarding such ideas as baptism, salvation, resurrection, and the general concept that Isis would help people with their difficulties in life and with healing.[26]

24. See above, pp. 50–51.
25. Donfried, *Paul*, 23.
26. While information regarding initiation into the Isis cult is sparse, the novel *Metamorphoses* (or *Golden Ass*) by the Latin writer Apuleius (born c. 125 CE) attests to the popularity of the worship of Isis. It tells the story of a Greek man, Lucius, who dabbled in magic and thereby turned into a donkey. He was rescued by Isis and returned to being human. Lucius then underwent the Isiac initiation rite. On similarities between the cult of Isis and many Christian practices, see, e.g., Stephen Benko, *The Virgin Goddess: Studies in the Pagan and Christian Roots of Mariology*, Numen Book Series, Studies in the History of Religions 59 (Leiden: Brill, 2004), 43–53.

Sometimes a devotee might receive a message from Isis in a dream. This could occur during the process of incubation, a period of sleeping in the temple at night. Both sexes participated in this hopeful waiting for the goddess to appear. Stephen Benko remarks that the "opportunity for vicious rumors, especially when incubation was practiced by women, was ever present, and sometimes illicit activities may have taken place."[27] Nevertheless, women's participation in the intense experience of incubation paralleled that of men. What might Paul have said about such a ritual, especially since Acts 16:9-10, if accurate, recounts that he himself had gone to Macedonia on the basis of a night vision?

Some of Isis's female followers were also priestesses,[28] although it appears not in the same numbers as men.[29] Neither their roles nor the duration of their duties are clear. Nevertheless, as Sharon Kelly Heyob has commented, "The fact that women did participate in the religion even to the small extent that they did is in itself significant, however, since their participation in the Greek and Roman religions was very narrowly limited."[30]

The Isiac women probably experienced an enabling and emphasis on gender equality at least on the level of some practices and with regard to females taking initiatives as did Isis in her myth. How would that have played out for Isiac women converting to Paul's community? Did those who joined his community transfer their cultic experiences of active participation and some leadership? If so, their transition into Christian leaders would accord with what is known from later letters to his other churches, namely, that women were important members and leaders in the nascent groups (see, e.g., Rom 16).

---

27. Ibid., 51. Benko reports that the best-known story about such an incident is that reported in Josephus, *Antiquities* 18.65–80. He also observes (52): "If occasional wrongs took place within the religion of Isis, that was not its outstanding characteristic. In fact, the opposite appears to be true."

28. On the participation of women in the cult of Isis, see, e.g., Sharon Kelly Heyob, *The Cult of Isis among Women in the Graeco-Roman World*, Études préliminaires aux religions orientales dans l'Empire romain 51 (Leiden: Brill, 1975), 81–110.

29. See Benko, *Virgin Goddess*, 48–49, where Benko offers this summary: "Although most of the principal priests appear to have been men, women priests became increasingly common from the first century A.D. onward, especially in the Roman sphere. Women devotees are frequently mentioned in inscriptions and are also depicted on the wall paintings of Herculaneum. The *Metamorphoses* (Chap. 11) mentions them several times, and there is much epigraphical information to show that they were present in the cult associations."

30. Heyob, *Cult of Isis*, 110.

An interesting feature of the Sarapeum or the Isiac Temple in Thessalonica that corresponds to various other temples of the cult known from western Asia Minor is that the architectural layout differs from traditional Greek temples, which functioned as the house of a god.[31] In contrast to the more conventional structures, these Isiac buildings had obvious spaces for the assembly of groups within, apparently in proximity to an image of the deity in the same space. Helmut Koester has thus commented, "Interior space, no longer the exclusive dwelling of the deity, had now become the place of worshippers."[32] He speculates that these religious structures, along with synagogue buildings, "appear as predecessors for the later Christian churches."[33] If indeed Isiac women were among Paul's converts, some may already have been accustomed not only to participatory roles and some cultic leadership but also to worship by a religious group within a relatively egalitarian space.

Considered together, this discussion of the popular cults of Demeter and Isis may have brought to the surface the types of tensions as well as a few lines of continuity possibly experienced by women moving from polytheism to Christianity. While I have only mused here at what the dynamics might have been like, Paul leaves no doubt that the Thessalonian believers paid a high price for the religious conversion they had embarked on.

31. Koester, "Egyptian Religion," 138–39.
32. Ibid., 139.
33. Ibid.

1 Thessalonians 4

Exhortations for the Living and about the Dead

In 1 Thess 4:1 Paul transitions from the extended thanksgivings of chapters 1–3 into the exhortations in chapters 4–5.[1] These two final chapters contain paraenesis as well as eschatological comments. Since the eschatological remarks are also paraenetic, or hortatory, all of chapters 4–5 can be considered paraenetic. Chapters 4 and 5 offer numerous clues about what Timothy must have reported to Paul was of concern in the Thessalonian church: these issues include sexual morality, relations among the believers as well as with their neighbors, and the fate of the dead and the living at the expected return of Jesus.

Paul's reference in 1 Thess 1:9 to the Thessalonians "turning to God from idols" had already foreshadowed his admonitions about sexual conduct in 4:3-8. Paul's concerns in these verses very likely include (probably along with other issues of sexual morality) that his converts, specifically the males in the group, should no longer participate in or revert to former, perhaps including cultic, sexual activity. Among the religious groups in Thessalonica, the cults of Cabirus and Dionysus, for example, incorporated a strong phallic and sexual character.[2] Issues of nonparticipation in cultic

---

1. See the general outline of the letter above, p. 22.
2. Jeffrey A. D. Weima, *1–2 Thessalonians*, BECNT (Grand Rapids, MI: BakerAcademic, 2014), 262.

1 Thess 4:1-18

⁴:¹Finally, brothers and sisters, we ask and urge you in the Lord Jesus that, as you learned from us how you ought to live and to please God (as, in fact, you are doing), you should do so more and more. ²For you know what instructions we gave you through the Lord Jesus. ³For this is the will of God, your sanctification: that you abstain from fornication; ⁴that each one of you know how to control your own body in holiness and honor, ⁵not with lustful passion, like the Gentiles who do not know God; ⁶that no one wrong or exploit a brother or sister in this matter, because the Lord is an avenger in all these things, just as we have already told you beforehand and solemnly warned you. ⁷For God did not call us to impurity but in holiness. ⁸Therefore whoever rejects this rejects not human authority but God, who also gives his Holy Spirit to you.

⁹Now concerning love of the brothers and sisters, you do not need to have anyone write to you, for you yourselves have been taught by God to love one another; ¹⁰and indeed you do love all the brothers and sisters throughout Macedonia. But we urge

sexual activity could be related to 2:14-16 as well, where, as suggested earlier, it is likely that the persecution of the believers included pressure to revert to their previous cultic involvement.

Paul's concern regarding sexual conduct is that the believers' holiness is at stake. Influenced by his Pharisaic background, he would have required of Gentile converts that same holiness that he as a Pharisee had always been expected to live with.[3] In Jeffrey Weima's view: "The holiness that previously has been the exclusive privilege and calling of Israel has now also become God's purpose for the Gentiles at Thessalonica who have 'turned to God from idols to serve a living and true God.'"[4] But Lone Fatum also sees in Paul's remarks a Jewish denigration of Gentile sexual morality. She comments: "For Paul, the former Pharisee, illegitimate and uncontrolled sexuality was tantamount to ungodliness and pagan impurity; idolatry and fornication were virtually synonymous in traditional Jewish interpretation. Thus Paul's argument in vv. 3-5 is loaded with stereotyped Jewish contempt of non-Jews in its caricature of pagan licentiousness."[5]

3. Lone Fatum, "1 Thessalonians," in *Searching the Scriptures*, vol. 2, *A Feminist Commentary*, ed. Elisabeth Schüssler Fiorenza (New York: Crossroad, 1993), 258.

4. Weima, *1–2 Thessalonians*, 265.

5. Fatum, "1 Thessalonians," 258.

you, beloved, to do so more and more, [11]to aspire to live quietly, to mind your own affairs, and to work with your hands, as we directed you, [12]so that you may behave properly toward outsiders and be dependent on no one.

[13]But we do not want you to be uninformed, brothers and sisters, about those who have died, so that you may not grieve as others do who have no hope. [14]For since we believe that Jesus died and rose again, even so, through Jesus, God will bring with him those who have died. [15]For this we declare to you by the word of the Lord, that we who are alive, who are left until the coming of the Lord, will by no means precede those who have died. [16]For the Lord himself, with a cry of command, with the archangel's call and with the sound of God's trumpet, will descend from heaven, and the dead in Christ will rise first. [17]Then we who are alive, who are left, will be caught up in the clouds together with them to meet the Lord in the air; and so we will be with the Lord forever. [18]Therefore encourage one another with these words.

The Rhetorical Function of Invective, or Negative-Stereotyping

Throughout Jewish literature, among the most popular *topoi*, or themes, used to slander non-Jews (τὰ ἔθνη, usually rendered "gentiles" or "pagans") were those related to sexual vice, which was associated with idolatry (see Wis 14:12-14, 21-27). Jews profiled gentiles as hyper-sexualized, sexually deviant people, given to every manner of sexual excess and depravity. This was an effective rhetorical strategy that functioned to underscore the distinction between Israel and all others and to showcase Jewish moral superiority (see, e.g., *Letter of Aristeas* 151–52; Philo, *Special Laws* 3.12). At 1 Thess 4:5, as elsewhere in his letters, Paul adopts a Jewish perspective and deploys stock sexual invective when he describes gentiles as those who act with "lustful passion." Paul expected Christ-believers, who were now integrated into Israel's salvation story, to distinguish themselves from nonbelievers by their sexual morality.

It is important to realize that sexualized invective, as all invective, depends on exaggeration. Certainly, not every non-Jew in Thessalonica, or elsewhere in the empire, was a depraved sex-maniac; nor was sexual constraint the hallmark and aspiration of Jews exclusively. Greco-Roman literature attests that many non-Jewish moralists of Paul's day also vigorously advocated sexual restraint, both within and outside of marriage (see, e.g., Musonius Rufus, Lecture XI, *On Sexual Indulgence* 85–89; Seneca, *Moral Letters to Lucilius* 94.26). Thus it is possible that in their

pre-Christian lives some, or
perhaps even most, of the newly
converted in Thessalonica had
already lived chastely.

It is also important to
recognize that invective,
whether sexualized, ethnicized,
or gendered, etc., was not an
exclusively Jewish rhetorical
device. Ancient rhetorical
handbooks advocated the use of
invective (Latin *vituperation*;
Greek ψόγος, considered the
inverted form of praise) as an
effective tool to attack the
character of a group or an
individual. Greco-Roman
orators frequently employed
sexual slander to defame their
political enemies. Cicero used
invective regarding sexual
excess and depravity to great
effect against Mark Antony (see
Philippic 2.6, 15, 44–45, 47, 58); in
two well-known court cases, he
used it against two women who

dared testify against his clients
(see *Pro Cluentio* 1.12; *Pro Caelio*
13–16).

Learning how to deploy
invective and choose the most
effective *topoi* for defaming a
person or group was part of
ancient rhetorical education, and
throughout the centuries, many
have masterfully employed this
rhetorical tool in the service of
numerous agendas. As testified
in various writings (see, e.g.,
John Chrysostom, *Eight Homilies
Against the Jews*), invective,
especially revolving around
sexual themes, was an effective
tool of early Christian anti-
Jewish rhetoric once Jews were
perceived as the other from
whom Christians needed to be
distinguished and over whom
Christians needed to assert their
superiority.

Maria Pascuzzi

In 1 Thess 4:3, Paul admonishes the Thessalonians to abstain from
πορνεία (NRSV, "fornication"). That warning is further explicated in 1
Thess 4:4 with the use of the term σκεῦος ("vessel"), resulting in probably
the most debated verse in this epistle. The NRSV renders σκεῦος as
"body," which can be understood either as a euphemism for a human
sexual organ or as a reference to the body in general. That translation
leads to an interpretation that suggests one needs to control one's body.
But σκεῦος has also been rendered as "wife," resulting in phrasing such
as "acquire a wife" (NAB). As is evident from the latter wording, one of
the uncertainties about this passage is whether it is addressed to all
Thessalonian believers or just the men.

Lindsey Trozzo, favoring the translation of σκεῦος as "vessel," that is,
as part of the body or the whole body, argues that Paul did have both

sexes in mind.[6] She reads Paul's admonishment as telling both men and women to gain control of their sexual conduct. Trozzo's approach is audience oriented; she reads all of 1 Thessalonians as directed by Paul to all of his mixed-gender audience throughout. As she sees it, for him to switch to speaking only to males in 4:4 (and using σκεῦος as a reference to a wife or exclusively male genitalia) "not only makes the female hearer invisible as a member of the audience, but it also transforms her from a participant to an object."[7]

For readers who "stand in front of the text" today, Trozzo's audience orientation is probably analogous to the most usual way of reading or hearing 1 Thess 4:3-8; i.e., it is generally heard now as a reminder to all Christians to be faithful to the norms of Christian sexual morality. With respect to that admonition now, in his recent commentary on 1 Thessalonians, Gary Shogren offers this sobering reflection:

> In 1995 I published a book on addiction and mentioned that beyond drugs and alcohol, some people might get addicted to pornography. I was visualizing magazines bought by a furtive customer at the convenience store. Roughly ten years later, I began to write this commentary and the new landscape was unrecognizable. People have exploited electronic media to expand the frontiers of Gentile [*sic*] sin far beyond what Paul could have imagined. Men and women can view sexual material or engage in sexual interaction of every variety without leaving their desk. It is likely that pornography is now the single greatest sin among Christians and their leaders. In addition, a friend who is writing a book on this topic informs me that American women have nearly caught up with the men in their use of pornographic material.[8]

While mixed-gender audiences certainly relate to 4:3-8 today, a strong argument against Trozzo's interpretation lies in the fact that women's sexual activity was severely restricted in Paul's era.[9] Trozzo would counter that point, however, by noting that libertine movements among female elites were increasing in the Roman eastern provinces and, she assumes, trickling

6. Lindsey M. Trozzo, "Thessalonian Women: The Key to the 4:4 Conundrum," *PRSt* 39 (2012): 39–52, at 51.

7. Ibid., 46.

8. Shogren, *1 and 2 Thessalonians*, 175.

9. See Monya A. Stubbs, "1 Thessalonians," in *Women's Bible Commentary*, ed. Carol A. Newsom, Sharon H. Ringe, and Jacqueline E. Lapsley, 3rd ed. (Louisville, KY: Westminster John Knox Press, 2012), 590: "Considering that Greco-Roman male privilege allowed sexual freedom for a married man that was out of the question for married women, it is reasonable to assume that this exhortation is primarily aimed at male converts."

down to the non-elites. While there is some reason to think that Paul would need to admonish new male converts about their sexual "excesses," as will be further discussed below, it is harder to imagine any significant number of female libertines in Paul's original church nucleus.

Contrary to Trozzo's preference to see Paul as addressing both genders, most interpreters, including many feminists, do assume Paul was focusing only on males in his use of σκεῦος, interpreted either as "wife" or "body." Further, the interpretation that σκεῦος is a euphemism for the male sex organ is regarded by many as Paul's probable meaning. The verse is thus read as a warning to male believers to exercise control over their own bodies. In tandem with that, 1 Thess 4:6, which bears a nuance of property rights, appears to forbid male believers' illicit sexual relations with females in another Christian's household. It is possible that if a relapse into forms of prior sexual activity is an element of Paul's concern in 4:3-8, 4:6 could imply he was forbidding any male believer to exploit, that is, to pressure, the members of another male's household to join in the recidivism.

Since the only people who were in complete control of their bodies sexually in the Pauline era were free or freed men, Paul's admonition recognizes the need for self-control on the part of such male believers.[10] The πορνεία referred to in 1 Thess 4:3 generally connotes a wide range of sexual misconduct; the word's meaning is not restricted to the narrow sense with which "fornication" is used today. While Paul leaves a reader wondering what he was specifically objecting to in the realm of sexual behavior, he reminds the Thessalonians in 4:3 that he had solemnly told them about this and had already admonished them about the avenging Lord.

However the term σκεῦος is interpreted, Paul is evidently urging the believers to adopt a stricter code of sexual conduct than they must have been observing. Raymond Collins summarizes Paul's concern this way: "There is little doubt that Paul excludes sexual liaisons other than that of

---

10. See Jennifer Wright Knust, "Paul and the Politics of Virtue and Vice," in *Paul and the Roman Imperial Order*, ed. Richard A. Horsley (Harrisburg, PA: Trinity Press International, 2004), 173, who contends that Paul assumed women to be naturally passive and slaves as having an inability to control desire, but held that "good" men, i.e., "good" believers, could control desire. She thus understands Paul's admonitions concerning male self-mastery as an indication that "he adopted the hierarchical sex-gender-status cultural presuppositions that had previously served to uphold imperial . . . claims to legitimacy. . . . [These were] hierarchical theories of sex and gender that, historically, had been used by Romans and Greeks to claim their own privileged status while undermining the claims of their rivals."

a man's sexual union with his wife."[11] Yet at the same time, it remains uncertain whether Paul's concern about male sexual activity included that between masters and slaves. The fact that Paul did not necessarily comment on master-slave sexual activity might not be unusual, nor can it be certain Paul even had it in mind with respect to male sexual activity. Even if he did, we could not assume that the Thessalonian believers would have thought of it as included within Paul's admonitions to them or have taken it seriously if it were. In this regard Margaret MacDonald and Carolyn Osiek have noted: "The fact that the sexual use of slaves—including slave children—was a common social expectation should guard against assuming that the practice disappeared in early Christian communities."[12]

Jennifer Glancy finds it surprising that Paul "did not explicitly reinforce a prohibition on the sexual use of slaves, if he believed that Christianity demanded such a discipline."[13] Glancy allows that during Paul's time with the Thessalonians he may indeed have forbidden the new believers to have sexual contact with their slaves. She thinks, however, that such a prohibition would have been so countercultural that surely Paul would have repeated it in admonishing the Christians to control themselves sexually. She therefore concludes that when contemporary scholars interpret Paul as telling the Thessalonian men to restrict their sexual activity to marriage, that actually goes beyond what Paul wrote to them. She further concludes that in the first century men who heard Paul's counsel to obtain "a vessel" (if that translation was favored) would have understood that as "consistent with reliance on slaves as morally neutral sexual outlets."[14]

The complexity of this situation regarding Paul's admonition to men and how it would have been received by the Thessalonian believers, especially if slaves were among them, is not easily resolved by a modern reader. As MacDonald and Osiek also point out, what a person today views as sexual exploitation of, for example, slave women would not necessarily have been seen that way by all slaves of Paul's time. "Many female slaves both Christian and not would have found a certain degree of status, security and perhaps even power in the relationship, as long

11. Raymond F. Collins, *Accompanied by a Believing Wife: Ministry and Celibacy in the Earliest Christian Communities* (Collegeville, MN: Liturgical Press, 2013), 99.

12. Margaret Y. MacDonald, Carolyn Osiek, and Janet Tulloch, *A Woman's Place: House Churches in Earliest Christianity* (Minneapolis: Fortress Press, 2006), 73.

13. Jennifer A. Glancy, *Slavery in Early Christianity* (Oxford and New York: Oxford University Press, 2002), 60.

14. Ibid.

as they were not mistreated and threatened by jealous wives. Some may have attained a great deal of power."[15] But they also point out that "from a modern perspective and perhaps an ancient one as well, even if the victim feels fortunate, it is still abuse."[16]

A different consideration concerning the question of sexual difficulties in transitioning from polytheism to monotheism can be seen in the work of Christine Thomas.[17] Her approach may be characterized as an analysis of persons moving from the concept of temples as sacred to the concept of bodies as sacred. She argues: "A tacit assumption seems to reign with New Testament scholarship that Gentiles possessed no independent system of moral values. . . . The standard anti-Gentile tropes employed by Paul are consequently taken at face value as a description of actual Gentile behavior."[18] Thomas sees the transition Paul's converts were making to be from lives where sexual purity, either maintained or recovered, was required as a condition for entering sacred spaces, such as temples, to their new situation where, according to Paul, purity was an ongoing imperative ever to be maintained—not as a condition for entrance to a temple, but in a believer's body. Thomas states: "Paul did not understand purity as a spatial practice, as would his Gentile audience, but rather as a bodily practice. Paul *somatized* the language of ritual purity."[19] Paul's approach starkly contrasts with Gentile values, which indeed maintained strong ethical admonitions about cultic purity requirements. As Thomas states: "In the logic of ancient Greek piety, purity was not really an absolute value but was related to access to sacred places or participation in sacred times such as festivals."[20]

Moving forward in 1 Thess 4, Paul transitions in 4:9 from concerns about sexual morality to a double admonition: the believers should increase their love for each other and relate properly toward outsiders, being dependent on no one. That dependency from which the group needed to be freed may also have been related to possible pressure to return to any abandoned cultic activity.

15. MacDonald, Osiek, and Tulloch, *A Woman's Place*, 113.
16. Ibid.
17. Christine M. Thomas, "Locating Purity: Temples, Sexual Prohibitions, and 'Making a Difference' in Thessalonikē," in *From Roman to Early Christian Thessalonikē: Studies in Religion and Archaeology*, ed. Laura Nasrallah, Charalambos Bakirtzis, and Steven J. Friesen (Cambridge, MA: Harvard University Press, 2010), 109–32.
18. Ibid., 118–19.
19. Ibid., 123. Her italics.
20. Ibid., 124.

In 1 Thess 4:13 Paul launches into eschatological themes that extend to 5:11. The length of these remarks suggests he had finally escalated his paraenesis to a point where he was ready to treat his major concern for and about the Thessalonians: their issues about the fate of believers at the Parousia of Jesus. Paul's comments fall into two large sections: 4:13-18, concerning the believers who had already died, and 5:1-11, treating the fate of the living believers.[21] The sustained remarks Paul composed suggest that Timothy had told Paul (3:6) that his teaching about these matters had been inadequate during his short time with the new believers ("we do not want you to be uninformed," 4:13).[22] Obviously a pressing issue for them, it appears the Thessalonians feared that dead believers would be disadvantaged at the return of the Lord compared with those who would still be alive. Paul's response in 4:13-18 is to sketch a scenario of the Parousia.

Paul had previously used the term Parousia (παρουσία) in 1 Thess 2:19 and 3:13 to describe Jesus' return, but in 4:15 he elaborates on the imagery surrounding his coming. With vivid details Paul evokes the visit of a Roman emperor or another important official, for whose advent παρουσία was the customary term. It must be kept in mind that the future event described by Paul, with its details of the Lord's descent, the raising of the dead, the seizure or assumption of the living, and the final reunion of all with the Lord in the clouds, is written to *comfort* the grieving Thessalonians. Interpreters thus warn against a too literal reading of this scenario, as has happened, for example, with some teaching on the so-called Rapture, seen as the sudden and literal "snatching up" of the living. Yet with all the literalist attention that has been applied to picturing Paul's scenario, Laura Nasrallah nevertheless cautions:

> The spatiality and politics of this passage [4:16-17] have sometimes been ignored. The dead, located in the cemeteries outside the city walls, rise along the way to greet Christ first in his *pompe* into Thessaloniki, while the living join the procession within the city walls. The image of the prominent and wealthy who emerge to greet the Roman emperor

21. Jennifer Houston McNeel, *Paul as Infant and Nursing Mother: Metaphor, Rhetoric, and Identity in 1 Thessalonians 2:5-8*, ECL 12 (Atlanta, GA: Society of Biblical Literature, 2015), 157, characterizes 4:13–5:11 as solidifying the identity of the believers "as those who live in the light rather than the darkness and who will be taken up with Christ forever—the ultimate in-group."

22. On theories concerning what Paul had taught in Thessalonica about the resurrection of believers, see John Gillman, "Signals of Transformation in 1 Thessalonians 4:13-18," *CBQ* 47 (1985): 263–81, esp. 268–71.

is replaced by the scene of some not-so-prominent Thessalonians who greet a different Lord.[23]

Nasrallah's point is worth considering. Many assume Paul envisioned a high-level delegation, such as a formal Hellenistic reception, with dignitaries going outside the city to greet the Lord and escort him into the community.[24] Yet the Parousia Paul describes is sudden, with no time for leading Christians to gather outside the city. As Nasrallah's comments about spatiality suggest, Christ's regal entrance to the city would pass by the dead first, for by long-standing custom they had to be buried outside the city. Then the living could join the entourage. Paul also adjusts the culmination of the event vertically into the clouds. What would this parade of saints have been like? How would an artist depict it?

In envisioning this "imperial" procession, we could note that the first wave of people, the dead, if we portrayed them *looking as they did when they died*, would include a high proportion of people whose lives had been tragically cut short. While the dead whom Christ called forth from Thessalonica would, of course, have included both men and women, elite and non-elite, who had lived full adult lives, far, far more numerous would have been the people who had died as infants, as small children, as women in childbirth, as impoverished, malnourished non-elites, and as maltreated slaves. In particular, the women in the procession would exemplify the whole social spectrum, extending from the elite to those women bound in slavery or impoverished or orphaned into degradation and begging.

This hypothetical parade could be compared to (and contrasted with) the extraordinary procession depicted on the tapestries created by John Nava for Our Lady of Angels Cathedral in Los Angeles.[25] Nava's twenty-five tapestries, created between 1999 and 2002, depict the Communion of Saints and adorn the side walls of the cathedral's nave. This provocative art implicitly invites a contemporary viewer to take his or her place within the visual Communion. If an artist created something similar mirroring a whole group of Thessalonians, but as they were at the age of their deaths, we could vividly confront for ourselves the Thessalonian demographics of Paul's era with all the fragility, pain, indignities, and inequities of their

23. Laura S. Nasrallah, "Empire and Apocalypse in Thessaloniki: Interpreting the Early Christian Rotunda," *JECS* 13 (2005): 465–508, at 500.

24. See, e.g., Abraham Smith, " 'Unmasking the Powers': Toward a Post-Colonial Analysis of 1 Thessalonians," in Horsley, *Paul and the Roman Imperial Order*, 48; Weima, *1–2 Thessalonians*, 333–34.

25. See John Nava, "John Nava Studio: The Cathedral of Our Lady of the Angels," http://www.johnnava.com/JNS%20Archive/COS/cos.htm.

existences. Perhaps we would also better comprehend the Christians' profound concern that at the Parousia of Jesus the faithful dead, some of whom in their lives had probably been persecuted for their belief, should not be disadvantaged when Christ returned. Because the Thessalonians' expressions of worried, fearful grief on the part of the dead believers had occasioned Paul's description of this peaceful scenario, he created it to reassure the living that both they and the dead believers, with no advantage reserved for the living, would ultimately be "with the Lord forever" (4:17).

In instructing the believers about grieving for the dead in 1 Thess 4:13, Paul distinguishes what their grief should be like compared with the grief of οἱ λοιποί ("the rest" or "the others") who have no hope. The identity of "the rest" is ambiguous, for Jews themselves and various Gentiles held a variety of hopeful expectations concerning an afterlife, although most people were resigned that there was nothing to expect beyond death. By referring to the "rest," Paul most likely denoted the latter. Much debate (which will not be rehearsed here) has occurred over whether Paul was telling the Thessalonians how *the content or quality* of their grief was to distinguish them from those others or whether Paul was *forbidding* Christians to express any grief. That Paul forbade all grief has been widely rejected, however, since Paul in various places comments on grieving himself (see, e.g., Rom 9:2).

What may be interesting from a feminist perspective to interject into the many aspects of the discussion about Paul's concern about grief in 1 Thess 4:13 is a consideration of *how* grief was manifested. It is possible that an element of Paul's admonition to not grieve as did those who had no hope concerned the *manner* in which lamentations were demonstrated, e.g., including displays of extensive wailing, because that in itself could communicate hopelessness. Is there perhaps a hint of aversion by Paul to such despairing noise a few sentences earlier in 4:11 where he tells the Thessalonians to "aspire to live quietly"?

Much of the expression of grief surrounding death and during funeral activities was carried on by loud wailing, that is, ululating female mourners. Paul may have disapproved of that practice among his believers. The wailing not only communicated despair rather than hope in the resurrection, but it could also bear idolatrous overtones, such as imitation of the weeping of the goddess Isis.[26] Yet how hard would it have been for

---

26. At one of the annual festivals honoring Isis, the Isia, her story was dramatically reenacted, including her wailing at the death of Osiris. In this mystery play, rejoicing also followed when the resurrection of Osiris was portrayed. See Bøgh, "The Greco-Roman Cult," 235.

female converts to Christianity to change their customary ways of expressing grief? And, if Paul was against such a commonly practiced activity, might this also have had an economic impact on some women, for whom performing as wailers at funerals was a paid service?

On the assumption that Roman funerary practice had some impact on the customs practiced in Roman Thessalonica during Paul's era, a study on gender and funeral ritual by Darja Šterbenc Erker is informative.[27] Regarding female mourning in funeral processions Erker notes that "*praeficae* [paid female mourners] were hired to increase the family's mourning and to augment the prestige of the family. Their performance consisted of tearing the cheeks, singing mourning songs (*neniae*) and screaming."[28] The gashing of the cheeks was to appease the spirits of the dead with their blood. Erker comments that these codified expressions of grief were considered excessive even by certain ancient authors.[29] She also states: "In general the performance of excessive gestures of mourning . . . [was] considered women's work. . . . It was women's work to be in closer contact with the dead and to mourn excessively; these practices enabled men to stay at a distance and to take part in public affairs."[30]

If Paul's indication that the Thessalonians ought not to grieve like "the rest" bore overtones of opposing loud manifestations of grief, it may have been that women's roles at funerals more than men's had to be adapted following their conversions. If so, with what would women have replaced their loud ululations? A hint, although from a later period, is found in Gregory of Nyssa's *Life of Macrina* (26–27), where at Macrina's death virgins were weeping and shouting her name. Gregory told them to "turn their lamentations into psalming in the same strain."[31]

It is likely that Paul's observance of the manner of grieving by οἱ λοιποί coupled with his belief in the resurrection of the dead caused him to form strong opinions about funeral customs. That he may especially have opposed the women's loud ululating may be indicated by 1 Cor 13:1, where he refers negatively to a clanging, that is, an ululating, cym-

27. Darja Šterbenc Erker, "Gender and Roman Funeral Ritual," in *Memory and Mourning: Studies on Roman Death*, ed. Valerie M. Hope and Janet Huskinson (Oxford: Oxbow Books, 2011), 40–60.

28. Ibid., 49.

29. Ibid.

30. Ibid., 57.

31. Éric Rebillard, *The Care of the Dead in Late Antiquity*, Cornell Studies in Classical Philology (Ithaca, NY: Cornell University Press, 2009), 129.

bal. Certainly it is known that in the next few centuries Christianity railed against observances it disliked, especially female singers.[32] Éric Rebillard summarizes, for example, some data about the preaching of John Chrysostom (c. 347–407) on this topic:

> In several sermons, preached at Antioch or Constantinople, John Chrysostom denounced what he called "the madness about funerals" [*In Iohannem homiliae* 85.5] and recalled that faith in the resurrection should turn Christians away from traditional mourning. Weeping, beating the breast, tearing the hair, requiring all the servants to mourn were all customs to be discarded by Christians. Calling upon professional mourners went even further, for those women were pagan.[33]

Rebillard cites yet another sermon of Chrysostom (*In epistulam ad Hebraeos homiliae* 4.7) wherein he said: "If it should happen, and anyone should hire these mourning women, believe me when I say . . . that I will exclude that person from the church for a long time. . . . We come, discoursing of the things concerning the resurrection . . . and you do bring those who overthrow our teachings?"[34] Chrysostom in his era was effectively echoing Paul's admonition to the Thessalonians in 4:13 that they should not grieve as did those who had no hope.

Paul follows his critique of excessive grief with his peaceful scenario of the Parousia. He rounds out his thought in 1 Thess 4:18 with a reminder to the believers to "encourage one another with these words," reflecting the importance he attached to Christians witnessing to faith among themselves in order to strengthen each other's hope. Having said that, Paul shifts his thought to sketch another set of dynamics about the Parousia, including aspects of it that might engender fear in some believers. A definite sense of the shift in mood in Paul's thought strikes the reader rather quickly in chapter 5. That is no doubt why centuries ago a division marking a new chapter was placed after 4:18.

32. Ibid., 128–34.
33. Ibid., 132.
34. Ibid., 133.

1 Thessalonians 5

A Warning about Coming Destruction: As Sudden and Inescapable as Labor Pains

In the first half of 1 Thess 5 Paul further expounds on the return of Jesus. While in 4:13-18 he had focused on the believers' concern about those who had already died, in 5:1-11 Paul considers the situation of the living at the Parousia. Reflecting that he knew the Thessalonians had concerns about "the times and the seasons" (5:1), that is, when Jesus would return, Paul indicates that they had already heard his thought on this. But, in the face of their (and Paul's?) apparent anxiety about how they would be judged by the Lord, Paul reminds them of what it meant to be "children of the light and children of the day" (5:5) destined "not for wrath but for obtaining salvation" (5:9).

Paul proceeds to narrate the return of Jesus, which in the previous scenario he had sketched with imperial overtones, with themes from the Day of the Lord (see, e.g., Isa 13:6-8; Amos 5:20). That concept in the Jewish Scriptures envisions the coming of God to punish evil and vindicate God's people. Perhaps in 5:2 Paul drew in that idea because "it better conveys the notion of judgment associated with Christ's return"[1]

---

1. Jeffrey A. D. Weima, *1–2 Thessalonians*, BECNT (Grand Rapids, MI: BakerAcademic, 2014), 346.

⁵:¹Now concerning the times and the seasons, brothers and sisters, you do not need to have anything written to you. ²For you yourselves know very well that the day of the Lord will come like a thief in the night. ³When they say, "There is peace and security," then sudden destruction will come upon them, as labor pains come upon a pregnant woman, and there will be no escape! ⁴But you, beloved, are not in darkness, for that day to surprise you like a thief; ⁵for you are all children of light and children of the day; we are not of the night or of darkness. ⁶So then let us not fall asleep as others do, but let us keep awake and be sober; ⁷for those who sleep sleep at night, and those who are drunk get drunk at night. ⁸But since we belong to the day, let us be sober, and put on the breastplate of faith and love, and for a helmet the hope of salvation. ⁹For God has destined us not for wrath but for obtaining salvation through our Lord Jesus Christ, ¹⁰who died for us, so that whether we are awake or asleep we may live with him. ¹¹Therefore encourage one another and build up each other, as indeed you are doing.

¹²But we appeal to you, brothers and sisters, to respect those who labor

than did the peaceful Parousia scenario he had sketched in 4:13-18. In 5:1-11 Paul intensifies the ominous specter of the Day of the Lord by describing the onset of Jesus' return as sudden, coming like a thief, a metaphor also found in the teaching of Jesus (Matt 24:43; Luke 12:39). Paul heightens the simile, however, by envisioning the thief coming "in the night," leading to his additional references to night in 1 Thess 5:5-6. What is the significance of Paul having added that phrase?

Paul, who was no stranger to danger (see 2 Cor 11:23-27), must have known well the fear sparked by being in the dark himself, often in strange places. In the unlit streets and widely unsafe dwelling places of the ancient world, night was a period of heightened vulnerability, especially for women and children if they were attacked by someone stronger than themselves. For men as well, the threat of violence during the night must have rendered them defensively alert. Danger at night was common and, ironically, not only hoodlums were a problem. Even individuals from among the elite, even an emperor such as Nero himself, could pose nocturnal hazards. This is apparent from Suetonius:

> As soon as night fell he [Nero] would snatch a hat or cap and make a round of the taverns, or prowl the streets in search of mischief—and not always innocent mischief either, because one of his games was to attack men on their way home from dinner, stab them if they offered resistance, and then drop their bodies down the sewers. He would also

among you, and have charge of you in the Lord and admonish you; [13]esteem them very highly in love because of their work. Be at peace among yourselves. [14]And we urge you, beloved, to admonish the idlers, encourage the fainthearted, help the weak, be patient with all of them. [15]See that none of you repays evil for evil, but always seek to do good to one another and to all. [16]Rejoice always, [17]pray without ceasing, [18]give thanks in all circumstances; for this is the will of God in Christ Jesus for you. [19]Do not quench the Spirit. [20]Do not despise the words of prophets, [21]but test everything; hold fast to what is good; [22]abstain from every form of evil.

[23]May the God of peace himself sanctify you entirely; and may your spirit and soul and body be kept sound and blameless at the coming of our Lord Jesus Christ. [24]The one who calls you is faithful, and he will do this.

[25]Beloved, pray for us.

[26]Greet all the brothers and sisters with a holy kiss. [27]I solemnly command you by the Lord that this letter be read to all of them.

[28]The grace of our Lord Jesus Christ be with you.

---

break into shops, afterwards opening a miniature market at the Palace with the stolen goods, dividing them up into lots, auctioning them himself, and squandering the proceeds. During these escapades he often risked being blinded or killed—once he was beaten almost to death by a senator whose wife he had molested.[2]

Paul was probably aware that people who knew Roman law viewed the punishment for thievery as needing to be weighed regarding when it occurred, i.e., during the day or during the night.[3] The Twelve Tables, the oldest code of Roman law (ca. 450 BC), many tenets of which had generally remained fundamental to subsequent developments in Roman legal formulations, envisioned circumstances in which the life of a thief was forfeit. Because in principle people had a right to protect themselves, it was seen as "lawful to kill the thief who came by night or burgled a house in the daytime and was found to be armed (XII Tables 1.17–18/8.12–13)."[4] At the same time, as Jill Harries has observed, "In a violent

---

2. Gaius Tranquillus Suetonius, *The Twelve Caesars*, trans. Robert Graves (Hammondsworth, UK: Penguin Books Ltd., 1957, repr. 1972), Nero (26), 222–23.

3. Jill Harries, *Law and Crime in the Roman World* (New York: Cambridge University Press, 2007), 50–51.

4. Ibid., 51. Killing an unarmed thief in the daytime may not have been viewed as commensurately justified. The observation of Harries (52) that according to Aulus Gellius (writing ca. 170 CE) in his *Noctes Atticae* 11.18.7, a thief "could be killed if it

and male-dominated society, rules on violence started from the premise that some forms of direct action were acceptable; the aim of regulation was to curtail its abuse."[5]

While Roman law confirms for us the danger people must have experienced from thievery in the night, other factors also complicated the situation for the innocent. For example, there was widespread lack of enforcement and bribery as well as the corruptive factor of the patronage system that allowed discretionary decision making about guilt and innocence to triumph over fair treatment.

As Paul thus qualified his warning about the foreboding onset of the Day of the Lord like a thief "in the night," he communicated that it would be a time of extraordinary danger, potential violence and destruction (1 Thess 5:3) for all, including the faithful, along with those whose life choices had been to live "in darkness" (5:4). Paul metaphorically urges the believers to remain awake and sober, probably an observation that drunkenness[6] contributed to the dangers and bad decisions of the night. He assures the faithful, however, saying, "you, beloved, are not in darkness" (5:4). Nevertheless, he had sounded his warning.

Paul continues arguing against moral complacency on the part of the believers, lest they be shocked or unprepared for the Day of the Lord, by quoting an apparently well-known stock phrase: "When they say, 'There is peace and security,' then sudden destruction will come upon them" (1 Thess 5:3). This reference to peace and security is widely understood to be a citation, but its source has been disputed. Some see it as echoing Hebrew prophetic warnings against, for example, false prophets. However, because the prophetic warnings about peace do not also mention security, it has been convincingly argued that the phrase is "a popular theme or slogan of the imperial Roman propaganda machine,"[7] which did link the two concepts. That Paul was making an imperial ref-

---

was night or if he defended himself from arrest in the daytime with a weapon" suggests the same principle had been maintained from the period of the Twelve Tables and forward into Paul's era.

5. Ibid., 132.

6. See Simon Hornblower and Antony Spawforth, *The Oxford Companion to Classical Civilization* (Oxford: Oxford University Press, 1998), 26: "The alcoholic beverage of choice for both the ancient Greeks and Romans was wine, customarily diluted with water, except perhaps in the case of the Macedonians who were reputed to drink their wine *akratos,* or unmixed. Distilled spirits, such as brandy and whisky, had not been invented, and beer was looked upon as a swinish potation better left to barbarians."

7. See a summary of the discussion in Weima, *1–2 Thessalonians,* 348–51.

erence here seems probable since it follows closely his description in 4:13-18 of the return of the Lord likewise portrayed as a Parousia, a term from the language of empire. James R. Harrison has argued that Paul is making a bold move in citing this propaganda. He observes that while the Thessalonian believers may have already moved away from the idolatrous imperial cult, known to be powerful in the city, some of them may have still been parasitically "tempted to rely upon the benefits that imperial patronage continued to bring."[8] Harrison continues:

> The implication of Paul's "hidden transcript" was clear: the return of the risen Christ to vindicate the Thessalonian believers eclipsed anything that the imperialistic benefactors had to offer (1 Thess 4:16-17). In a bold move Paul's reference to εἰρήνη καὶ ἀσφάλεια in 1 Thessalonians 5:3—a familiar slogan of the imperial propaganda—functioned as a prophetic oracle announcing the demise of the self-satisfied Julio-Claudian clients in the eastern Mediterranean provinces.[9]

The analysis by those who find anti-imperialistic tones in what Paul has written prompts one to ask *why* Paul was opposed to the empire. While that broad question is beyond the scope of this commentary, it is instructive to note the importance of that extensive ongoing debate. And, to cite one succinct answer to the question of *why*, Néstor Oscar Míguez may be quoted. Analyzing 1 Thessalonians from a primarily Latin American socio-political but also feminist perspective and assessing what he terms "the counterhegemonic value of Pauline symbolism,"[10] Míguez defends this hypothesis regarding Paul's groups:

---

8. James R. Harrison, *Paul and the Imperial Authorities at Thessalonica and Rome: A Study in the Conflict of Ideology*, WUNT 273 (Tübingen: Mohr Siebeck, 2011), 327; see also Abraham Smith, " 'Unmasking the Powers': Toward a Post-Colonial Analysis of 1 Thessalonians," in *Paul and the Roman Imperial Order*, ed. Richard A. Horsley (Harrisburg, PA: Trinity Press International, 2004), 65, who comments: "What Paul guarantees for his assembly is an alternative society of mutual love and support, dramatically different from the security in their dominant positions sought by the Thessalonian elite."

9. Harrison, *Paul*, 327. See further Maria Pascuzzi, *Paul: Windows on His Thought and His World* (Winona, MN: Anselm Academic, 2014), 255: "In reality, the imperial program of 'peace and security' was accomplished through war and violence and benefitted the propertied classes, whose assets and interests were safeguarded. What peace and security the conquered experienced came at the price of colonization and loss of autonomy."

10. Néstor Oscar Míguez, *The Practice of Hope: Ideology and Intention in First Thessalonians*, Paul in Critical Contexts (Minneapolis: Fortress Press, 2012), 1.

Christianity opposed the empire, namely, in regard to its pretension to hold an integrating, absolute power from a center of dominion that saw itself as the unique and eternal regulator of human relations. This momentum of economic and political centralization of the empire coincided with the religious centralization that presupposed the divinization of the empire (the goddess Roma and the *divus Caesar*) and the use of the image of "the household" (*domus, dominus, dominio*) as encompassing the entire empire. We really find ourselves with a "political" struggle by peripheral groups (national and social) against the project of the empire's domination. These groups disputed the symbolic (ideological) space.[11]

With respect to the rhetoric of anti-imperialistic overtones in Paul's scenario of the Parousia, another interesting avenue to consider involves material evidence. In what may be interpreted as an ironic reversal, it appears that the future local readers of 1 Thessalonians within the city of Thessalonica employed what Paul may have cast as antihegemonic to positively underscore imperial power in their day. This has been proposed in an analysis of the mosaics of the dome of the Rotunda in Thessalonica by Laura Nasrallah.

The Rotunda, originally part of the palace complex of the Emperor Galerius (ruled 305–311 CE), who was notable for persecuting Christians, was converted to a Christian church by the late fourth or early fifth century. The transformation of Galerius's structure to a church may have seemed in itself ironic. Nasrallah muses: "Did the itinerant Christian, traveling the footsteps of Paul in 410 CE or so, stand at the intersection of Thessaloniki's main avenue with the road from the imperial palace to the Rotunda and shake her head in disgust at the convergence of the kingdom of God with this sort of empire?"[12] In any case, mosaics were added to the dome then. Now only partially preserved, the three tiers of scenes present Christ striding forth in the apex, surrounded by four angels bearing him aloft, encircled in the tier beneath by twenty-four figures and, in the lowest band below that, by martyrs with arms outstretched in prayer. Nasrallah's analysis concludes that 1 Thess 4:13–5:11 was a significant, although not the only, literary influence on the design of the mosaics. Her observation is that "a revolution in meaning occurred because the early Christian Rotunda can be interpreted as having borrowed from an apocalyptic rhetoric that formerly subverted empire, turning this around in order to articulate a Christian Roman identity

11. Ibid., 38.
12. Laura S. Nasrallah, "Empire and Apocalypse in Thessaloniki: Interpreting the Early Christian Rotunda," *JECS* 13 (2005): 465–508, at 467.

continuous with a supportive Roman Empire."[13] She finds this to be evidence of an ongoing Thessalonian conversation, that is, a convergence of "civic pride, literary texts associated with a city, and building programs and iconography within this one city."[14]

With respect to the in-breaking of the day of the Lord, Paul then draws on a metaphor used widely in the Hebrew prophets: the sudden onset of a pregnant woman's labor pains (1 Thess 5:3). He elaborates on this by stating that such pains signal an event from which there is no escape. By relating the day of the Lord, destruction, and the resurrection of the dead to birth pangs, Paul echoes, for example, Isa 13:6-9 and 26:16-19.[15]

> Wail, for the day of the LORD is near;
>   it will come like destruction from the Almighty!
> Therefore all hands will be feeble,
>   and every human heart will melt,
>   and they will be dismayed.
> Pangs and agony will seize them;
>   they will be in anguish like a woman in labor.
> They will look aghast at one another;
>   their faces will be aflame.
> See, the day of the LORD comes,
>   cruel, with wrath and fierce anger,
> to make the earth a desolation,
>   and to destroy its sinners from it. (Isa 13:6-9)

> O LORD, in distress they sought you,
>   they poured out a prayer
>   when your chastening was on them.
> Like a woman with child,
>   who writhes and cries out in her pangs
>   when she is near her time,
> so were we because of you, O LORD;
>   we were with child, we writhed,
>   but we gave birth only to wind.
> We have won no victories on earth,
>   and no one is born to inhabit the world.
> Your dead shall live, their corpses shall rise.
>   O dwellers in the dust, awake and sing for joy!
> For your dew is a radiant dew,
>   and the earth will give birth to those long dead. (Isa 26:16-19)

13. Ibid., 468.
14. Ibid., 469.
15. See also Isa 21:3; Jer 4:31; 22:23; Hos 13:13; 1 En 62:4.

The onslaught of birth pangs and the inescapability of going through the birth process were existential comparisons for Paul to use in teaching Gentile converts about the coming of the Day of the Lord. Ancient women, even apart from references to the prophets, undoubtedly personally experienced the moments before and during birth as an apocalyptic time. Paul's use of the metaphor was apt, not only because he was steeped in the thought of the Jewish Scriptures, but because his converts' lives regularly dealt with birth—and the foreboding results it might bring about. In his urban lifestyle and regular presence in house churches, Paul must have been very aware of women's apocalyptic moments leading up to giving birth.[16] While the intensity of Paul's imagery may have been mitigated for the males he addressed, many of them would have resonated with their own experiences of being suddenly thrust into helpless waiting during labors and deliveries in which they might lose wives and children. One wonders, however, who the women and men are today who can truly grasp the apocalyptic nature of Paul's reference to the suddenness of birth pangs. Have we become too anesthetized to grasp the metaphor? For whom is childbirth still apocalyptic?

An answer to my latter query has to take much into account, including where people live and their access to modern medicine. That entails a complicated assessment, since the lack of maternal and child care today is not solely determined by, for example, geography and poverty; it is also, and some argue predominantly, political will that problematically does not always prioritize saving mothers. As Nicholas Kristof and Sheryl WuDunn have pointed out: "Maternal mortality is an injustice that is tolerated only because its victims are poor, rural women."[17] For many women, childbirth is still personally apocalyptic.[18] In contrast, can

16. See Margaret Y. MacDonald, Carolyn Osiek, and Janet Tulloch, *A Woman's Place: House Churches in Earliest Christianity* (Minneapolis: Fortress Press, 2006), 50–67.

17. Nicholas D. Kristof and Sheryl WuDunn, *Half the Sky: Turning Oppression into Opportunity for Women Worldwide* (New York: Alfred A. Knopf, 2009), 122.

18. See this excerpt from an op-ed filed from Ndjamene, Chad, by Nicholas D. Kristof, "Terror of Childbirth," *New York Times*, March 20, 2004, http://www.nytimes.com/2004/03/20/opinion/20KRIS.html: "Zara Fatimé, a 15-year-old girl, was in labor for four days before her family loaded her onto public transportation—the back of a truck—and took her to the dilapidated National General Reference Hospital here on Tuesday. Her blood pressure was high, 170/80, and she soon lapsed into a coma. The baby arrived stillborn. Zara needed oxygen, but the hospital had none to spare. 'We have the knowledge to save these people,' Dr. Grace Kodindo, Chad's first female obstetrician, said with a sigh. 'But we lose them because of a lack of tiny amounts of money.' When she started, Dr. Kodindo was one of only 2 obstetricians serving a

people accustomed to good health care, including the option for anes-
thesia and Caesarean deliveries, possibly hear Paul's imagery as did the
people of his day for whom even a C-section (at least not a maternally
survivable one) was not an option?[19]

In the ancient world, the onset of labor pains may have been particularly ominous for first-time mothers. As the words of the prophet em-
pathize in Jer 4:31: "For I heard a cry as of a woman in labor, anguish as
of one bringing forth her first child, the cry of daughter Zion gasping
for breath, stretching out her hands, 'Woe is me! I am fainting before
killers!' " Paul may well have observed many women's reactions to the
onset of labor, their realization that their time from which there is no
turning back had come, which for some descended on them with an
excruciatingly painful swiftness. He would have been no stranger to the
nervousness of expectant mothers and their thoughts of possible impending death for their child or themselves. In his world, such fears were
based on the cruel reality of maternal and child mortality rates.[20] For that
reason, Paul's comparison of the arrival of the Day of the Lord with the
onset of labor pains must have been sobering imagery for his listeners,
themselves immersed in family as well as household slave situations
where the screams of labor and birth were only too often *not* followed
by cries of relief, joy, and attention given to a new child.[21]

---

country of nine million people; now there are 15. Each year, 500,000 women die, almost
one per minute, in pregnancy or childbirth in the third world. Childbirth is terrifying
for most of the world's people. As a local proverb here in Chad puts it: A woman
who is pregnant has one foot in the grave."

19. See Beryl Rawson, *Children and Childhood in Roman Italy* (Oxford and New York:
Oxford University Press, 2003), 99, who observes that "Caesarean section deliveries
were known from an early date (but perhaps not from live women), although the
procedure does not appear in medical texts until the fourteenth century, and the association with the birth of Julius Caesar is doubtful." She also indicates that, if a
woman died while pregnant (including before being ready to give birth), her burial
could not take place until the fetus had been taken from her body to preclude any
viable child from being buried.

20. See Cornelia B. Horn and John W. Martens, *"Let the Little Children Come to Me":
Childhood and Children in Early Christianity* (Washington, DC: The Catholic University
of America Press, 2009), 21: "Some conservative estimates place the rate at about
twenty-eight infant deaths per one hundred births. This phenomenon crossed all
class, ethnic and gender boundaries."

21. On the birthing practices that generally would have been familiar to the Thessalonians, see Soranus, *Soranus' Gynecology*, trans. Owsei Temkin (Baltimore, MD: Johns
Hopkins University Press, 1956; repr., 1991), 70–76. Soranus offers detailed directions
for assisting a birthing mother. He assumes that normally a midwife would be present
and would have brought with her a birthing stool for the mother to sit on. The stool,

In 1 Thess 5:12-22 Paul shifts away from eschatological concerns and offers a series of final, briefly stated exhortations concerning the group as a congregation. These issues touch on respecting the leaders and ministering to idlers, the fainthearted, and the weak. He follows this with an admonition about rejoicing and praying, and finally a comment about prophecy.

With respect to the leaders, Paul lodges an appeal that they should be esteemed highly in love because of their effort on behalf of the church. They are characterized as having three functions: laboring among the group, being in charge in the Lord, and being admonishers. First Thessalonians offers no clue about who these people were or what their gender was. From Acts 17 it could be inferred that the leaders included Jason and some of "the leading women" (17:4), perhaps because those individuals might have had enough resources to host the church.[22] Pheme Perkins has argued, however, that despite Acts 17:4, which assumes some elite women's presence, "the poverty and largely artisan population of Thessalonica would make it less likely to have had women of sufficient wealth or education to act as patrons such as we find in other Pauline churches."[23]

From a postcolonial interpretive stance, Efrain Agosto observes that since the assembly is composed of those who work with their hands (1 Thess 5:11), Paul's commendation of the leaders can be seen to "differ dramatically from the typical letter of recommendation among the impe-

---

he notes, had to be supportive of a woman's back and weight, yet with a large crescent cut out of the seat so that the movement of the fetus could be "in a straight line" (71). If no stool was available he recommends the mother should sit on another woman's lap, a woman who was robust enough to support her and able to "hold her firmly during the pangs of labor" (74) while keeping her own legs spread apart. Soranus also says that the mother should be advised to channel her breathing into the flanks, not screaming but rather groaning. The importance of directing screaming into groaning, he comments, matters since "some inexperienced women, keeping the breath in the upper parts and not driving it downwards have brought about a tumor of the bronchus" (74).

22. Monya A. Stubbs, "1 Thessalonians," in *Women's Bible Commentary*, ed. Carol A. Newsom, Sharon H. Ringe, and Jacqueline E. Lapsley, 3rd ed. (Louisville, KY: Westminster John Knox Press, 2012), 591, comments: "Although no women are mentioned, we cannot assume that the Thessalonian leadership is all male. Paul does not list any particular male leaders either. In fact, it might be more accurate to imagine female leadership in the congregation, since Acts suggests that a number of Thessalonica's 'prominent women' were among the converts (Acts 17:4)."

23. Pheme Perkins, "1 Thessalonians," in *The Women's Bible Commentary*, ed. Carol. A. Newsom and Sharon H. Ringe (Louisville, KY: Westminster John Knox Press, 1992), 350.

rial elite."[24] In this respect Paul identifies them neither by name nor by distinguished family ties nor, for example, by their financial status or political connections. Agosto interprets Paul's recommendation of the leaders as rather "one component among many in his urging the solidarity of the assembly in its struggle against its hostile political environment in Thessalonica."[25]

The possibility nevertheless remains that some elite women were among the group's leaders, especially when one considers the vibrancy of the seaport city of Thessalonica within Roman Macedonia. Even apart from the question of the historical veracity of Acts 17:4, given the leadership roles Thessalonian women would have been accustomed to hold as patrons, or the roles they may have played in various cult celebrations such as the all-female Thesmophoria or in the worship of Isis, one could expect that their skills as leaders transferred with them into the Christian group. Of course, it remains possible that Paul's female converts were patriarchally demoted upon their conversions, but nothing in the letter either suggests or confirms that, and Paul's other authentic letters attest to his collaboration with many female leaders.[26]

Paul's comment about respecting leaders suggests Timothy had reported various difficulties on their part. Speculation on what those dynamics were could run rampant, given all the subjects Paul touches on in 1 Thessalonians. Certainly among the issues, especially in light of the comments Paul directs to men in 4:3-8, may have been relapses into sexual practices he had forbidden. That would have required the leaders to function also as admonishers (5:12). Female converts in mixed marriages with unbelievers may also have been especially problematic for leaders to deal with; they would have easily been prey to cultic backsliding. In contrast, Christian men married to pagan women would have exercised more social control over their spouses and household members. On this general situation in the early church Margaret MacDonald has commented (alluding to imagery from Jas 1:6-8): "Despite the accounts of heroic determination in the literature, one wonders how many of those who were married to unbelievers were a source of frustration for church

---

24. Efrain Agosto, "Patronage and Commendation, Imperial and Anti-Imperial," in Horsley, *Paul and the Roman Imperial Order*, 112.

25. Ibid.

26. See Florence Morgan Gillman, *Women Who Knew Paul* (Collegeville, MN: Liturgical Press, 1992), *passim*.

leaders who saw in their behaviour the instability of a wave of the sea that is driven and tossed by the wind."[27]

Converts to any group may require a time of thorough conversion, and during that immersive period they can be most challenging to leaders and other members. One cannot assume that new believers' social and political views and customs, not to speak of their changing beliefs and practices, instantly move into total conformity. As H. A. Drake has observed (although commenting on the second century and later), "Even the rigorous preparation for membership required by the early Church could not prevent the introduction of heterodoxy as well as heterogeneity. In this sense, converts represent a destabilizing element, one that can seem threatening to established norms."[28] How complex must have been the leadership of the earliest believers in Thessalonica when even the norms were yet being solidified.

As Paul closes his letter with a final prayer (1 Thess 5:23-24), contrary to what a reader might expect, he does not repeat the hope he had mentioned in 3:10 that he might somehow see the Thessalonians again. No doubt he was very wary of ever safely reentering their city. But he also ends his missive by praying for their blamelessness at the coming of Jesus (5:24), an indication that his own focus, as felt so strongly in chapters 4 and 5, was not on his own or their traveling future but upon an imminent return of the Lord.

In 1 Thess 5:25-28, Paul then makes a few last recommendations. These include an order that the letter should be read to all the believers (5:27) and a concluding salutation (5:28). One wonders if Paul's need to insist that his message be communicated to the whole group emerged from prior experience where that had not happened, perhaps confirming that 1 Thessalonians was a product of Paul as a very experienced evangelizer and letter writer.[29] It also reflects his ongoing concern for and nonhierarchical approach to each of his converts.

27. Margaret Y. MacDonald, "Early Christian Women Married to Unbelievers," *SR* 19 (1990): 221–34, at 221.
28. H. A. Drake, "Models of Christian Expansion," in *Spread of Christianity in the First Four Centuries: Essays in Explanation*, ed. William V. Harris (Leiden: Brill, 2005), 10–11.
29. See above, p. 6 n. 3.

Afterword

Courage and Complexities in Believing in "the Gospel of God" (2:2)

A s profound and liberating as conversion to belief in the living God may have been, this commentary has sought to stress that it must have been very hard for the earliest Thessalonian believers, both women and men, to experience the limitations monotheism imposed on them relative to their earlier lives as polytheists. And the passing of time, even in the few months reflected in 1 Thessalonians that had elapsed between Paul's initial visit in 49 CE and his letter to them in 50, may have made their lives increasingly difficult. As the first Christians in Thessalonica were converted to belief in Jesus, they were imbued with apocalyptic fervor. But the Parousia of Christ had not occurred, and implementing new practices and leaving behind former ways would have immersed them in unforeseen cultural and personal complexities, even local persecution. The lure of recidivism must have been constant.

Throughout this commentary attention has been consistently drawn to both certain as well as possible issues concerning the Thessalonian believers' rejection of their idols. I have repeatedly mused about how Paul's small contingent of early believers may have navigated their radical move from polytheism to monotheism. Some of the material I have brought into dialogue with 1 Thessalonians has been treated in the *probability* that it relates to the earliest Thessalonian Christian women. That is how it is with studying much about ancient women. In these concluding remarks I would like to echo an observation made by Nicola Denzey (regarding her work on the Via Latina catacomb)[1] that I think applies to many attempts, including mine, to better uncover ancient women's experience:

> These are speculative thoughts, of course, perhaps overly sentimental for some historians who refuse to look beyond proof and paper trails and smoking guns. But women's history grants few of those, more often offering only silence from which to extrapolate lives and relationships and moments.[2]

We can be certain, of course, that the women and men to whom Paul wrote had accepted what he had to offer, "the gospel of God," "the living and true God" to whom they had turned in imitation of Paul and the Lord Jesus. God was the reality to which they had converted; that God, whom they experienced "in power and in the Holy Spirit and with full conviction" (1:1), was the enabling factor in changing their own identities.

In reflecting similarly on this process Christopher Kavin Rowe has summarized the transition of the early Christians well:

> To see that the contour of their life derived from their understanding of God is to penetrate to the core of the conflict that surrounded their birth and growth. From 1 Thessalonians (1:9) through Pliny's famous epistle (10.96) to the persecution under Decius and beyond, the clash of the gods ultimately determined the shape of the collision between (emerging) Christianity and paganism. . . . But the conflict as a whole and the instantiation of a new culture—for that is what it was—are utterly inconceivable apart from the clash between the exclusivity of the Christian God and the wider mode of pagan religiousness. . . . Christian ecclesial life, in other words, was the cultural explication of God's identity.[3]

---

1. See above, pp. 63–64.
2. Nicola Denzey, *The Bone Gatherers: The Lost Worlds of Early Christian Women* (Boston: Beacon Press, 2007), 42.
3. Christopher Kavin Rowe, *World Upside Down: Reading Acts in the Graeco-Roman Age* (New York and Oxford: Oxford University Press, 2011), 17–18.

As I reflect on my experience of thinking about 1 Thessalonians for the past few years while researching and writing this text, I agree with Rowe's use of the terms "clash" and "conflict." I too think Paul's converts lived within a momentous collision between polytheism and monotheism. I also think the Thessalonians were plunged into far more complicated lives than they had ever anticipated while they faithfully awaited the Parousia. One finishes a commentary on Paul's letter to them with profound admiration for their courage and, as Paul himself put it, their steadfastness of hope (1:3).

2 Thessalonians

Authors' Introduction

Feminism, Apocalyptic, and 2 Thessalonians

Thessalonica (modern-day Thessaloniki, Greece) was named after the stepsister of Alexander the Great, wife of the general Cassander who founded the city in 316–315 BCE.[1] The poet Antipater called Thessalonica the mother city of Macedonia (*Anthologia Palatina* 4.428); it was personified by a city goddess with a crown of turrets.

Figure 1: Thessalonian City Goddess[2]

The book of Acts (17:1-9) describes the mission to Thessalonica as Paul's second stop in Macedonia after Philippi, inspired by the apostle's dream of a Macedonian man begging for help (16:9-10). After Paul and

---

1. Ben Witherington III, *1 and 2 Thessalonians* (Grand Rapids, MI: Eerdmans, 2006), 2.
2. Source: Printed with permission of wildwinds.com, http://www.wildwinds.com/coins/greece/macedonia/thessalonica/Moushmov_6591.jpg.

Silas arrive in the city, Paul spends three Sabbaths arguing "from the scriptures" that Jesus is the Messiah (17:2). According to Acts, some synagogue members heeded the message of the missionaries, "as did a great many of the devout Greeks and not a few of the leading women" (17:4). "Devout Greeks" (σεβομένων Ἑλλήνων) probably refers to "God-fearers"—Gentiles attracted to Jewish beliefs and worship. The reference to "leading women" recalls the account in Acts 16:11-15 of the conversion of Lydia, "a worshiper of God" in the Macedonian city of Philippi, who gathered with other women on the Sabbath in a "place of prayer" and who founded the first church in Europe when she had the members of her household baptized. While it is unclear whether she was wealthy, it is evident that she owned a home and had servants, which means she had economic resources to support the mission of Paul upon her conversion. We may also speculate that her leadership reflects the religious leadership of other women of that time at Philippi.[3] It is in this context that the writer of Acts refers to "leading women."

The Thessalonian letters show little apparent relationship to the events related in Acts.[4] Jason, one of the supporters of Paul and Silas who is said to have welcomed them to his house (Acts 17:7), is mentioned in neither letter, nor is Aristarchus of Thessalonica, a member of Paul's missionary circle (Acts 19:29; 20:4; 27:2). More germane to the focus of this commentary, except for a cryptic and, from a contemporary perspective, slighting and sexist reference in 1 Thess 4:4,[5] there are no explicit references to women in either letter. Perhaps this is the reason why one of the earliest commentators on 2 Thessalonians, John Chrysostom (ca. 347–407), assumed that the Thessalonian letters were written to men only (see, e.g., *Homily on 1 Thessalonians* 113:345).[6] This makes feminist interpretation of the letter challenging, since the usual avenues of approach are not espe-

3. Carol Myers, Toni Craven, and Ross S. Kraemer, eds., *Women in Scripture: A Dictionary of Named and Unnamed Women in the Hebrew Bible, The Apocryphal/Deuterocanonical Books, and the New Testament* (Boston: Houghton Mifflin, 2000), 111.

4. Acts was written decades after Paul's death, and its account of early church history is questioned by many scholars.

5. See Florence Gillman's commentary on 1 Thessalonians in this volume.

6. See Peter Gorday, ed., *Ancient Christian Commentary on Scripture, New Testament IX: Colossians, 1–2 Thessalonians, 1–2 Timothy, Titus, Philemon* (Downers Grove, IL: InterVarsity, 2000), 81. See also contemporary NT scholar Richard Ascough's thesis that 1 Thessalonians was addressed primarily to a men-only trade association, although he admits that this would make the Thessalonian church atypical among Pauline communities ("The Thessalonian Christian Community as a Professional Voluntary Association," *JBL* 119 [2000]: 325–27).

cially applicable. For example, of six areas of feminist interpretation of the Bible identified by Alice Ogden Bellis, only one—the reassessment of translation principles relating to women's concerns—is ostensibly germane to the task.[7] Another feminist approach not explicitly listed by Bellis is also germane: the critique of biblical passages and interpretations that have been used to limit or oppress women and other marginalized people, or that have functioned to the detriment of peace, justice, and ecological well-being. However, like other works of feminist interpretation, our commentary proceeds with a "hermeneutic of suspicion" that "scrutinizes the presuppositions and interests of interpreters" (i.e., "traditional" understandings of the Bible) as well as "the androcentric [male-centered] strategies of the biblical text itself."[8] That is, our commentary recognizes that like other biblical texts, 2 Thessalonians was written by men, and its "authoritative" interpreters have been male; therefore it can be assumed that, to some extent, the letter and its interpreters reflect male/patriarchal bias (androcentricity). Our commentary applies a gynocentric ("woman-centered") perspective to 2 Thessalonians and is cognizant of the French feminist understanding of *le feminin* as any force resistant to and disruptive of traditional patriarchal symbolic structures.

In the four one-volume feminist Bible commentaries that have been published in the past two decades, the author of two of the four chapters on 2 Thessalonians is one of the co-authors of this volume, Mary Ann Beavis, and the chapter on 2 Thessalonians in *A Feminist Companion to the Deutero-Pauline Epistles* was also written by Beavis.[9] Thus our commentary will inevitably expand, reflect on, and sometimes critique this previous work. It will also engage with other feminist work on the letter,

---

7. The others are: investigations of the status and role of women in biblical times; the rediscovery and reassessment of overlooked biblical traditions about women; the reassessment of well-known biblical texts relating to women; the discovery of female images of the divine in the biblical texts; explorations of the history of the cultural reception and appropriation of biblical texts about women, e.g., in art, cinema, literature, and music. See Alice Ogden Bellis, *Helpmates, Harlots and Heroes* (Louisville, KY: Westminster John Knox, 2007), 119.

8. Ibid., 23.

9. Mary Ann Beavis, "'If Anyone Will Not Work, Let Them Not Eat': 2 Thessalonians 3:10 and the Social Support of Women," in *A Feminist Companion to the Deutero-Pauline Epistles*, ed. Amy-Jill Levine (London and New York: T & T Clark, 2003), 29–36. See also Sheila E. McGinn and Megan Wilson-Reitz, "2 Thessalonians vs. the *Ataktoi*: A Pauline Critique of White-Collar Welfare," in *By Bread Alone: The Bible Through the Eyes of the Hungry*, ed. Sheila E. McGinn, Lai Ling Ngan, and Ahida Pilarski (Minneapolis: Fortress Press, 2014), 185–208.

notably with Marlene Crüsemann's chapter in the recent volume of European feminist commentaries on the Bible and related literature.[10] Since feminist scholarship is often overlooked by "malestream" commentators, it is important that these works receive specific attention here.

The co-authors of this commentary are Canadian biblical scholar Mary Ann Beavis, whose feminist exegesis structures the volume, and HyeRan Kim-Cragg, a Korean-Canadian theologian whose approach to the text is informed by postcolonial feminist theology, practical theology of worship, and religious education. Contributing author Pia Sison reflects on the theme of suffering (2 Thess 1:4, 5, 6) from the perspective of a Filipina feminist biblical scholar. The approach to the text is thus cooperative, multidisciplinary, and multicultural, weaving together the threads of historical and literary approaches, feminist and postcolonial critique, and theological reflection into a tapestry that reflects the different academic, ecclesial, ethnic, and geographical locations of the contributors.

Date and Authorship

In contrast to 1 Thessalonians, which is widely regarded by scholars as Paul's first extant letter, the oldest document in the Christian canon (ca. 49–52 CE), 2 Thessalonians belongs to a handful of New Testament letters attributed to Paul but whose authorship is disputed. The others are Colossians, Ephesians, 1–2 Timothy, and Titus. However, 2 Thessalonians does not have much in common with these other Deutero-Pauline letters except for its canonical attribution to Paul. Colossians and Ephesians, on the one hand, and 1–2 Timothy and Titus, on the other, show literary affinities with one another; Ephesians appears to be a literary expansion of Colossians, and the letters to Timothy and Titus are classified together as "Pastoral Epistles," apparently written after Paul's death, in order to adapt the apostle's teachings to the circumstances of the late

10. E. Elizabeth Johnson, "2 Thessalonians," in *The Women's Bible Commentary*, ed. Carol A. Newsom and Sharon H. Ringe (Louisville, KY: Westminster John Knox, 1992), 351–52; Mary Ann Beavis, "2 Thessalonians," in *Searching the Scriptures*, vol. 2: *A Feminist Commentary*, ed. Elisabeth Schüssler Fiorenza (New York: Crossroad, 1994), 263–73; Marlene Crüsemann, "2 Thessalonians: Hope in God's Last Judgment," in *Feminist Biblical Interpretation: A Compendium of Critical Commentary on the Books of the Bible and Related Literature*, ed. Luise Schottroff and Marie-Theres Wacker (Grand Rapids, MI, and Cambridge: Eerdmans, 2012), 821–29; Mary Ann Beavis, "2 Thessalonians," in *Women's Bible Commentary*, ed. Carol A. Newsom, Sharon H. Ringe, and Jacqueline E. Lapsley, 3rd ed. (Louisville, KY: Westminster John Knox, 2012), 592–94.

first or early second century. Second Thessalonians, in contrast, closely resembles 1 Thessalonians to the extent that over a hundred years ago William Wrede surmised that 2 Thessalonians was a post-Pauline forgery, dated between 100 CE and 110 CE, precisely because of its lack of originality.[11] Conversely, it has often been argued that the similarities between the two letters point to the authenticity of the second epistle; it is reasonable to assume that two documents written to the same addressees by the same authors (Paul, Silvanus, and Timothy)[12] within a short interval would show stylistic and thematic similarities, although, as E. Elizabeth Johnson noted, "Paul is not found quoting himself from one letter to another."[13] Indeed, similarities can be found. For example, an expression of thanksgiving (1 Thess 1:2; 2:13; 3:9; 2 Thess 1:3; 2:13) and intercessory prayer (1 Thess 3:11-13; 2 Thess 2:16-17) are found in both letters. However, this does not lead to a definite conclusion that the two letters were written by the same author. In fact, there are many differences between them. Abraham Smith, citing Daryl D. Schmidt, contends that the excessive and redundant styles of expression found in 2 Thessalonians' opening thanksgiving are not in line with the Pauline corpus.[14]

Another striking difference between the two letters that is often mentioned as evidence of the questionable authenticity of the second is the difference in eschatology between the two. Both letters look forward to a near-future return (παρουσία) of Jesus Christ to vindicate the faithful. First Thessalonians 4:13-18 reassures the members of the church, who are concerned that some members of their group have died and Jesus has not yet arrived, that at the parousia the faithful "dead in Christ" will "rise first," that is, be resurrected, "to meet with the Lord in the air; and so we will be with the Lord forever" (1 Thess 4:17). In the second letter the situation is quite different: the addressees are concerned because they have received "by word or by letter" a message that "the day of the Lord is already here" (2 Thess 2:2). This is usually taken to mean that at least

11. William Wrede, *Die Echtheit des zweiten Thessalonicherbriefs* (Leipzig: Hinrichs, 1903), 95–96. For a summary of the parallels between the two letters, see Witherington, *1 and 2 Thessalonians*, 11–12.

12. 1 Thess 1:1; 2 Thess 1:1.

13. Johnson, "2 Thessalonians," 351.

14. Abraham Smith, "The First and Second Letters to the Thessalonians," in *A Postcolonial Commentary on the New Testament Writings*, ed. Fernando F. Segovia and R. S. Sugirtharajah, The Bible and Postcolonialism 13 (New York: T & T Clark, 2007), 305, citing Daryl D. Schmidt, "The Syntactical Style of 2 Thessalonians: How Pauline Is It?," in *The Thessalonian Correspondence*, ed. Raymond F. Collins (Leuven: Leuven University Press, 1990), 382–93.

some members of the audience had heard that the parousia had arrived and they had missed it, although, as the comments on 2 Thessalonians 2 below will show, other interpretations are possible. The authors respond by reminding the addressees that certain events must happen before Jesus arrives: there will be a rebellion when "the lawless one" will be revealed and install himself in the temple of God, presumably in Jerusalem. However, for the present he is being restrained, so that he will be revealed "when his time comes" (2 Thess 2:6). Only when the restraint is removed will the "lawless one" be exposed and destroyed by Jesus "by the manifestation of his coming" (2:7-8). That is, 1 Thessalonians promises that Christ will return abruptly "from heaven"; no series of preliminary events is expected. In contrast, 2 Thessalonians presupposes a well-known apocalyptic timetable that must ensue before the Day of the Lord (2:2).

The distinct eschatologies of the two documents do not conclusively prove that they originate from different authors, times, and places. One way of explaining the discrepancy between the two is to question the canonical ordering of the letters and assume that 2 Thessalonians was written first, in response to a rumor, perhaps conveyed in a letter falsely attributed to Paul, Silvanus, and Timothy, that the parousia had already arrived (2 Thess 2:2). The missionaries comfort the congregation by insisting that certain events must happen before the coming of the Lord and that they must hold fast to their teaching (2 Thess 2:15). A short time later the missionaries receive word that the Thessalonians have heeded their teaching but that in the interim some of the faithful have died, leading them to question whether the deceased will share in the glories of the parousia. The missionaries write back, extravagantly praising the believers for their firm faith in Jesus (1 Thess 1:2-10) and reassuring them that their deceased loved ones will be raised up to be with Christ even before the living (1 Thess 4:13-18). This explanation, originally made by T. W. Manson and more recently supported by Charles A. Wanamaker[15] is intriguing but has received little scholarly acceptance. Moreover, the discrepancy between the eschatologies of the two letters is not definitive proof that they were written by different authors. The synoptic eschatological discourses (Mark 13:1-36; Matt 24:1-44; Luke 21:5-36) are capable of asserting both that believers must keep alert because the date of the parousia is known to God alone (e.g., Mark 13:32-37) and that a series

15. T. W. Manson, "St. Paul in Greece: The Letters to the Thessalonians," *BJRL* 35 (1952–53): 428–47; Charles A. Wanamaker, *Commentary on 1 and 2 Thessalonians* (Grand Rapids, MI: Eerdmans, 1990), xxx.

of end-time events must happen before the sudden arrival of the Son of Man (e.g., Mark 13:14-31).

In light of the arguments against Pauline authorship mentioned above and other reasons that will be discussed below, we accept the majority view that 2 Thessalonians is pseudonymous. However, this begs the question of why a letter, specifically addressed to the church at Thessalonica, would be relevant, or of persuasive force, decades later.[16] Presumably the Thessalonian church of the time would have preserved and valued the first letter and would have been suspicious of a second letter suddenly unearthed to illumine their contemporary situation. Conversely, the prophecies of 2:1-12 do fit the events surrounding the destruction of the temple in 70 CE in a general way, although, as supporters of the letter's authenticity have often remarked, 3:3-4 does not accurately reflect the details of the invasion of Jerusalem.[17] However, it is questionable whether Thessalonian christians,[18] living far from Judea and without recourse to the historical accounts accessible by contemporary biblical scholars, would have had detailed knowledge of events in Jerusalem; nonetheless, they would have found reports of those events disturbing and anxiety-provoking. In other words, we take the Thessalonian destination of the letter seriously, although we regard the letter as Deutero-Pauline (inspired by the example of Paul) rather than as having been written by the apostle himself.

On this hypothesis, then, someone other than Paul wrote 2 Thessalonians in order to address the concerns and anxieties of the church at Thessalonica about two decades after the writing of the first epistle—and probably after the death of the apostle. Like 1 Thessalonians, however, the second letter claims multiple authorship, by Paul, Silvanus, and Timothy (2 Thess 1:1). Although it may have been written by none of these missionaries (or by one or both of the latter, invoking Paul's name), the attribution of joint authorship reminds us that the anonymous author(s) are not the only voices that can be discerned in the letter. Other persons involved in the formulation of the letter might include the scribe

16. See Witherington, *1 and 2 Thessalonians*, 11.

17. See ibid., 12–13.

18. Since the term "Christian" was not commonly used in the first century (in the NT it is found only in Acts 26:28 and 1 Pet 4:16, referring to followers of Christ, not to devotees of a religion), and "Christianity" did not exist as a religion, the term "christian" will be used with reference to the earliest members of the kingdom of God movement, including the author and audience of 2 Thessalonians.

to whom the letter was dictated,[19] the prophets behind the apocalyptic teachings in 2 Thess 1:5-9 and 2:1-12, and the recipients of the letter whose needs and concerns indirectly shaped the discourse. The putative anonymity of 2 Thessalonians leaves open the possibility of female authorship; as Virginia Woolf remarked in a letter to her husband, "I would venture to guess that Anon, who wrote so many poems without signing them, was often a woman."[20] Furthermore, the notion of unknown authorship frees us to imagine the plethora of unnamed people among the founders of the early church, many of whom were women. Whether such anonymity or omission is intentional or not, resulting "from literary strategy, biblical androcentrism . . . or some other reason," it enables us to wonder, ponder, and imagine what might have happened.[21] Unknowing also creates ambiguity in which other meanings and interpretations can emerge that may shed new light, otherwise hidden.

If 2 Thessalonians, as discussed above, is a pseudepigraphal letter modeled on the first letter, this makes 2 Thessalonians the first stage in the reception history of 1 Thessalonians. Steven J. Friesen calls the disguised author of 2 Thessalonians "the first New Testament scholar, the first specialist in Pauline studies," whose forgery was so successful that it eventually became part of the Christian canon.[22] It should be noted, however, that, contrary to Friesen's assertion that by feigning Pauline authorship the anonymous author embedded the apostle's authority in the letter rather than in his personal presence, the author of 2 Thessalonians chose to imitate the multiple authorship of the first letter—"Paul, Silvanus, and Timothy" (1:1)—and to ground the authority of their teachings in the apocalyptic oracles of anonymous prophets.

Women, Religion, and Thessalonica

In view of the questionable authenticity of the letter, its Thessalonian context is debatable, although, as argued above, it is also defensible. In an essay on the "invisible" women of the Thessalonian church, Melanie

19. See comment on 2 Thess 3:17 below at 184.

20. Virginia Woolf, *A Room of One's Own* (New York: Harcourt, Brace & World, 1957; first pub. 1929), 51.

21. Myers, et al., *Women in Scripture*, xi.

22. Steven J. Friesen, "Second Thessalonians, the Ideology of the Epistles, and the Construction of Authority: Our Debt to the Forger," in *From Rome to Early Christian Thessalonikē: Studies in Religion and Archaeology*, HTS 64, ed. Laura Nasrallah, Charalambos Bakirtzis, and Steven J. Friesen (Cambridge, MA: Harvard University Press, 2010), 207–8.

Johnson-DeBaufre discusses three areas of archaeological research that can be drawn upon to bring the female recipients of the Thessalonian letters to visibility. First, women participated extensively in the religious life of the city. In her 1948 article "Cults of Thessalonica," Johnson-DeBaufre notes, "Charles Edson catalogues priestesses, wives, daughters, and empresses—some with names—without comment and without indication that their presence is either surprising or problematic."[23] Second, women participated significantly in voluntary associations—professional and religious associations offering friendship and mutual support to their members.[24] Third, Johnson-DeBaufre discusses the way in which the focus of contemporary interpreters on the imperial ideology reflected in the eschatological teachings of 1 Thess 4:13–5:11[25] assumes that "Thessalonian experiences of imperial rule are uniform and uninflected by status or gender."[26] Johnson-DeBaufre further observes that "by not actively discussing wo/men in regard to other aspects of everyday life, we thus miss an opportunity to imagine them variously resisting, surviving, negotiating, and resignifying the ideologies of empire."[27] For that reason, we have been attentive throughout this discussion to the task of bringing the women of the Thessalonian church to visibility. Attention is also paid to the everyday life of the women and men as a way of putting the apocalyptic (otherworldly) message in context. We also use the lens of the liturgy, i.e., "a common art of the people of God,"[28] to look at how the people of Thessalonica put their faith into practice, commingling the cries of suffering and expectation with praise and thanksgiving, evoking both the already-here and the not-yet kin-dom of God,[29] a new world social order.

23. Melanie Johnson-DeBaufre, " 'Gazing Upon the Invisible': Archaeology, Historiography, and the Elusive Wo/men of 1 Thessalonians," in Nasrallah, et al., *From Roman to Early Christian Thessalonikē*, 73–108, at 83, citing Charles Edson, "Cults of Thessalonica," *HTR* 41 (1948): 153–204.

24. Johnson-DeBaufre, "Gazing," 87–90.

25. See also 2 Thess 1:5-12; 2:1-11.

26. Johnson-DeBaufre, "Gazing," 91.

27. Ibid.

28. Don E. Saliers, "Human Pathos and Divine Ethos," in *Primary Sources of Liturgical Theology: A Reader*, ed. Dwight W. Vogel (Collegeville, MN: Liturgical Press, 2000), 277.

29. This term, "kin-dom of God," was coined by Ada Maria Isasi-Diaz. See her article, "Solidarity: Love of the Neighbor in the 1980s," in *Lift Every Voice: Constructing Christian Theologies from the Underside*, ed. Susan Brooks Thistlethwaite and Mary Potter Engel (San Francisco: Harper and Row, 1990), 31–40.

Testament of a Thessalonian Priestess

Charles Edson provides this translation and paraphrase of a third-century CE funerary inscription recording the last wishes of a Dionysian priestess, Euphrosyne, whose cult title was "Evia," the feminine form of a common designation of the god, Dionysos Evios:

Being priestess Evia of Prinophoros, I bequeath for the perpetuation of my memory two plethra of vineyard, together with the adjacent irrigation ditches in order that sacrifices may be burned for me from the income thereof to the value of not less than five denarii. The mystai, each and every one, are to bear a crown of roses at the ceremony. The mystes who does not bear such a crown is to have no share in the income from my bequest. If the Prinophoroi do not fulfill these conditions, the bequest is to devolve to the thiasos of the Dryophoroi, subject to the same conditions. And if the other thiasos does not carry out the terms of the bequest, then the vineyard is to become the property of the city.[30]

Among other goddesses and gods worshiped in Thessalonica were Isis and Serapis, Zeus, Asclepius, Aphrodite, Demeter, Roma, Cabirus, and Theos Hypsistos ("God Most High"), a title associated especially with Gentile "God-fearers."[31] In addition there was a highly developed imperial cult, resulting from Thessalonica's status as a free city within the Roman Empire.[32]

Mary Ann Beavis

Feminism and Apocalyptic

As an intrinsic part of the christian canon, 2 Thessalonians has contributed disproportionately to the development of doctrines about the end of the world, particularly the appearance of the "Antichrist"—even

30. Edson, "Cults," 170.

31. See Karl P. Donfried, *Paul, Thessalonica, and Early Christianity* (London: T & T Clark, 2002), 21–49; Ekaterini G. Tsalampouni, "The Cult of Theos Hypsistos in Roman Thessalonica and the First Christian Community of the City," paper presented at the SBL International Meeting, July 5, 2011.

32. See Donfried, *Paul*, 31–38, and especially Holland Hendrix, "Thessalonicans Honor Romans" (ThD diss., Harvard Divinity School, 1984).

though the term ἀντίχριστος does not appear in the text.[33] From a feminist standpoint, the lurid and violent apocalyptic imagery that takes up so much of the letter (2 Thess 1:5–2:12) provokes initial distaste, perhaps more due to the way such texts have been interpreted through the centuries than for their enigmatic canonical expressions. Most saliently for our times, as feminist theologian Catherine Keller observes, literalist readings of biblical apocalyptic literature undergird the Western cultural conviction that the destruction of the earth and her inhabitants is inevitable and even desirable: "The religious habit of imagining the world out of existence would not seem to be irrelevant to material habits of world-waste ruining our civilization; in right-wing religious anti-environmentalism, for instance, the expectancy that Our Father will make us a shiny new world when this one breaks explicitly correlates with a willingness to dump this one."[34] Ironically, she observes, "environmentalists resort to apocalypse as well, predicting premature points of no return or declaring the 'end of nature.'"[35]

Historically, women have not been immune to the appeal of apocalyptic thought. The second-century CE movement known as the "New Prophecy" (later called "Montanism" by its opponents, after the prophet Montanus) revered the oracles of female prophets[36] who predicted the imminent arrival of the New Jerusalem in Phrygia, Asia Minor. In the fourth century the heresiologist Epiphanius of Salamis reported that "in Pepuza either Quintilla or Priscilla . . . had been asleep . . . and the Christ came to her and slept with her in the following manner, as that deluded woman described it: 'Having assumed the form of a woman,' she says, 'Christ came to me in a bright robe and put wisdom (*sophian*) into me, and revealed to me that this place is holy, and that it is here that Jerusalem will descend from heaven'" (*Or.* 11 in Epiphanius, *Panarion* 49.1).[37] What remains of the oracles of the New Prophecy is fragmentary and transmitted through hostile witnesses, but their extant prophecies do not share the fear-inspiring imagery of the canonical apocalypses.

33. See Anthony C. Thiselton, *1 & 2 Thessalonians through the Centuries* (Chichester, UK: Wiley, 2011), 211–30.

34. Catherine Keller, *Apocalypse Now and Then: A Feminist Guide to the End of the World* (Minneapolis: Fortress Press, 1996), 2.

35. Ibid., citing Bill McKibben, *The End of Nature* (New York: Random House, 1989).

36. The names of three of these prophets survive: Priscilla, Maximilla, and Quintilla.

37. Susanna Elm, "Montanist Oracles," in Schüssler Fiorenza, *Searching the Scriptures*, 2:131–38, at 133.

Although it would be anachronistic to project feminism onto this ancient prophetic movement, it seems to have been gender-egalitarian, featuring a central ritual in which seven white-clad virgins prophesied to the people, and where women not only baptized and celebrated the Eucharist but also served as elders and bishops.[38] According to Marcella Althaus-Reid and Lisa Isherwood, this new prophecy of the end of time was not simply predicted but faithfully practiced in reality. Revisiting the story of Thecla, who dressed as a man following her baptism, they speculate that her gender-bending performance, rooted in Montanism, is an example of a practice aimed at subverting the hierarchy of class, race, and gender. It was a lived practice of faith based on the belief that there is no longer any difference between the sexes in the apocalyptic age, a belief inspired by proclamations such as the one found in Gal 3:27-28. As Althaus-Reid and Isherwood explain, "In taking seriously the message of equality of the Christian gospel, [the women of the Montanist movement] queered gender-performance in order to find a way of living the radical equality they professed to believe."[39] Our early church sisters teach us that baptism "is the foundation for justice within the church. It is the sacrament of equality."[40] Their view of the end of time is of an alternative way to resist oppressive structures, actualizing the faith that is taught. Not so surprising, then, that despite the fragmentary nature of the Montanist women's prophecies that survive, more oracles attributed to Priscilla, Maximilla, and Quintilla are extant than oracles attributed to named women in the entire New Testament.

Feminist historians and theologians have restored scholarly attention to the work of one of the most influential women in the Western church of her time, the medieval abbess Hildegard of Bingen (1098–1179).[41] One of her most famous visions, redolent of both 2 Thess 2:1-12 and Rev 12:1-5, but applying very much to her own time, is her bizarre and disturbing account of the birth of the Antichrist:

38. Ibid., 135, citing Epiphanius, *Panarion* 49.2; can 11 Laodicea.

39. Marcella Althaus-Reid and Lisa Isherwood, *Controversies in Feminist Theology* (London: SCM Press, 2007), 21.

40. James F. White, *Sacraments as God's Self-Giving* (Nashville, TN: Abingdon, 1983), 96.

41. E.g., Sabina Flanagan, *Hildegard of Bingen, 1098–1179: A Visionary Life* (New York and London: Routledge, 1998); Barbara Newman, ed., *Hildegard of Bingen: Voice of the Living Light* (Berkeley: University of California Press, 1998); Barbara Newman, *Hildegard of Bingen: The Woman of Her Age* (New York: Doubleday, 2001); Barbara Newman, *Sister of Wisdom: St. Hildegard's Theology of the Feminine* (Berkeley: University of California Press, 1987).

And I saw again the figure of a woman whom I had previously seen in front of the altar that stands before the eyes of God; she stood in the same place, but now I saw her from the waist down. And from her waist to the place that denotes the female, she had various scaly blemishes; and in that latter place was a black and monstrous head. It had fiery eyes, and ears like an ass's, and nostrils and mouth like a lion's; it opened wide its jowls and terrible clashed its horrible iron-colored teeth. And from this head down to her knees, the figure was white and red, as if bruised by many beatings; and from her knees to her tendons where they joined her heels, which appeared white, she was covered with blood. And behold! That monstrous head moved from its place with such a great shock that the figure of the woman was shaken all through her limbs. And a great mass of excrement adhered to the head; and it raised itself up upon a mountain and tried to ascend the height of heaven. (*Scivias*, Book 3, Vision 11)[42]

As Allison Jaines Elledge observes, the imagery in Hildegard's vision is both violent and apocalyptic,[43] and a contemporary reader might regard her revelation with the kind of puzzlement and aversion provoked by biblical apocalyptic. However, this account of the birth of the Antichrist should not be taken literally as an event in a horrific eschatological timetable but as shaped by the political and ecclesiastical context of her own time. Joseph L. Baird and Radd K. Ehrman describe her time in the following way: "The age into which Hildegard was born was a turbulent, disorderly age, a time of petty wars, and fierce struggles, of unruly secular leaders and undisciplined Church officials . . . in short, of bloody conflict between Church and State. . . . The struggles between the Empire and Church continued throughout Hildegard's lifetime."[44] For Hildegard, the woman giving birth symbolizes the church, and her monstrous offspring is ecclesiastical corruption: "The Church herself is corrupt, especially 'at the place that denotes the female,' and as excrement covered the head of Evil as it came out of her body. Even though this image suggests that all hope is lost and the recovery of the Church is now impossible, Hildegard left room for hope and the anticipation of reform: *Ecclesia*'s shoes are white, which

---

42. Translation in Allison Jaines Elledge, "Contextualizing Hildegard of Bingen's Violent and Apocalyptic Imagery," *Academia* (May 3, 2010), 45, https://www.academia.edu/494645/Contextualizing_Hildegard_of_Bingens_Violent_and_Apocalyptic_Imagery.

43. Ibid., 3.

44. Joseph L. Baird and Radd K. Ehrman, eds., *The Letters of Hildegard of Bingen*, vol. 1 (Oxford: Oxford University Press, 1994), 10–11.

indicates a time of goodness and spiritual reform."[45] However, Elledge's interpretation of this image, regarding the color white as "good and spiritual," is problematic today, even if Hildegard might have intended it that way. When whiteness is assumed to connote goodness or purity, questions need to be raised about racial assumptions at play. Given the historical, cultural, and theological treatment of blackness as bad and evil, this kind of color-coded interpretation should be contested.

Contesting Color in Biblical Art

Feminist liturgical theologian Ruth Duck, who carefully attends to the power of language used in liturgy, warns that constant use of certain symbols or colors regularly linked to race or gender helps perpetuate current social injustices.[46] When images are rooted in and based on biblical texts, like Hildegard's vision of the Antichrist, the impact becomes particularly painful and dangerous for those who live in a context heavily influenced by religion. William Blake's painting, *Naomi Entreating Ruth and Orpah* (1795), is another such example. In this painting, Ruth, who is counted as righteous and faithful for turning to the God of Judah, is painted as having white skin and blond hair, while Orpah, supposedly bad because of her decision to turn away from that God, is given darker skin and black hair.[47] The racial overtones of an ideology of Israel as the chosen race—although both the biblical Ruth and Orpah are Moabite women—is implicit in this visual interpretation. One should note that postcolonial feminist and biblical scholars have contested the interpretation of Orpah as a bad woman without true faith.[48]

45. Elledge, "Contextualizing Hildegard," 45; see also Richard K. Emmerson, "The Representation of Antichrist in Hildegard of Bingen's *Scivias*: Image, Word, Commentary, and Visionary Experience," *Gesta* 41, no. 2 (2002): 95–110.

46. Ruth C. Duck, "Expansive Language in the Baptized Community," in Vogel, *Primary Sources*, 286–94, at 294.

47. William Blake, "Naomi Entreating Ruth and Orpah to Return to the Land of Moab," 1795, *Galleria opere d'arte di William Blake*, Settemuse.it: per condividere la conoscenza, http://www.settemuse.it/pittori_scultori_europei/blake/william_blake_015_naomi_ruth_1795.jp.

48. Laura E. Donaldson, "The Sign of Orpah: Reading Ruth through Native Eyes," in *Ruth and Esther*, FCB, 2nd ser., ed. Athalya Brenner (Sheffield: Sheffield Academic Press, 1999), 130–44; Musa Dube, "The Unpublished Letters of Orpah to Ruth," in the same volume, 145–50; Judith E. McKinlay, *Reframing Her: Biblical Women in Postcolonial Focus* (Sheffield: Sheffield Phoenix Press, 2004), 37–56.

In this context, critique of paintings of Jesus is necessary, given his centrality to Christianity. Such paintings exemplify the power that images have in reinforcing certain assumptions and prejudices. Randall C. Bailey argues that attempts to justify images of Jesus with blond hair, blue eyes, white skin, and able body are often made "under the guise of scientific and rational objectivity."[49] Rosemary Radford Ruether, commenting on Neil Macgregor's *Seeing Salvation: Images of Christ in Art*, similarly contends that Christ (as well as Mary and the disciples) has been depicted as "luminously pure white" in European and American art from the Middle Ages to the present. Such (mis) representation, she writes, reflects a viewpoint—the superiority of whiteness and the inferiority of non-whites—and was used to this effect during the enslavement of Africans and the conquest of indigenous people of the Americas from the sixteenth to the twentieth century.[50]

HyeRan Kim-Cragg

Hildegard's violent and apocalyptic portrayal of the Antichrist, admittedly grotesque and demonic, is not a horrific fantasy but a poignant and astute critique of the church. Marcella Althaus-Reid, feminist/queer theologian, elaborates on how demonology can be rethought and reconfigured in the context of contemporary theology. In her (re)construction of demonology, she claims that demonologies help us to be attentive to rebellious spirits that have rejected the "light" for the "darkness." In her queer theological thinking, the line between saint and demon is blurred; "saint" is not necessarily good and "demon" is not necessarily bad, nor are "light" and "dark" mutually exclusive opposites correlated with good and evil. This way of thinking defeats dualism and dichotomy. On the contrary, sainthood is a category that exemplifies an idea of "good humanity" that is sustained by excluding the other, using a given system (ecclesial, economic, capitalist), while demonology is "a prophetically inspired rebelliousness" that disrupts the system.[51] R. S. Sugirtharajah

49. Randall C. Bailey, "In Danger of Ignoring One's Own Cultural Bias in Interpreting the Text," in *The Postcolonial Bible*, ed. R. S. Sugirtharajah, The Bible and Postcolonialism 1 (Sheffield: Sheffield Academic Press, 1998), 66–90, at 75.

50. Rosemary Radford Ruether, "Is Christ White? Racism and Christology," in *Christology and Whiteness: What Would Jesus Do*, ed. George Yancy (New York: Routledge, 2012), 101–13, at 102.

51. Marcella Althaus-Reid, *The Queer God* (New York: Routledge, 2003), 152, 142.

supports her claim in his own argument that we should pay attention to noncanonical writings that have been labeled "esoteric" and "weird," though "conveying sacred mystical knowledge." Rather, he says, these express "an anti-imperial stance."[52] Hildegard's demonic vision is then about invoking the rebellious spirits that challenge and disrupt the corrupted ecclesial and political group in power, offering a resistant stance that ushers in an alternative vision. As Elledge notes, the vision encapsulates Hildegard's critique of the evils of "clerical abuse, secular corruption, heresy, simony, and spiritual decline."[53] However, far from being an expression of apocalyptic determinism, her vision was an expression of hope for future church renewal, while exposing the monstrous and greedy reality of the church's corruption. Perhaps her rather idiosyncratic view of the church portrayed in the painting below can be considered a lens through which we can get a glimpse of both a twelfth-century world of political unrest and the world beyond that time.

Figure 2: Hildegard, Birth of the Antichrist[54]

It would be difficult to argue that the apocalyptic teachings of 2 Thessalonians do not anticipate a series of horrific end-time events that must

---

52. R. S. Sugirtharajah, "Postcolonial and Biblical Interpretation: The Next Phase," in Segovia and Sugirtharajah, *A Postcolonial Commentary on the New Testament Writings*, 455–65, at 456.

53. Elledge, "Contextualizing Hildegard," 46.

54. Norman Cohn, "Apocalypticism Explained: The Antichrist Legend," *PBS WGBH: Frontline*, http://www.pbs.org/wgbh/pages/frontline/shows/apocalypse /explanation/legend.html. Printed with permission of Lessing Images.

transpire before the parousia: "that day will not come unless the rebellion comes first and the lawless one is revealed, the one destined for destruction" (2 Thess 2:3b). However, like Hildegard's shocking biblical revision, the prophetic language of 2 Thessalonians must be interpreted from within the letter's own historical, social, and religious contexts, insofar as those can be reconstructed.

From a feminist perspective it should be noted that the biblical apocalyptic tradition is the ancestor of a wave of contemporary feminist apocalyptic, or counter-apocalyptic, writing that both "echoes and parodies apocalypse in order to disarm its polarities" but "also savors its intensity, its drive for justice, its courage in the face of impossible odds and losses."[55] As Tina Pippin puts it, the feminist gaze at biblical apocalyptic enables women to gaze at the "contemporary apocalypse"[56] and to imagine alternative utopias that differ from the static perfection of the biblical vision of the New Jerusalem. The feminist predilection for post/counter-apocalyptic writing is illustrated in the novels of writers like Octavia Butler, Margaret Atwood, Jeanette Winterson, Doris Lessing, Maggie Gee, and Liz Jensen.[57] Susan Watkins observes that contemporary women's apocalyptic novels avoid "the tragic, fundamentalist narrative of blame, judgment, the sheep and the goats."[58] Rather, they offer narratives that are plural and hybrid and that expose human fallibility and corrigibility rather than sacrifice and redemption.[59] However, even counter-apocalypse tends to imagine the future in terms of the inevitability of cataclysm and reconstruction rather than the less dramatic and even more difficult prospect of gradual, partial, and incremental projects conducive to social and ecological justice, equality, peace, and health.

55. Keller, *Apocalypse*, 20.
56. Tina Pippin, "The Revelation to John," in Schüssler Fiorenza, *Searching the Scriptures*, 1:109–30, at 127.
57. See Susan Watkins, "Future Shock: Rewriting the Apocalypse in Contemporary Women's Fiction," *Literature Interpretation Theory* 23 (2012): 119–37. Watkins does not discuss the novels of Octavia Butler, *The Parable of the Sower* (New York: Four Walls Eight Windows, 1993) and *The Parable of the Talents* (New York: Seven Stories Press, 1998), or Margaret Atwood's *Maddaddam* (Toronto: McClelland and Stewart, 2013).
58. Watkins, "Future Shock," 135.
59. From another angle, see Mary Ann Beavis, "Women and the 'City of Tomorrow': Feminist Transformations of the City in the New Millennium," in *Reclaiming the Future: Women's Strategies for the 21st Century*, ed. Somer Brodribb (Charlottetown, PEI: Gynergy, 1999), 23–47.

Structure

The internal structure of 2 Thessalonians is fairly well captured by the traditional canonical chapter divisions. The outline below uses the terminology of Greco-Roman rhetoric, following the works of several contemporary scholars who have attempted to situate the letter within its contemporary literary context.[60] Overall, in ancient rhetorical terms, the letter belongs to the genre of deliberative rhetoric used to convince an audience to pursue or to avoid a certain course of action. In the case of 2 Thessalonians, the recipients are exhorted to reject the teaching that the Day of the Lord has already arrived (2:2) and to adhere to the "traditional" eschatological timetable laid down in 2:3-12. In addition, the members of the ἐκκλησία ("church") must avoid "idleness" and follow the work ethic modeled by the senders (3:6-15). From a feminist standpoint "the nature of rhetoric as a means of ideological domination and manipulation—of imposing the rhetorician's position upon the audience—makes the rhetorical approach a useful tool for exposing some of the power plays that underlie the text."[61] In addition, the rhetorical approach recognizes that the letter was shaped by ancient literary conventions, adapted to the social and situational context of the authors and their intended audience.

Outline of 2 Thessalonians

Epistolary Prescript (1:1-2)

Exordium (1:3-12) — an introduction, seeking the goodwill of the audience

Partitio (2:1-2) — statement of the problem to be discussed

Probatio (2:3-12) — proof of the author's position and refutation of the opponent's

Peroratio (2:13–3:5) — summation of the author's arguments

Exhortatio (3:6-15) — moral exhortation of the audience

Epistolary Closing (3:16-18)

---

60. See references in Beavis, "2 Thessalonians," in Schüssler Fiorenza, *Searching the Scriptures*, 2:263–71, at 271, and more recently Witherington, *1 and 2 Thessalonians*.
61. Beavis, "2 Thessalonians," in Schüssler Fiorenza, *Searching the Scriptures*, 2:265.

2 Thessalonians 1

Resistance and Suffering

The epistolary greeting of 2 Thess 1:1 is similar but not identical to that of the first letter. The senders in both are identified as Paul, Silvanus, and Timothy. On the hypothesis of pseudepigraphal authorship, it is significant that the author (or authors) has (have) not chosen to claim the sole authority of Paul but to imitate the multiple authorship of 1 Thessalonians.[1] In fact, co-authorship is often claimed in Pauline letters,[2] contrary to the focus of much contemporary scholarship on the personality and theological contribution of the "great man" Paul as a dominant individual who left his decisive imprint on the history of Christianity,[3] if not of the world. Consistently with the claim of

---

1. Sean A. Adams makes a distinction between co-authors and co-senders and suggests that Paul carefully chose to claim co-sendership with persons well known to and respected by the recipients in order to enhance the authority of the letter ("Paul's Letter Opening and Greek Epistolography: A Matter of Relationship," in *Paul and the Ancient Letter Form*, ed. Stanley E. Porter and Sean A. Adams [Leiden: Brill, 2010], 33–55, at 40–44). See also Abraham J. Malherbe's discussion of the use of the "authorial we" (*The Letters to the Thessalonians: A New Translation with Introduction and Commentary* [New York: Doubleday, 2000], 86–89).

2. See 1 Cor 1:1; 2 Cor 2:2; Phil 1:1; Phlm 1:1; cf. Gal 1:1; Col 1:1.

3. For an interesting example of this kind of thinking about Paul, see Herman Westerink, "The Great Man from Tarsus: Freud on the Apostle Paul," *PsychoanalQ* 76 (2007): 217–35.

2 Thess 1:1-12

¹·¹ Paul, Silvanus, and Timothy, to the church of the Thessalonians in God our Father and the Lord Jesus Christ: ²Grace to you and peace from God our Father and the Lord Jesus Christ. ³We must always give thanks to God for you, brothers and sisters, as is right, because your faith is growing abundantly, and the love of every one of you for one another is increasing. ⁴Therefore we ourselves boast of you among the churches of God for your steadfastness and faith during all your persecutions and the afflictions that you are enduring.

⁵This is evidence of the righteous judgment of God and is intended to make you worthy of the kingdom of God, for which you are also suffering. ⁶For it is indeed just of God to repay with affliction those who afflict you, ⁷and to give relief to the afflicted as well as to us,

multiple authorship, the first person plural is used to denote the authors throughout the letter, with few exceptions.[4] Where the first-person singular is used, it is to remind the recipients of previous teaching by one of the missionaries (2:5), or to explain a change in handwriting (3:1).

The remainder of the prescript (2 Thess 1:1-2) echoes the first letter (1 Thess 1:1-2), with some amplification. Similarly to many translations, the NRSV renders the term ἐκκλησία as "church," a translation that masks the political origins of the term as an assembly of citizens, as well as the feminine form of the word, which lends itself to female personification.[5] In the early christian context the assembly was often held in the house of a member or members.[6] Among women whose names are associated with house churches are Prisca (Rom 16:3; 1 Cor 16:19), Chloe (1 Cor 1:11), Nympha (Col 4:15), Mary of Jerusalem (Acts 12:2), Lydia (Acts 16:11-14), and Apphia (Phlm 1:2). Apart from the names of Paul, Silvanus, and Timothy, no personal names of members of the ἐκκλησία, male or female, appear in the letter.

In addition to the feminine understanding of ἐκκλησία, vocational and pedagogical dimensions of ἐκκλησία are worth exploring. Feminist practical theologian and religious educator Joyce Ann Mercer delineates the meaning of vocation in relation to identity in the context of ἐκκλησία. She

4. See also 1 Thess 2:18; 3:5; 5:27.

5. See, e.g., 2 John 1:1, where the assembly is addressed as "the elect lady and her children."

6. See, e.g., Rom 16:5; 1 Cor 16:9; Phlm 1:2; Col 4:15; Acts 2:46; 12:2.

when the Lord Jesus is revealed from heaven with his mighty angels [8]in flaming fire, inflicting vengeance on those who do not know God and on those who do not obey the gospel of our Lord Jesus. [9]These will suffer the punishment of eternal destruction, separated from the presence of the Lord and from the glory of his might, [10]when he comes to be glorified by his saints and to be marveled at on that day among all who have believed, because our testimony to you was believed. [11]To this end we always pray for you, asking that our God will make you worthy of his call and will fulfill by his power every good resolve and work of faith, [12]so that the name of our Lord Jesus may be glorified in you, and you in him, according to the grace of our God and the Lord Jesus Christ.

writes, "Vocation as the 'call from God' is something that every Christian receives through baptism, through which we 'put on a new identity in Christ.' . . . Paul's linguistic way of conveying this link between the call and identity was to use the Greek term *klēsis,* or call as a *name.* . . . Being called becomes their name, their identity. In fact, the very word used for church in the New Testament, ἐκκλησία, literally means 'the called-out ones.' "[7]

An egalitarian view of ἐκκλησία as the assembly of the ones called by God provides strength and encouragement for resistance. Richard Horsley makes an argument that Paul's message and mission feature "decolonizing cultural resistance."[8] Criticizing the standard essentialist, individualistic, and depoliticized Augustinian-Lutheran Paul, Horsley reconstructs Paul as "an activist movement-builder" who was almost obsessive about "building" what he calls "assemblies," ἐκκλησίαι, as an alternative society in resistance to the Roman imperial order.[9] Whether we agree with Horsley's reconstruction of Paul or not, it is notable that the ἐκκλησία was not an apolitical body. Elisabeth Schüssler Fiorenza, while broadly agreeing with Horsley's reading, complicates the meaning of ἐκκλησία by highlighting sociopolitical conflicts and religio-cultural tensions that existed within the ἐκκλησία. Such tensions were evident

7. Joyce Ann Mercer, "Call Forwarding: Putting Vocation in the Present Tense with Youth," in *Compass Points: Navigating Vocation,* Institute for Youth Ministry (Princeton, NJ: Princeton Theological Seminary, 2002), 29–43, at 32.

8. Richard A. Horsley, "Submerged Biblical Histories and Imperial Biblical Studies," in *The Postcolonial Bible,* ed. R. S. Sugirtharajah, The Bible and Postcolonialism 1 (Sheffield: Sheffield Academic Press, 1998), 152–73, at 164.

9. Ibid., 169.

between those who "advocate the ethos of *ekklēsia* both as a '*basileia* discipleship of equals' and as 'a community of freedom in the spirit' . . . and those that advocate the kyriarchal leadership of elite male power and the kyriarchal institutionalization of the *ekklēsia*."[10] Schüssler Fiorenza successfully reminds us that ἐκκλησία, when it sought to resist imperial rule and build an alternative society, was not without flaws or limitations. In fact, the very community that dismantled the barriers of oppression and discrimination among people is the same body that built walls of exclusion and subordinated wo/men, slaves, and barbarians to a higher class made up of men. Paul, who might be seen as "an activist movement-builder," on the one hand, is implicated in this othering process and even benefited from it. What is needed is a hermeneutic of ἐκκλησία that unveils what Schüssler Fiorenza calls a conflictive egalitarian politics of interpretation that "no longer needs to privilege the authorial master-voice of Paul . . . but can position its own inquiry on the side of the historical victims whose subjugated knowledges have left traces in the canonical text."[11] One may even contest a politics of interpretation of the ἐκκλησία restricted to the early writings and readings. Instead, Schüssler Fiorenza suggests that "such emancipatory rhetorical practices and sociopolitical religious struggles for freedom began long before the Christian movements emerged on the scene" and are related to struggles that "are still going on today."[12] Biblical texts, critical scholarship, and rhetorical research on these ancient texts are not removed from current struggles. Thus, as Musa Dube poignantly argues, "to divorce biblical interpretation from current international relations, or to discuss it primarily as an ancient text, becomes another Western ideological stance that hides its direct impact on the postcolonial world and maintains its imperial domination of Two-Thirds World countries."[13]

The prescript deviates slightly from the wording of 1 Thessalonians by referring to "God *our* Father and the Lord Jesus Christ" (2 Thess 1:1) as opposed to "God *the* Father and the Lord Jesus Christ" (1 Thess 1:1). In order to disrupt the expectedness of these formulas in the NRSV, we sug-

---

10. Elisabeth Schüssler Fiorenza, "Paul and the Politics of Interpretation," in *Paul and Politics: Ekklesia, Israel, Imperium, Interpretation; Essays in Honor of Krister Stendahl*, ed. Richard A. Horsley (Harrisburg, PA: Trinity Press International, 2000), 40–57, at 56.
11. Ibid., 57.
12. Ibid.
13. Musa W. Dube, *Postcolonial Feminist Interpretation of the Bible* (St. Louis, MO: Chalice Press, 2000), 20.

gest an alternate translation of 1:1: "Paul and Silvanus and Timothy to the Thessalonian house-assembly in God our Father-Mother and Kyrios Jesus Christ." Second Thessalonians 1:2 expands on the simple "grace to you and peace" of 1 Thess 1:1 with the fuller "grace to you and peace from God our Father-Mother and Kyrios Jesus Christ." The translation of the Greek word for "father" (πατήρ) with "Father-Mother" reminds us that God is not a literal divine male parent; "father" is a theological metaphor that is one of many expressions of biblical God-language—including God as Mother.[14] The transliteration of the term *kyrios* (usually translated as "Lord") highlights both the kyriarchal nature of the language and its embeddedness in Greco-Roman religion and society. Here, following Schüssler Fiorenza, we conceive kyriarchy ("rule by lord") as "a complex system of structural dependencies and individual oppressions, as the life-destroying power of Western society and religion. Kyriarchy is not to be understood solely in terms of male supremacy and misogynist sexism but must be seen in terms of the systemic interaction of racism, classism, and sexism in Western militarist societies."[15] Although the authors of the letter may be straining to express an alternative to the "lordly" rule of Rome, especially with reference to its destructive impact on first-century Judea, the use of imperial language to express the "lordship" of Christ inevitably reinforces the relationships of domination and oppression inherent in kyriarchy. The double invocation of *Kyrios* Jesus Christ, as Raymond E. Collins observes, is consistent with the preference for this title throughout the letter; it appears twenty-two times in three short chapters: "nine times associated with 'Jesus Christ' (2 Thess 1:1, 2, 12; 2:1, 14, 16; 3:6, 12, 16), four times with 'Jesus' (2 Thess 1:7, 8, 12; 2:8), eight times by itself (2 Thess 1:9; 2:2, 13; 3:1, 3, 4, 5, 16), and once in the expression 'the Lord of peace' (2 Thess 3:16)."[16] This is almost as many as in the first letter (twenty-three times), with its two additional chapters, indicating that for 2 Thessalonians κύριος ("lord"), with all its kyriarchal associations, is "the christological title par excellence."[17]

14. See Virginia Ramey Mollenkott, *The Divine Feminine: The Biblical Imagery of God as Female* (New York: Crossroad, 1987).

15. Elisabeth Schüssler Fiorenza, *Changing Horizons: Explorations in Feminist Biblical Interpretation* (Minneapolis: Fortress Press, 2013), 232.

16. Raymond F. Collins, *Letters That Paul Did Not Write: The Epistle to the Hebrews and Pauline Pseudepigrapha* (Wilmington, DE: Michael Glazier, 1988), 227.

17. Ibid.

Contrary to the speculations of some ancient and modern commentators with respect to the gender composition of the Thessalonian community (see our introduction),[18] we take the position here that the recipients of the letter probably were based in a small domestic assembly made up of both women and men and agree with the NRSV's translation of the false generic ἀδελφοί ("brothers") with the more inclusive "brothers and sisters" (2 Thess 1:3; 2:1, 13, 15; 3:1, 13). This does not mean that the Thessalonian community was free of the gender and class hierarchies of the dominant culture, although it can be argued that, insofar as Jesus is conceived as sole κύριος, other kyriarchal relationships are displaced, or at least relativized. Both the letters' thanksgivings (1:3-4; 2:13) use familial imagery to strengthen the bonds between the senders and the recipients, who represent themselves as part of the family of ἀδελφοί and ἀδελφαί ("sisters"), bound together by ties of trust (πίστις) and the growing "love of every one of you for one another" (1:3).

Brothers . . . and Sisters?

With reference to 1 Thessalonians, Melanie Johnson-DeBaufre shows how the presence of women has been highlighted and suppressed in contemporary interpretations.[19] For example, Karl P. Donfried envisions Thessalonian women engaging in orgiastic religious rites as the occasion for Paul's admonitions to self-control, especially with reference to the sexual immorality mentioned in 1 Thess 4:3.[20] Robert Jewett, in contrast, compares the supposed orgiastic practices of Thessalonica to egalitarian millenarian movements featuring sexual freedom and openness to low-status men and women.[21] Although he admits

18. Among recent commentaries that choose a gender-exclusive translation of ἀδελφοί as "brothers" is Malherbe, *Letters*, 109–10, although he does not deny the presence of women in the Thessalonian ἐκκλησία (58, 64).

19. Melanie Johnson-DeBaufre, " 'Gazing Upon the Invisible': Archaeology, Historiography, and the Elusive Wo/men of 1 Thessalonians," in *From Roman to Early Christian Thessalonikē: Studies in Religion and Archaeology*, HTS 64, ed. Laura Nasrallah, Charalambos Bakirtzis, and Steven J. Friesen (Cambridge, MA: Harvard University Press, 2010), 73–108.

20. Ibid., 84, referring to Karl Donfried, "The Cults of Thessalonica and the Thessalonian Correspondence," *NTS* 31 (1985): 336–56.

21. Johnson-DeBaufre, "Gazing," 85–86, referring to Robert Jewett, *The Thessalonian Correspondence: Pauline Rhetoric and Millenarian Piety* (Philadelphia: Fortress Press, 1986), 172–74.

that there are ample records of women's involvement in ancient trade associations, Richard Ascough hypothesizes that the christian trade association of Thessalonica participated in Paul's trade of tent-making or leatherworking, meaning that the assembly would have been made up primarily of men.[22] Ascough uses Lone Fatum's feminist commentary on 1 Thessalonians, which stresses the androcentric point of view of the letter, to buttress his case, irrespective of the fact that all the Pauline letters are androcentric.[23]

Like the first letter, 2 Thessalonians contains no explicit references to women—or even to activities, like sexual practices, that might imply the presence of women. However, at the very least the simple fact that, except for the Thessalonian

letters, all the other Pauline (and Deutero-Pauline) letters refer to women[24] overwhelmingly implies that women were indeed there. As Johnson-DeBaufre observes, "If one adjusts for the kyriocentric nature of the texts and materials of antiquity, which ignore or mask the presence of wo/men, then the sheer number of times that women's presence in the ἐκκλησίαι becomes visible—in names, direct addresses, discussion of 'women's issues,' and efforts to circumscribe women's speech, clothing, and bodies—should weigh heavily against any counterargument. . . . This wide-ranging evidence should overcome the androcentric silence of any one Pauline text."[25] This includes the relentlessly androcentric 2 Thessalonians.

Mary Ann Beavis

Rhetorically, the authors' assertion that "we ought" (ὀφείλομεν; 2 Thess 1:3) to give thanks for the faith and love of the brothers and sisters might suggest that the thanksgiving is offered from a sense of duty, since, as the content of the letter shows, some members of the assembly were being influenced by teaching unapproved by the missionaries.

22. Johnson-DeBaufre, "Gazing," 87–89; see Richard Ascough, *Paul's Macedonian Associations: The Social Context of Philippians and 1 Thessalonians* (Tübingen: Mohr Siebeck, 2003), 186–87, but cp. Act 18:3.

23. Johnson-DeBaufre, "Gazing," 89, referring to Lone Fatum, "1 Thessalonians," in *Searching the Scriptures*, vol. 2: *A Feminist Commentary*, ed. Elisabeth Schüssler Fiorenza (New York: Crossroad, 1994), 250–62.

24. For example, Rom 16:1, 3, 6, 7, 12, 13, 15; 1 Cor 1:11; 7:1-16; 11:2-16; 14:34-36; 16:19; 2 Cor 6:18; Gal 3:28; Phil 4:2-3; Phlm 1:2; Col 4:15; 3:18-21; Eph 5:22-33, 6:1-3; 1 Tim 2:8-15; 3:11-12; 5:1-16; 2 Tim 1:5; 4:19, 21; Titus 2:3.

25. Johnson-DeBaufre, "Gazing," 92–93.

Alternatively, the "we ought" could be taken to mean that the audience is deserving of praise—but only if they continue to acknowledge the gospel message preached by the missionaries in the past.[26]

The initial thanksgiving concludes with a reference to the community's "steadfastness and faith during all your persecutions and the afflictions that you are enduring" (2 Thess 1:4). We can only speculate on the nature of the difficulties envisioned by the authors, which could range from the kind of political incitement described in Acts, where Paul and Silas are accused of "turning the world upside down" and acting contrary to the decrees of the emperor, "saying that there is another king called Jesus" (Acts 17:5-8), to social and familial rejection of converts to a new and outlandish religion. We can also only imagine that such loyalty (to Jesus and not to the emperor) felt real and urgent among the audience of this letter, even if they might not have been subject to persecution or imprisonment at the time of writing. Their convictions might, nonetheless, have been dangerous from the imperial Roman point of view. The meanings embedded in both of the words ὑπομονῆς, "steadfastness," and πίστεως, "faith," (1:4) are important. Feminist theologian Dorothee Sölle asserts that we need a "revolutionary patience" anchored in hope and understood not as a naïve optimism but as a painstaking labor of endurance.[27] The key to steadfastness is faith, which is persistence fueled by hope. This steadfastness can be strengthened through the cultivation of habits and practices. Though revolutionary in nature, the Day of the Lord will not come overnight. Thus learning to be patient is a necessary part of keeping the fire of steadfastness and faith going. Here a lesson from Lu Xun, a Chinese philosopher, is illustrative: "Hope can be neither affirmed nor denied. Hope is like a path in the countryside: originally there was no path—yet, as people are walking all the time in the same spot, a way appears."[28] Xun's insight on the appearance of a way is illuminating here. Juxtaposing παρουσία (presence) with the advent of Jesus, the authors of 2 Thessalonians portray the coming of Jesus as ἐπιφάνεια (2:8),[29] translated as

26. See Mary Ann Beavis, "2 Thessalonians," in Schüssler Fiorenza, *Searching the Scriptures*, 2:266.

27. Dorothee Sölle, *Revolutionary Patience*, trans. Rita and Robert Kimber (Maryknoll, NY: Orbis Books, 1997).

28. Cited in Catherine Keller, *Apocalypse Now and Then: A Feminist Guide to the End of the World* (Minneapolis: Fortress Press, 1996), xvi.

29. Abraham Smith, "The First and Second Letters to the Thessalonians," in *A Postcolonial Commentary on the New Testament Writings*, ed. Fernando F. Segovia and R. S. Sugirtharajah, The Bible and Postcolonialism 13 (New York: T & T Clark, 2007), 310.

"the appearance of his coming," or "the revelation of Christ's presence" (*Inclusive Bible*).[30] As a way emerges with steady and persistent walking, Jesus as the Way appears in the midst of our revolutionary patience, equipped with faith and hope.

If, as suggested earlier, the distinctive apocalyptic theme of the letter was occasioned by the events surrounding the First Jewish War, the recipients not only would be anxious about the violent events unfolding in faraway Judea but could be under suspicion locally for having embraced a form of Judaism (or Judean-ism) and for their lack of participation in the religious life of the city, especially the imperial cult.[31] In view of the strong ties between Thessalonica and Rome, and particularly the prominence of the cult of the emperor in the city,[32] it can be imagined that the Thessalonian christians suffered from divided loyalties and fears occasioned by reports of apocalyptic-like events—including the rumor that the "Day of the Lord" had already arrived (2 Thess 2:2).

Second Thessalonians 1:3-12 is an exordium, introducing the main theme of the letter, the futurity of the parousia. In rhetorical terms an exordium seeks "to influence or even manipulate the audience by securing their interest and goodwill."[33] The co-authors encouragingly compliment the "steadfastness and faith" of the community in the face of afflictions (although 2:1-12 indicates that they were actually "shaken in mind" and "alarmed"). Steadfastness and faith, the authors assert, evidence "the righteous judgment of God," intended to make them worthy of the reign of God for which they are suffering (1:5), and promise that God will "repay with affliction those who afflict you" (1:6). Jouette M. Bassler has argued that the "sign" (ἔνδειγμα) of the righteous judgment of God mentioned in 1:5 consists in the sufferings of the ἐκκλησία, in line with the Jewish apocalyptic teaching that the sufferings of the faithful were a kind of chastisement or atonement for their transgressions that

30. Priests for Equality, *The Inclusive Bible: The First Egalitarian Translation* (Lanham, MD: Rowman & Littlefield, 2009).

31. See Marlene Crüsemann, "2 Thessalonians: Hope in God's Last Judgment," in *Feminist Biblical Interpretation: A Compendium of Critical Commentary on the Books of the Bible and Related Literature*, ed. Luise Schottroff and Marie-Theres Wacker (Grand Rapids, MI, and Cambridge: Eerdmans, 2012), 825.

32. See Karl P. Donfried, *Paul, Thessalonica, and Early Christianity* (London: T & T Clark, 2002), 37–38.

33. David E. Aune, *The New Testament in its Literary Environment* (Philadelphia: Westminster, 1987), 199; Beavis, "2 Thessalonians," in Schüssler Fiorenza, *Searching the Scriptures*, 2:267.

would make them worthy of future glorification.[34] From a feminist stand-point the portrayal of God as a harsh disciplinarian who tests the faithful by afflicting them with undeserved persecution but punishes the perse-cutors who apply the discipline by annihilating them is extremely dis-turbing. Here the arrival of the reign of God is described in vivid and apocalyptic language: Kyrios Jesus will "be revealed" (ἀποκαλύψει) from heaven with his "mighty angels" in "flaming fire," "inflicting vengeance on those who do not know God and on those who do not obey the gospel of our Lord Jesus" (1:7-8).

Suffering and Resistance

The apocalyptic notion of atoning through suffering has been compared to Gandhian passive resistance[35]—or, perhaps better, peaceful resistance. However, with respect to an apocalyptic text like 2 Thessalonians, it has a dark side in that the hope of atonement through suffering implies "that the misery of the oppressed is acceptable to God, and that concrete, secular action to remedy this is unnecessary, even impious."[36] Marlene Crüsemann sees the situation of the Thessalonian ἐκκλησία as an instance of the resistance of a group that has been forcibly marginalized and instructed to await liberation by an "unarmed Messiah"[37] (however,

cp. 1:8-9). Admittedly, insofar as the letter does not incite violence on the part of the recipients it is preferable to the alternative.

Crüsemann points out that although the letter does not advocate the personal use of violence, for women this does not provide an alternative for their expected role of "continual accommodation and submission to those who are always stronger."[38] Jewish feminist theologian Melissa Raphael, speaking of the women of Auschwitz, provides an example of women in the midst of extreme suffering responding to oppression with an active and nonviolent resistance that has been practiced by women throughout history:

34. Jouette M. Bassler, "The Enigmatic Sign: 2 Thessalonians 1:5," *CBQ* 46 (1984): 496–510. See also Beavis, "2 Thessalonians," in Schüssler Fiorenza, *Searching the Scriptures*, 2:268.

35. See William Klassen, "Vengeance in the Apocalypse of John," *CBQ* 28 (1966): 300–311.

36. Beavis, "2 Thessalonians," in Schüssler Fiorenza, *Searching the Scriptures*, 2:267.

37. Crüsemann, "2 Thessalonians," 827.

38. Ibid., 828.

The maternal posture . . . a capacity to bend over and cover, stroke, warm, feed, clean, lift and hold the other, was an embodied resistance to Auschwitz which had institutionalized the exposure, breakage and waste of bodies. Yet there, mothers had mothered daughters; daughters, mothers; sisters, sisters; friends, friends; and mothers, other mothers. That mothering was in many senses futile and pitifully ineffectual to the scale of loss, terror and deprivation. But in none of the memoirs I have read for this study were its comforts incidental or peripheral to meaning and hope, then or now. On the contrary, many women's sheer bodily presence to one another, carrying [the other's] burden at whatever . . . cost, mirrored and sustained the deathless promise of covenantal love between God and Israel, knowable in God's presence as a suffering Mother in Auschwitz.[39]

Perhaps, in the Thessalonian ἐκκλησία, women's resistance consisted in the sharing and networking characteristic of women's leadership patterns.[40] For an understanding of how this kind of resistance plays out in the more recent context of global capitalism one may look to Guatemala. The women's movement in this Central American nation in solidarity with people in Canada is an example of women coming together across differences to make life better for themselves and their children. Kathryn Anderson, trained as an adult Christian educator, co-founded Breaking the Silence (BTS), a solidarity network between Canada and Guatemala, when she first encountered indigenous Guatemalan women during the World Council of Churches General Assembly in 1983.[41] In her book *Weaving the Relationships: Canada-Guatemala Solidarity*, she provides numerous stories and examples that demonstrate networking as a way of practicing women's leadership for relationship building, a matter "of the heart

---

39. Melissa Raphael, *The Female Face of God in Auschwitz* (New York: Routledge, 2003), 10.

40. Ibid., 97. Here, of course, Raphael is speaking of women's activities in the mid-twentieth century, but examples of this kind of women's "relational resistance" can be easily located in early Christian literature, e.g., in the relationship between the missionary Thecla and her adoptive mother, Tryphaena (see Sheila E. McGinn, "The Acts of Thecla," in Schüssler Fiorenza, *Searching the Scriptures*, 2:800–828, at 818–19.

41. See more at Tatamagouche Centre, "Partnerships: Breaking the Silence," *Tatamagouche Center: Make Your Connection*, https://www.tatacentre.ca/index.php /partnerships/bts.

and of faith."[42] Reflecting on this BTS work, HyeRan Kim-Cragg has suggested a theology of resistance as remembrance, relationship-building, and reclaiming of space.[43] In particular, a theology of resistance as relationship-building is fed by "the embodiment of love" that "hangs together" in the web of living interactions.[44] Despite the suffering, instead of reacting to it with hatred through the vicious cycle of violence, this "hanging together"—that is, in the words of Raphael, "many women's sheer bodily presence to one another, carrying her burden at whatever its cost"—is another name for relationship building that can help respond to suffering and resist violence. Perhaps we can perceive in this an example of an unfolding of the Thessalonian reality into the present.[45] After all, from a postcolonial perspective the past is connected to and continues to haunt the present reality of suffering and oppression. Hence inquiry into the past starts by posing the question: what might this past reality mean for our lives today in our work for the future?—as though the lives of those of the past matter in the future. It is important to feel "the touch of the past," Canadian educator and scholar Roger Simon argues, because it "is an encounter with difficult knowledge and the welcome given to the memories of others as a teaching."[46]

Mary Ann Beavis and
HyeRan Kim-Cragg

42. Kathryn Anderson, *Weaving the Relationships: Canada-Guatemala Solidarity* (Waterloo, ON: Wilfred Laurier University Press, 2003), 199. She cites Marta Gloria de la Vega, a lawyer who worked closely with Guatemalan Nobel Peace Prize winner Rigoberta Menchu, who said, "Solidarity is revolutionary and is of the heart, of faith."

43. HyeRan Kim-Cragg, "A Theology of Resistance in Conversation with Religious Education in Unmasking and Unmaking Violence," *RelEd* 110 (August 2015): 420–34.

44. Catherine Keller and Laurel Schneider, "Introduction," in *Polydoxy: Theology of Multiplicity and Relation*, ed. Catherine Keller and Laurel Schneider (New York: Routledge, 2011), 3–4.

45. Patrick Williams and Laura Chrisman, "Colonial Discourse and Post-Colonial Theory: An Introduction," in *Colonial Discourse and Post-Colonial Theory: A Reader*, ed. Patrick Williams and Laura Chrisman (New York: Columbia University Press, 1994), 1–20, at 12; HyeRan Kim-Cragg, *Story and Song: A Postcolonial Interplay between Christian Education and Worship* (New York: Peter Lang, 2012), 31.

46. Roger Simon, *The Touch of the Past: Remembrance, Learning and Ethics* (New York: Palgrave/MacMillan, 2005), 9–10.

As many scholars have observed, this account of the parousia is reminiscent of Mark's apocalyptic discourse,[47] which is often dated during or slightly after the Jewish-Roman war.

> But in those days, after that suffering, the sun will be darkened, and the moon will not give its light, and the stars will be falling from heaven, and the powers in the heavens will be shaken. Then they will see "the Son of Man coming in clouds" with great power and glory. Then he will send out the angels, and gather his elect from the four winds, from the ends of the earth to the ends of heaven. (Mark 13:24-27)

However, in contrast to the Markan apocalypse's focus on the exaltation of the elect, the authors of 2 Thessalonians describe in some detail the vengeance that will be visited on the disobedient: "These will suffer the punishment of eternal destruction, separated from the glory of his might" (1:9)—a cruel fate for the unbelieving family members, neighbors, and fellow citizens of the Thessalonian ἐκκλησία.

While the authors of 2 Thessalonians do not describe Jesus in the light of crucifixion and resurrection, they do present him as the one who will overthrow, destroy (1:8), and condemn those who have not believed in truth (1:12). These revelations of "the greatness of God," Abraham Smith observes, are dependent on the writings of the Jewish prophets Isaiah and Zechariah. They borrow the image of a "flaming fire" (1:8) from the LXX translation of Isa 2:10 and the image of angels (1:7) from Zech 14:5 to describe an eschatological vision.[48] Feminist commentator Marlene Crüsemann rightly argues that this lurid apocalyptic language must be interpreted within the context of an ancient Jewish theology of suffering, "a theological perspective emerging from the Jewish war and the

---

47. E.g., Kevin L. Hughes, *Constructing Antichrist: Paul, Biblical Commentary, and the Development of Doctrine in the Early Middle Ages* (Washington, DC: The Catholic University of America Press, 2005), 12; Crüsemann, "2 Thessalonians," 825; Charles A. Wanamaker, *Commentary on 1 and 2 Thessalonians* (Grand Rapids, MI: Eerdmans, 1990), 226; Malherbe, *Letters*, 403, 415; Earl J. Richard, *First and Second Thessalonians*, SP 11 (Collegeville, MN: Liturgical Press, 2007), 315. The term παρουσία (*parousia*) occurs frequently in the NT (twenty-four times) with reference to the "second coming" of Jesus; in Greek literature it often refers to the arrival of a royal personage or a God (*LSJ*). Here, as in 1 Thess 1:15-17, the term evokes the image of "the visit of a high-ranking official or ruler to a city, with his entourage, where he would be met by a deputation of leading citizens and escorted into the city" (James D. G. Dunn, *The Theology of Paul the Apostle* [Grand Rapids, MI: Eerdmans, 2006], 299).

48. Smith, "1 and 2 Thessalonians," 311.

destruction of Jerusalem in 70 CE, a perspective that encounters and interprets the suffering of the Jewish people that these evoked."[49]

This theological perspective has its roots in the Jewish Scriptures.

> . . . the hand of the Lord is with his servants,
>   and his indignation is against his enemies.
> For the Lord will come in fire,
>   and his chariots like the whirlwind,
> to pay back his anger in fury,
>   and his rebuke in flames of fire.
> For by the fire will the Lord execute judgment,
>   and by his sword, on all flesh;
> and those slain by the Lord shall be many. (Isa 66:14b-16)[50]

Later it is crystallized in works like 2 Baruch[51] and in the school of Rabbi Akiba,[52] offering consolation to those who suffer for their faithfulness to Torah with the prospect of eschatological reversal:

> And as for the righteous, what will they do now?
> Rejoice you in the suffering which you now suffer:
> For why do you look for the decline of your enemies?
> Make ready your soul for that which is reserved for you,
> And prepare your souls for the reward which is laid up for you. (2 Bar 52:5-7)

Crüsemann focuses on the joy and hope offered the suffering members of the Thessalonian community: that 2 Thessalonians is a message promising the end of oppression at the glorious appearing of Jesus.

Resilience and Faith: Filipina Perspectives 1

The Filipino translation of the Greek text of the Bible, *Ang Banal na Biblia* (The Holy Bible),[53] translates "afflictions" (θλίψεσιν) as *kapighatian*[54] and "suffering" (πάσχετε) as *pagtitiis*.[55] Both Filipino words embody not just the physical dimension of the

---

49. Crüsemann, "2 Thessalonians," 824.

50. The phrase "in flaming fire" (2 Thess 1:8) uses the exact wording of Isa 66:15 LXX, ἐν πυρὶ φλογός.

51. See, for example, 2 Bar 13:1-12; 48:48-50; 52:5-7.

52. Crüsemann, "2 Thessalonians," 824.

53. Jose C. Abriol, *Ang Banal na Biblia*, rev. (Boston, MA: Paulines, 2000). Also see "Rectors: Msgr. Jose C. Abriol" *Manila Cathedral Basilica*, http://manilacathedral.ph /msgr-jose-c-abriol-1962-1975/.

54. 2 Thess 1:4.

55. 2 Thess 1:5.

English rendering but more descriptively characterize the intensity of the experience these words represent. Hence, when a Filipino reads the vernacular translation of 2 Thessalonians, *damang-dama niya*, he or she can deeply feel it. *Kapighatian* and *pagtitiis* are words that resonate strongly with the people of the Philippines, a developing country that "has been through five centuries of colonial rule under three different nations,"[56] and was described in news headlines as "The Most Storm-Exposed Country on Earth,"[57] and has had "more than its share of disasters."[58] In spite of the overwhelming challenges the Philippines faces almost unremittingly and in apocalyptic proportions, Filipinos in general are lauded for their amazing resilience. We are able to rise above painful, often unimaginable circumstances. We hardly ever lose hope.

What is the secret of the resilience of the Filipinos? Fr. Horacio de la Costa, a Jesuit historian, writer, priest, religious, and nation-alist, provides an insight. He says that the Filipino has two treasures: music and faith, *la musica e la fede*. Our melodies make our spirits soar above the trag-edies of life. Our faith makes us stand up again and again after deadly fires, earthquakes, typhoons, and wars. And now, as many of our poor people are just beginning to rise from recent natural and human-made calamities, as we are struggling, you, Holy Father, came to us.[59]

These were the words of Philippine Cardinal Luis Antonio Tagle, archbishop of Manila, in his welcoming address to Pope Francis during the pontiff's visit to the country in January 2015. His pastoral visit took place thirteen months after catastrophic typhoon Haiyan bulldozed whole towns and cities in the eastern and central Visayas regions in November 2013. Approximately two million people lost their homes, and more than six thousand lost their lives. An online news article

---

56. Nila Bermisa, *That She May Dance Again: Rising from the Pain of Violence Against Women in the Philippine Church* (Philippines: WGC-AMRSP, 2011), 105.

57. Sophie Brown, "The Philippines Is the Most Storm-Exposed Country on Earth," *Time*, November 11, 2013, http://world.time.com/2013/11/11/the-philippines-is-the-most-storm-exposed-country-on-earth/.

58. Hillary Whiteman, "Philippines Gets More Than Its Share of Disasters," *CNN*, December 5, 2014, http://edition.cnn.com/2013/11/08/world/asia/philippines-typhoon-destruction/.

59. "Message of Luis Antonio Cardinal Tagle to Pope Francis, Manila Cathedral," *PTV*, January 16, 2015, https://www.youtube.com/watch?v=DvBwTJMt_Hw.

reported that Haiyan was "the strongest tropical cyclone ever to make landfall anywhere in the world in recorded history."[60] In spite of the devastation it caused, it did not hinder survivors from gathering in roofless, dilapidated churches to thank God that they were spared and to pray that they would be reunited with loved ones whom they hoped were still alive. A female survivor expressed her deep gratitude in this way: "I wish to thank the Lord. We asked for his help for all the people who survived this typhoon to be able to eat and continue a life that is hopefully more blissful. The Lord has strengthened our faith and made us stronger in order for us to survive and start off all over again."[61] For millions of Catholic and non-Catholic Filipinos, Pope Francis's presence was a palpable reminder that God hears and answers prayers.

Pia Sison

Certainly early christians sporadically suffered great hardships and persecution within the general time frame of the Thessalonian letters. Acts mentions that Priscilla and Aquila were expelled from Rome at the order of Emperor Claudius, who had ordered all the Jews (including christians) out of the city (18:2). According to Tacitus, Nero's attack on the christians of Rome subsequent to the great fire of 64 CE was so gratuitous that it excited the compassion of the Roman populace for these practitioners of what he regarded as a pernicious superstition (*Annals* 15.44). Pliny's famous account of his interrogation of two women "ministers" accused of being christians in early second-century Bithynia-Pontus indicates that believers were under suspicion at that time—and that they could lose their lives for refusing to offer sacrifices to the gods and to the emperor (*Epistle to Trajan* 10.96). However, the "suffering with affliction" being experienced by the Thessalonian ἐκκλησία, and the framing of that suffering within the prophetic-apocalyptic theological tradition, qualifies but does not excuse the harshness of the sentence of "eternal destruction, separated from the presence of the Lord and from the glory of his might" (2 Thess 1:9): "The 'us against them' mentality of this section falls short of the love of 'enemies' that constitutes the best

---

60. Whiteman, "Philippines."

61. BBC, "Philippine Typhoon Survivors Attend Church Services," *BBC News*, November 17, 2013, http://www.bbc.com/news/world-asia-24977113.

of early Christian paraenesis (Matt 5:44; Luke 6:27, 35); the faith and love cited in the thanksgiving ([2 Thess] 1:3) are for believers only."[62]

Contemporary, post-Shoah Jewish theologies of suffering have developed the theme of protest against God, or of divine absence or hiddenness. Jewish feminist theologian Melissa Raphael, however, finds the female *presence* of God (*Shekinah*) in the stories of four women imprisoned at Auschwitz-Birkenau, who, she argues, made the divine visible through the material and spiritual care they exercised on behalf of other prisoners in situations of extreme suffering and abuse.[63] In Raphael's feminist revisioning of the Jewish theology of suffering, rather than anticipation of vindication through the intervention of a divine warrior or denial of the divine presence in suffering, God's love is experienced in the divine presence throughout salvation history, and especially in the midst of suffering. Raphael quotes an ancient Jewish tradition that portrays the female divine presence with Israel in times of hardship:

> Come and see how beloved Israel is before God; for wherever they went into exile the Shekhinah went with them. When they were exiled to Egypt, the Shekhinah went with them, in Babylon the Shekhinah was with them, and in the future, when Israel will be redeemed, the Shekhinah will be with them. (Megillah 29a)[64]

Second Thessalonians 1:10, in contrast, portrays the parousia of Kyrios Jesus as a future, glorious event "to be marveled at on that day among all who have believed, because our testimony to you was believed." The phrase "on that day" evokes many prophetic passages in which the Day of the Lord brings both judgment and salvation to the people of God, to the nations,[65] and even, in a beautiful passage in Hosea, to the natural world:

> I will make for you a covenant on that day with the wild animals, the birds of the air, and the creeping things of the ground; and I will abolish the bow, the sword, and war from the land; and I will make you lie down in safety. (Hos 2:18)

---

62. Mary Ann Beavis, "2 Thessalonians," in *Women's Bible Commentary*, ed. Carol A. Newsom, Sharon H. Ringe, and Jacqueline E. Lapsley, 3rd. ed. (Louisville, KY: Westminster John Knox, 2012), 593.

63. The four women are Olga Lengyel, Lucie Adelsberger, Bertha Ferderber-Salz, and Sara Nomberg-Przytyk; see Raphael, *Female Face.*

64. Quoted in Raphael, *Female Face*, 128.

65. See, e.g., Isa 2:11, 17, 20; 10:20; 11:10-11; Jer 4:9; 25:33; 39:16-17; Ezek 29:21; 30:9; Joel 3:18; see also Mark 13:17, 19, 20, 24, 32.

Here the use of the phrase emphasizes that the Day is a future expectation, anticipating the argument in 2 Thess 2:1-12 refuting the rumor that "the day of the Lord is already here" (2:2).

Resilience and Faith: Filipina Perspectives 2

Eucharistic celebrations at which the Pope officiated, especially in Tacloban City, which was most affected by typhoon Haiyan, were reminiscent of scenes from the Exodus narrative when God's divine presence or *Shekinah* dwelt in the midst of the Israelites as they journeyed through the wilderness toward the promised land (Exod 3:17; 25:8-9). The pope was like a Moses figure sent by God to liberate Filipinos from their suffering. The Hebrew word *Shekinah* (שכינה), although not explicitly used in the Hebrew Scriptures, shares the same root as *mishkhan* (משכן, "dwelling" or "tabernacle") in Exod 25:9. The root is שכן, which, according to Jon D. Levenson, means "to set up tent" or "to dwell." Levenson describes the *Shekinah* as "a delicate tabernacling presence, on the move with His people."[66] For feminist theologians the *Shekinah* is not just God's divine presence but God's divine *female* presence. To feminize Levenson's description, the *Shekinah* is God's "delicate tabernacling *female* presence, on the move with Her people."

Pia Sison

Once again the postcolonial understanding of history as a nonlinear ordering of time finds its relevance in a reconsideration of 2 Thessalonians' eschatology. We are reminded of the theological and biblical understanding of the καιρός, the "opportune time," expressed in the paradox of the Kin-dom of God "already-here" and "not-yet," briefly mentioned in the introduction. Furthermore, the postcolonial epistemology of history as "a spatial plurality" emphasizes a space in which heterogeneous people can coexist without glossing over conflicts and divisions in the struggle to build a community. In other words, a postcolonial community recognizes and accepts differences while resisting totalitarian homogenous forces of assimilation and uniformity.[67] Here

---

66. Jon D. Levenson, "The Jerusalem Temple in Devotional and Visionary Experience," in *Jewish Spirituality: From the Bible through the Middle Ages*, vol. 1, ed. Arthur R. Green (New York: Crossroad, 1994), 33.

67. Bill Ashcroft, Gareth Griffiths, and Helen Tiffin, *The Empire Writes Back: Theory and Practice in Post-Colonial Literatures* (London: Routledge, 1989), 36–37.

heterogeneity points to power differentials and different social locations, understanding that not everyone comes to a place on an equal footing or at one and the same time. However, as an alternative to a "temporal lineality" in which history (as the past) and ancestry are major references for identity, a "spatial plurality" seeks to open up a possibility of co-dwelling with one an/other out of respect and in right relationship, even though our places of origin and our ancestry are different or even in conflict and tension (e.g., slaves vs. masters). A recognition of the place of *Shekinah* in the guise of her sister *Sophia* in the Wisdom tradition lends itself to an understanding of postcolonial space, a dwelling place of God's presence, a co-dwelling of heterogeneous people with God. *Shekinah* becomes a place where peace defeats violence and suffering ends with redemption. It is a tent, a moving home, protecting and providing shelter to people on a journey. In this sense of *Shekinah*, a journey of faith inhabits both a sense of home and of homelessness. A Korean-American theologian, reflecting on his own migrant life, puts it this way: "My journey is not over yet, but I am at home. And home is not only the place to relax, but also the place to struggle, challenge, and grow."[68]

Sophia and Shekinah

Although the term *Shekinah* does not appear in the Jewish Scriptures, the figure of Ḥochmah/*Sophia*, the female-personified presence of God, plays a similar role in the Wisdom tradition. For example, the book of Wisdom/*Sophia* portrays *Sophia* as accompanying the people of God from the creation of the world to the wilderness wanderings of Israel.

She protected the first-
    formed father of the
    world,
when he alone had been
    created, . . .
When the earth was flooded
    because of him,
Wisdom again saved it,
steering the righteous man
    by a paltry piece of
    wood.
She also, when the nations
    in wicked agreement
    had been put to
    confusion,
recognized the righteous
    man
and preserved him blame-
    less before God,

68. Andrew Sung Park, "Church and Theology: My Theological Journey," in *Journeys at the Margin: Toward an Autobiographical Theology in American-Asian Perspective*, ed. Peter C. Phan and Jung Young Lee (Collegeville, MN: Liturgical Press, 1999), 172.

and kept him strong in the
face of his compassion
for his child.
She rescued a righteous
man when the ungodly
were perishing . . .
Wisdom rescued from
troubles those who
served her. . . .
When a righteous man was
sold,
she did not desert him, but
delivered him from sin.
She descended with him
into the dungeon,
and when he was in prison
she did not leave him,
until she brought him
the scepter of a kingdom
and authority over his
masters.
. . .
A holy people and a blameless race Wisdom deliv-
ered from a nation of
oppressors.

She entered the soul of a
servant of the LORD,
and withstood dread kings
with wonders and
signs,
she guided them along a
marvelous way, and
became a shelter to them
by day,
and a starry flame through
the night.
She brought them over the
Red Sea, and led them
through deep waters;
. . .
She prospered their works
by the hand of a holy
prophet.
They journeyed through an
uninhabited wilderness,
and pitched their tents
in untrodden places.
(Wis 10:1, 4, 5, 6, 13,
15-18; 11:1-2)

Mary Ann Beavis

Rhetoric is the art of persuasive speech and, by extension, writing. Persuasion can easily morph into manipulation, as it often does in 2 Thessalonians; the rhetoric here tends toward coercion, taking advantage of the dominant position of the authors relative to the audience.[69] In 2 Thess 1:10-11, the authors use their rhetorical skills to insist that the community must continue to believe in their previous "testimony," presumably the eschatological teaching of the first letter, the source document and model for the second, which had emphasized the imminence and futurity of the parousia (see 1 Thess 4:13-18). The reference to "our testimony [μαρτύριον] to you" (2 Thess 1:10) insists that the members of the ἐκκλησία must hold fast to the missionaries' witness, which they had believed and must continue to believe in light of the prospect of the

---

69. Beavis "2 Thessalonians," in Schüssler Fiorenza, *Searching the Scriptures*, 2:270.

return of Kyrios Jesus "to be glorified by his saints and to be marveled at on that day among all who believed." The implied threat is that the "saints" ("holy people") who are tempted to deviate from the received testimony, which they had "believed," are in danger of suffering the fate of "those who do not obey the gospel [εὐαγγέλιον] of our [Kyrios] Jesus" (1:8)—eternal destruction and estrangement from the divine glory (1:9). The reference to the authors' continual prayer on behalf of the audience, "asking that our God will make you worthy of his call and will fulfill by his power every good resolve and work of faith" (1:11), insinuates that the addressees may not be altogether worthy of the divine call and that they are in need of God's power and the constant intercession of the missionaries to maintain their faithfulness and resolution. As Abraham Malherbe observes, "It is through their conduct now, as they are empowered by God, that the name of the Lord Jesus will be glorified. The *en hymin* ('in you') describes the ground of the glorifying, that is 'by virtue of you,' as it did in v. 10 (cf. *en tois hagiois*, 'in his saints' . . .)."[70]

The unuttered warning that concludes this section of 2 Thessalonians is that the name of Kyrios Jesus will *not* be glorified in "you"—the audience—and they in him if they do not adhere to the missionaries' teaching (1:12), and they will fail to be worthy of the reign of God for which they "are suffering" (1:5). Presumably, failure to remain worthy will result in the same dire consequences as those in store for the unknowing and disobedient.

70. Malherbe, *Letters*, 411.

2 Thessalonians 2

Eschatological Birth Pangs

In rhetorical terms, 2 Thess 2:1-2 constitutes a *partitio*, a statement of the main issue to be discussed in the ensuing section (2:3-12): "the coming of our Kyrios Jesus Christ and our being gathered together to him" (2:1). The authors presuppose that the ἐκκλησία has received some communication—"by spirit or by word or by letter, as though from us"—to the effect that the Day of the Lord had already arrived (2:2). As noted in the previous chapter, the prophetic vision of the Day evokes both judgment and salvation; here the emphasis is on the catastrophic signs that must occur before the parousia.

> ### Eschatological Fulfillment in Early Christian Interpretation
>
> Although most interpreters presuppose that 2 Thess 2:2 conceptualizes the Day of the Lord in traditional, futuristic terms, it is possible that the authors were countering a contemporary doctrine that living believers had already spiritually ascended to the "heavenly places" with Christ, as expressed in the Deutero-Pauline letters Colossians and Ephesians (Eph 2:6; Col 3:4).[1] This belief is similar to the notion of "realized

1. Stephen L. Harris speculates that "it is possible that the visionary Spirit of prophecy that Paul encouraged the Thessalonians to cultivate (1 Thess 5:19-22) had come back to haunt him. Empowered by private revelations, a few Christian prophets may have interpreted the Spirit's presence—made possible by Jesus' resurrection and ascension to heaven—as a mystical fulfillment of the Parousia" (*The New Testament: A Student's Introduction* [Boston: McGraw-Hill, 2002], 360).

2 Thess 2:1-17

2:1As to the coming of our Lord Jesus Christ and our being gathered together to him, we beg you, brothers and sisters, 2not to be quickly shaken in mind or alarmed, either by spirit or by word or by letter, as though from us, to the effect that the day of the Lord is already here. 3Let no one deceive you in any way; for that day will not come unless the rebellion comes first and the lawless one is revealed, the one destined for destruction. 4He opposes and exalts himself above every so-called god or object of worship, so that he takes his seat in the temple of God, declaring himself to be God. 5Do you not remember that I told you these things when I was still with you? 6And you know what is now restraining him, so that he may be revealed when his time comes. 7For the mystery of lawlessness is already at work, but only until the one who now restrains it is removed. 8And then the lawless one will be revealed, whom the Lord Jesus will destroy with the breath of his mouth, annihilating him by the manifestation of his coming. 9The coming of the lawless one is apparent in the working of Satan, who uses all power,

eschatology" developed by C.H. Dodd with reference to the Gospel of John, where the notion of "eternal life" characteristic of that gospel is interpreted to mean a quality of existence lived in spiritual relationship with the risen Christ. Based on this notion, the parousia is not seen as a future event:

> His followers will enter into union with Him as their living Lord, and through Him with the Father, and so enter eternal life. That is what He meant when He said, "I will come again and receive you to myself, that where I am you too may be" (cf. also xvii. 24). This is the true "epiphany," and it is essentially an epiphany of the love of God, as the evangelist has set forth clearly and emphatically in xiv.21-4.[2]

However, the detailed chronology of end-time events sketched in 2 Thess 2:3-12 makes these spiritualized interpretations of the Day of the Lord unlikely.

Mary Ann Beavis

2. C. H. Dodd, *The Interpretation of the Fourth Gospel* (London and New York: Cambridge University Press, 1953), 447.

signs, lying wonders, [10]and every kind of wicked deception for those who are perishing, because they refused to love the truth and so be saved. [11]For this reason God sends them a powerful delusion, leading them to believe what is false, [12]so that all who have not believed the truth but took pleasure in unrighteousness will be condemned.

[13]But we must always give thanks to God for you, brothers and sisters beloved by the Lord, because God chose you as the first fruits for salvation through sanctification by the Spirit and through belief in the truth. [14]For this purpose he called you through our proclamation of the good news, so that you may obtain the glory of our Lord Jesus Christ. [15]So then, brothers and sisters, stand firm and hold fast to the traditions that you were taught by us, either by word of mouth or by our letter.

[16]Now may our Lord Jesus Christ himself and God our Father, who loved us and through grace gave us eternal comfort and good hope, [17]comfort your hearts and strengthen them in every good work and word.

The reference in 2 Thess 2:2 to a letter purporting to be from Paul, Silvanus, and Timothy has received a great deal of scholarly commentary, since it seems to refer to a pseudepigraphal epistle conveying eschatological doctrine contrary to that of the missionaries. Frank Witt Hughes, for example, concludes that the author of 2 Thessalonians was infuriated by "the authoritative claims of his adversaries, as evidenced by their publishing ventures, which our author dismissed as forgeries."[3] In order to counter the claims of the forgers, the author used the venerable 1 Thessalonians as a model, composing "a powerful and well-argued reply, full of apocalyptic fire and yet chillingly cold, but clearly a polished piece of religious rhetoric."[4] Ironically, Hughes observes, the author had "all too much in common" with the excesses of his adversaries.[5] Another possibility is that the "letter" purporting to be from the authors is actually 1 Thessalonians, "an interpretation of which . . . could have been responsible for the erroneous doctrine."[6] However, the source of the

---

3. Frank Witt Hughes, *Early Christian Rhetoric and 2 Thessalonians*, JSNTSup 30 (Sheffield: Sheffield Academic Press, 1989), 95.

4. Ibid.

5. Ibid.

6. Abraham J. Malherbe, *The Letters to the Thessalonians: A New Translation with Introduction and Commentary* (New York: Doubleday, 2000), 416, 429–30.

unauthorized teaching is left deliberately vague by the authors—it could have been conveyed by a "spirit" (πνεῦμα) of prophecy, a "word" (λόγος) of preaching, or a "letter" (ἐπιστολή—which the authors assume is a characteristic means of early christian communication). The first-person address in 2 Thess 2:5—"Do you not remember that *I* told you these things when *I* was with you?"—invokes the authority of Paul, by now a respected figure in the memory of the Thessalonian assembly (see 3:17). It also suggests that, in fact, the highly unusual teaching in 2:3-12 is an artifact of anxieties provoked by the war in Judea a generation after the composition of the first letter.[7]

The description of the events that must precede the Day of the Lord in the *probatio* ("proof") is filled with mysterious references, beginning with prophecies of the "rebellion" and the revelation of the "lawless one" who is "destined for destruction" (2 Thess 2:3), who resists and elevates himself above "every so-called god or object of worship," even to the extent of taking his seat in "the temple of God, declaring himself to be God" (2:4).

TRANSLATION MATTERS:
LAWLESS OR LOST?

It is difficult, if not impossible, to get a clear sense of what or to whom the "lawless one" of 2 Thess 2:3 is referring. In a Korean translation "lawless one" is rendered "against-law-person," which implies that the person is "illegal" or "anarchistic."[8] In the Korean cultural context this indicates that the person is not afraid of the law or lives and acts above the law, which could be understood as heroic and bold in a positive sense when the law and those who enforce it are unjust. This person is also referred to in the Korean translation as "son," rather than "man." In another English translation, the *Inclusive Bible*, the "lawless one" is translated as "the Lost One." This reminds us of the parables of the Lost, including that of the Lost Son, in Luke 15:1-32, which leaves room for love and

---

7. Malherbe notes that "There is nothing like 2 Thess 2:1-12 anywhere else in Paul's writings or in the NT" (*Letters*, 427). The fact that the eschatological teaching is subordinate to the authors' intention to calm the fears of the audience does not obviate its distinctiveness (see ibid., 427–28).

8. *NIV Explanation Korean-English Bible* (Seoul: Agape Publishing Company, 2003). "불법" (read as *buhlbup*) in Korean comes from the Chinese 不法, meaning "no law."

forgiveness, even though this person is clearly referred to as "The Enemy."[9] But the *Inclusive Bible* translation would nonetheless evoke the sense that, just as the Lost Son in Luke 15:11-21 did wrongful (illegal) things yet deserves forgiveness, this "lawless one," "the enemy," "destined for destruction" might also be worthy of forgiveness and redemption.

While the enemy is the demonic (satanic) force alluded to in 2 Thess 2:9 rather than a person in an anthropomorphic sense, the translation of the *Inclusive Bible*, "The Lost One," encourages us to speculate about other possible meanings in this ambiguous (and odd) text. As the editors of the *Inclusive Bible* point out, the particular choice of word in the translation indeed challenges us "to confront the limits of our language and to ask what baggage is attached to our proclamation of scripture." Furthermore, the meaning (culturally embedded and otherwise) behind such a translation challenges us to "consider how we think . . . and how our concepts influence the way we treat other people"[10] who are deemed to be "the enemy."

Such self-critical and ethical awareness of the limitations of the translation is also raised by Tat-Siong Benny Liew, a New Testament scholar. In commenting on the passage of the widow's offering in Mark 12:41-44, Liew contends that there is a big gap between linguistic and cultural translations to the point that it is virtually impossible to translate. However, he argues, "an inability to translate spells not only loss but also possibilities of gain, or moments of dynamic creativity."[11] To some extent the work of translation itself and that of digging into different translations to compare in order to get culturally, contextually, and possibly correct understanding are more than a linguistic matter. The art of translation (read as caring about words) requires and extends to ways of living, as Ludwig Wittgenstein, philosopher of language, wisely notes.[12] One may, then, be encouraged to speculate further about how to understand and practice the teaching of Jesus—to love your enemy in the form of "the lawless one" who is identified as "the enemy" in this text. Within the context of the community in Thessalonians, the destructive, violent, and illegal acts committed by the enemy may have happened inside the community, while the external demonic force,

9. Priests for Equality, *The Inclusive Bible: The First Egalitarian Translation* (Lanham, MD: Rowman & Littlefield, 2009), 768.

10. Ibid., vi.

11. Tat-Siong Benny Liew, "Lost in Translation? Tracing Linguistic and Economic Transactions in Three Texts," in *Planetary Loves: Spivak, Postcoloniality, and Theology*, ed. Stephen D. Moore and Mayra Rivera (New York: Fordham University Press, 2011), 116.

12. Ludwig Wittgenstein, *Lectures and Conversations on Aesthetics, Psychology, and Religious Belief*, ed. Cyril Barrett (Berkeley: University of California Press, 1967), 11–18.

the Roman Empire, as a possible example, is certainly also a threat to their survival, as pointed out further below. The one who "restrains the lawless one" is
God, but the work of restraining him is also the work of the people.

The understanding of how to define who the enemy is in 2 Thessalonians is
not necessarily the concern of the authors, but how to treat the enemy seems to
be a concern in terms of how this enemy has acted in the community. Abraham
Smith thinks that the author of 2 Thessalonians is exhorting the community not
to treat one another as enemies.[13] Here the enemy is understood as a kind of
group that lacks discipline and self-control. For this reason it often hurts others
within the community. If the enemy is a person or group of people within the
community, then he/she/they is/are not necessarily strange or "other" in the
sense of an "us versus them" mentality. That is to say, the enemy can be with
and among us, and we ourselves, as both good and bad, coexist in the community
and in society. However, when a member of the group becomes an enemy, she
or he goes through a kind of othering process, which means that this person or
this group becomes "othered" by being expelled by the group that labels that
person or group as "enemy." This imposition, or "the rhetoric of othering," using
Smith's words, "presupposes what was considered an androcentric goal, that is
self-control."[14]

Although the identity of the "temple" (ναός) here is not specified, most
commentators take it to be a reference to the temple in Jerusalem[15] and
see allusions both to the figure of Antiochus IV Epiphanes,[16] who in-
stalled the "abomination that makes desolate" there and defied God,
and his latter-day antitype, the Roman general Titus (later emperor),
who demolished both the holy city and the temple in 70 CE.[17] That is,
for the Thessalonian ἐκκλησία, the despoliation of the temple by Rome—
evoking the "Day of the Lord"—had recently occurred, provoking their
hopes of salvation and fears of disappointment.

13. Abraham Smith, "The First and Second Letters to the Thessalonians," in *A Postcolonial Commentary on the New Testament Writings*, ed. Fernando F. Segovia and R. S.
Sugirtharajah, The Bible and Postcolonialism 13 (New York: T & T Clark, 2007), 317.

14. Ibid.

15. As noted by Malherbe, *Letters*, 420.

16. See 1 Macc 1:29-40, 54-61; see also Dan 9:27; 11:31, 36-37; 12:11.

17. See Mark 13:14; Matt 24:15-16; Luke 20:20-21.

Josephus on the Destruction
of the Temple

The Jewish historian Flavius Josephus wrote this account of the destruction of the temple by Titus less than a decade after the event:

Now, as soon as the army had no more people to slay or to plunder, because there remained none to be objects of their fury (for they would not have spared any, had there remained any other such work to be done), [Titus] Caesar gave orders that they should now demolish the entire city and temple, but should leave as many of the towers standing as were of the greatest eminency; that is, Phasaelus, and Hippicus, and Mariamne; and so much of the wall as enclosed the city on the west side. This wall was spared, in order to afford a camp for such as were to lie in garrison [in the Upper City]; as were the towers [the three forts] also spared, in order to demonstrate to posterity what kind of city it was, and how well fortified, which the Roman valor had subdued; but for all the rest of the wall [surrounding Jerusalem], it was so thoroughly laid even with the ground by those that dug it up to the foundation, that there was left nothing to make those that came thither believe it [Jerusalem] had ever been inhabited. This was the end which Jerusalem came to by the madness of those that were for innovations; a city otherwise of great magnificence, and of mighty fame among all mankind.

. . . And, truly, the very view itself of the country was a melancholy thing; for those places which were before adorned with trees and pleasant gardens were now become desolate country every way, and its trees were all cut down; nor could any foreigner that had formerly seen Judea and the most beautiful suburbs of the city, and now saw it as a desert, but lament and mourn sadly at so great a change; for the war had laid all signs of beauty quite waste; nor, if anyone that had known the place before, had come on a sudden to it now, would he have known it again; but though he [a foreigner] were at the city itself, yet would he have inquired for it notwithstanding.[18]

---

18. Josephus, *Jewish War* 7.1.1; 6.1.1.; William Whiston, trans., *The Works of Josephus* (Peabody, MA: Hendrickson, 1987), 750–51, 727.

Figure 3: Judea Capta Coin[19]

Writing in the name of Paul, Silvanus, and Timothy from their post-70 CE perspective, the anonymous author(s) reassure the ἐκκλησία that the recent Roman triumph in Jerusalem, interpreted metaphorically as imperial usurpation of the prerogatives of the God of Israel (2:4), is indeed part of the divine plan that is coming to fruition in their own time, the conclusion of an age in which evil was being manifested on a cosmic scale and in which the good present in the world would soon be realized when the forces of evil had run their course.[20] In the time of the putative authors, the "mystery of lawlessness" was already operating "until the one who now restrains it is removed" (2 Thess 2:7). Second Thessalonians 2:6-7 speaks of both "that which restrains" (τὸ κατέχον) and "he who restrains" (ὁ κατέχων) the "lawless one" who will be revealed, "apparent in the working of Satan, who uses all power, signs, lying wonders, and every kind of wicked deception for those who are perishing, because they refused to love the truth and so be saved" (2:9-10). The "restraining force" and the figure embodying that force were, ironically, identified as the empire and its emperor by early christian interpreters, beginning with Tertullian of Carthage (ca. 200 CE).[21] In reality, it was Rome and its emperor who had unleashed destruction

---

19. Coin minted to commemorate the victory of Rome in Judea, pictured as a humiliated woman seated under a palm tree, a traditional symbol of Israel (printed with permission of Lessing Images). See Marlene Crüsemann, "2 Thessalonians: Hope in God's Last Judgment," in *Feminist Biblical Interpretation: A Compendium of Critical Commentary on the Books of the Bible and Related Literature*, ed. Luise Schottroff and Marie-Theres Wacker (Grand Rapids, MI, and Cambridge: Eerdmans, 2012), 827.

20. Malherbe, *Letters*, 418. Also see 4 Ezra 5:1-13; 4:27-29; 14:16-18; 2 Bar 27; 1 Enoch 91:5-7; 1 QPHab 2:1-10.

21. Earl J. Richard, *First and Second Thessalonians*, SP 11 (Collegeville, MN: Liturgical Press, 2007), 337–38.

and despoliation on the holiest place on earth, as the forces of Antiochus had done in the time of the Maccabees.

> For the citadel became an ambush against the sanctuary,
>> an evil adversary of Israel at all times.
> On every side of the sanctuary they shed innocent blood;
>> they even defiled the sanctuary.
> Because of them the residents of Jerusalem fled;
>> she became a dwelling of strangers;
>> she became strange to her offspring,
>> and her children forsook her.
> Her sanctuary became desolate like a desert;
>> her feasts were turned into mourning,
>> her sabbaths into a reproach,
>> her honor into contempt.
> Her dishonor now grew as great as her glory;
>> her exaltation was turned into mourning. (1 Macc 1:36-40)

Forgiveness for the Lost

The movie *Dead Man Walking* (1995) provokes theological and soteriological questions similar to those raised in 2 Thessalonians. In the movie, parents of murdered teenagers demand "absolute justice," meaning the death sentence, while Catholic Sister Helen Prejean believes that redemption is possible even for the person who brutally killed two innocent children.[22] The story leaves the question of forgiveness largely unresolved. What does it mean to forgive the enemy, the lawless one, even if he is a murderer? What is justice in this sense? It is indeed a difficult question when one faces the conundrum of how to treat others whose violent acts have caused great harm. Biblically and theologically speaking, the abundant grace of God is bigger than the weight and influence of sin (Rom 5:12). God is the one who redeems, forgives, and offers mercy and grace, whether deservedly or not. The theological issues of justification and sanctification or judgment and grace are never clear-cut.

Over two millennia many christian theologians, including the apostle Paul, Augustine of Hippo, Martin Luther, Karl Rahner, and Karl Barth have argued that grace is an unconditional gift from God, manifested in Jesus, while at the same time trying to come to terms with human sin. Christian

---

22. *Dead Man Walking*, directed by Tim Robbins, 1995.

ecclesial bodies also have wrestled with the issues of sin in light of grace, and of law in light of Gospel. The *Joint Declaration on the Doctrine of Justification between the Lutheran and Catholic Church* is one such contemporary example.[23] Shannon Craigo-Snell, systematic theologian, and

Shawnthea Monroe, a pastoral theologian, suggest that we should not avoid the reality of sin because it holds the truth about us, that though we are fallen we are also the children of a God who forgives.[24]

HyeRan Kim-Cragg

A more plausible explanation is that "that which restrains" the end-time events is the early christian mission itself: the gospel must be spread throughout the world before the parousia (2 Thess 3:1).[25] In this case the "restrainer" would be God, as 2 Thess 2:11-12 suggests: "For this reason God sends them a powerful delusion, leading them to believe what is false, so that all who have not believed the truth but took pleasure in unrighteousness will be condemned." This interpretation is supported by the allusion to Isa 66:14b-16, mentioned in the last chapter; in the LXX, Isa 66:19 reads: "From them I will send [those who are saved] to the nations."[26] As Roger Aus observes, "It is the mission to the Gentiles, to the coastlands and afar off, which could be the (neuter) restraining factor of the author of 2 Thessalonians. It is *God's will or plan* that the gospel first be carried to all . . . before the Day of the Lord arrives."[27] This interpretation does not contradict the imminent eschatological expectation held by the authors and recipients of the letter; in the Gospel of Mark, also written during or shortly after the Jewish War, the disciples/audience are assured that "there are some standing here who will not taste death" before the arrival of the reign of God (Mark 9:27) and are

23. Lutheran World Federation and the Catholic Church, "Joint Declaration On The Doctrine Of Justification," *The Holy See*, 1999, http://www.vatican.va/roman_curia/pontifical_councils/chrstuni/documents/rc_pc_chrstuni_doc_31101999_cath-luth-joint-declaration_en.html.

24. Shannon Craigo-Snell and Shawnthea Monroe, *Living Christianity: A Pastoral Theology for Today* (Minneapolis: Fortress Press, 2009), 93–94.

25. See also Mark 13:10; Matt 28:8.

26. See Roger Aus, "God's Plan and God's Power: Isaiah 66 and the Restraining Factors of 2 Thess 2:6-7," *JBL* 96 (1977): 537–53, at 540.

27. Ibid.

exhorted to live in a state of preparedness (13:32-36), although the necessity of the Gentile mission is affirmed (13:10).

Following Aus, Marlene Crüsemann detects a birth image from Isa 66:7-9 embedded in 2 Thess 2:7.[28]

> Before she was in labor
> > she gave birth;
> before her pain came upon her
> > she delivered a son.
> Who has heard of such a thing?
> > Who has seen such things?
> Shall a land be born in one day?
> > Shall a nation be delivered in one moment?
> Yet as soon as Zion was in labor
> > she delivered her children.
> Shall I open the womb and not deliver?
> > says the LORD;
> shall I, the one who delivers, shut the womb?
> > says your God.

If the tribulations of 2 Thess 2:3-11 are understood as the eschatological birth pangs alluded to by Isaiah,[29] then God is the divine midwife so remarkably skilled that she is able "to shut the womb and slow down the birth process."[30] The powerful contractions being experienced by the Thessalonian assembly signify that the labor process is well underway and that Lady Zion will soon be delivered from her travails. Then the sufferings of the ἐκκλησία will be reversed in the glory of the parousia.

> Rejoice with Jerusalem, and be glad for her,
> > all you who love her;
> rejoice with her in joy,
> > all you who mourn over her—
> that you may nurse and be satisfied
> > from her consoling breast;
> that you may drink deeply with delight
> > from her glorious bosom.
> For thus says the LORD:

---

28. Crüsemann, "2 Thessalonians," 827.

29. See Isa 13:8; Mic 4:9-10; 5:3; Rom 8:22; John 16:21-23.

30. Crüsemann, "2 Thessalonians," 827. See 1 Thess 5:3, where the sudden advent of the Day of the Lord is compared to the suddenness of labor pains.

I will extend prosperity to her like a river,
and the wealth of the nations like an overflowing stream;
and you shall nurse and be carried on her arm,
and dandled on her knees.
As a mother comforts her child,
so I will comfort you;
you shall be comforted in Jerusalem. (Isa 66:10-13)

The birth imagery of the section is carried through in 2 Thess 2:13, where the audience is addressed as "the first fruits of salvation."[31]

The assurance that the addressees become the firstfruits of salvation points to a new beginning, anchored in hope, despite the suffering of the ἐκκλησία. It gives them a new way of knowing the world, a new way of seeing their lives. Many feminist developmental theorists, including Carol Gilligan and Mary Field Belenky, claim that giving birth is a catalyst to seeing new things.[32] In the process of becoming a mother (in a biological sense) a woman gains a new understanding of life, self, and world. To some extent she becomes a new person, and she generates by renewing and transforming her community. Indeed, her waters have broken as the morning has broken for the new day. Through "nursing" from "her consoling breast" as a mother carrying her offspring in her arms, beholding the vision of Isaiah, she "holds up half the sky" and "reproduces the world," as practical theologian Bonnie J. Miller-McLemore says in her poetic description of the role of a nursing mother.[33] This work of holding up is far from easy or light. Thus we should not indulge too much in the fantasy of an omnipotent mother who endures and bears all our physical, emotional, spiritual, and pedagogical demands. As a matter of fact, the life-giving and life-nurturing power of motherhood expressed in 2 Thessalonians is not free from danger or difficulty. The work of sanctification requires pain sometimes akin to birth pangs as we do our best at "standing firm and holding fast to the tradition that you were taught" (2:13, 15).

---

31. See "Fruit," in *Dictionary of Biblical Imagery*, ed. Leland Ryken, James C. Wilhoit, and Tremper Longman III (Downers Grove, IL, and Leicester, UK: InterVarsity, 1998), 310. See also Gen 49:3; Exod 13:12-16; Jas 1:18.

32. Carol Gilligan, *In a Different Voice: Psychological Theory and Women's Development* (Boston: Harvard University Press, 1982); Mary Field Belenky, Blythe McVicker Clinchy, Nancy Rule Goldberger, and Jill Mattuck Tarule, *Women's Ways of Knowing: The Development of Self, Voice, and Mind* (New York: Basic Books, 1986), 76.

33. Bonnie J. Miller-McLemore, *Also a Mother: Work and Family as Theological Dilemma* (Nashville, TN: Abingdon, 1994), 134, 144.

However, the maternal imagery submerged in the authors' lurid account of the eschatological birth pangs does not fully obviate the violence and vindictiveness of the scenario sketched here, where powerful male forces—God, Christ, Satan, the "man of lawlessness/son of destruction"—vie for cosmic supremacy. Or, to put it differently—in Christianity, suffering has been treated as holy when it is involved in "sacred violence," chiefly "the cross," as the symbolic event of the suffering of God. Such elevation of violence creates and sacralizes "destructive sadomasochistic impulses," says Mark Lewis Taylor.[34] The term "sadomasochistic" implies that a kind of pleasure is derived both from inflicting pain on others and from being abused by others. Gayatri Spivak speaks about "enabling violence" and "enabling violation" as a paradox of a postcolonial condition or as a vicious cycle of oppression.[35] While her observations of the colonial reality do not excuse the one who committed violence or suggest that the power differentials between the one who commits violence and the one who is victimized by violence are inconsequential, she nonetheless points to a condition that leads the victimized to allow further violence to occur against themselves. This colonial violence not only creates a dynamic reality but is passed down to future generations. Like a contagious disease, violence is transmitted to the one who is susceptible and already vulnerable. The documented example that women who grow up being abused by their fathers or brothers tend to find partners who also abuse them is a horrifying case in point. Rather than the cycle of violence being cut off from generation to generation, it often continues and reoccurs, even if the manner of that violence changes.

> **Resilience and Faith:**
> **Filipina Perspectives 3**
>
> Is there such a thing as "Filipino resilience" and "faith" when the afflicted is a sexually abused woman and her perpetrator—the cause of her *kapighatian* ("affliction") and *pagtitiis* ("suffering")—is a member of the clergy? One might ask, "Where is the *Shekinah* in that?" Where is God's "gentle tabernacling female presence" in a woman's

34. Mark Lewis Taylor, *The Executed God: The Way of the Cross in Lockdown America* (Minneapolis: Fortress Press, 2001), 2.
35. Gayatri Chakravorty Spivak, "Bonding in Difference: Interview with Alfred Arteaga," in *The Spivak Reader*, ed. Donna Landry and Gerald MacLean (New York: Routledge, 1996), 15–28, at 19.

experience of abuse, especially by a man perceived by the community as "pious"? Interestingly, there is something valuable to be learned from *Iggeret Ha-Kodesh* ("The Holy Letter," thirteenth century) that gives a Kabbalistic view of sexuality. While technically the text is not halakhic in nature, Rachel Biale states that *Iggeret Ha-Kodesh* was "a popular treatise and exercised considerable influence on the way pious [Jewish] men related to sexuality."[36] Pertaining to sexual relations between a husband and wife, *Iggeret Ha-Kodesh* instructs husbands:

> And you shall not possess her against her will nor force her because in that kind of a union there is no divine presence [*Shekinah*] because your intentions are opposite to hers and her wish does not agree with yours. And do not quarrel with her nor beat her for the sake of having intercourse. The rabbis say in Tractate

Yoma: "As a lion smashes and eats and has no shame, so a boor beats and possesses and has no shame."[37]

Although one could misogynistically argue against that statement by quoting another Jewish source that says "no spot on earth is devoid of the Presence,"[38] it can be deduced from *Iggeret Ha-Kodesh* that when women (in general) are possessed against their will there is no *Shekinah* in that oppressive act. As Elizabeth A. Johnson puts it, "When violence is done to women, to their bodies or their spirits, it is an insult to divine glory."[39] Hence, where is the *Shekinah* in the Filipino woman's experience of abuse? It is in her ability to be resilient through her strong faith in God. According to Nila Bermisa, even in the midst of *kapighatian* and *pagtitiis*, resilience and faith are what liberate sexual abuse victims from their pain. These are the keys to their survival. Bermisa, a feminist nun, was part of a research team that documented

---

36. Rachel Biale, citing *Iggeret Ha-Kodesh* (traditionally ascribed to Nachmanides) in *Women and Jewish Law: The Essential Texts, Their History, and Their Relevance for Today* (New York: Schocken Books, 1984), 140.

37. Biale, citing *Iggeret Ha-Kodesh* chap. 6, "The Fifth Way—Concerning the Quality of Intercourse," in ibid., 142.

38. Numbers Rabbah 12:4; Hayim Naman Bialik and Yehoshua Hana Ravnitzky, eds., *The Book of Legends (Sefer Ha-Aggadah): Legends from the Talmud and Midrash* (New York: Schocken Books, 1992), 503:6.

39. Elizabeth A. Johnson, *Quest for the Living God: Mapping Frontiers in the Theology of God* (New York and London: Continuum, 2008), 96.

cases of abuse committed by priests in the Philippines. She recounts:

> This Filipino resilience and deep religiosity (faith), so innate in the Filipino, have been the saving grace for the many Filipino women who have survived sexual abuses in the past. Their bodies and spirits may have been broken but they survived and lived on, struggling for life not only for themselves but also for others.[40]

For the author, Filipino resilience is best articulated in the expression *"bahala na."* Bermisa explains:

> *Bahala na* can be interpreted in different ways within the Filipino context. It can mean "The heck with it, let's just do it." Or it can be a bold abandonment of logic and reason in order to follow one's instinct or intuition: "throwing all cares to the wind," let chance fall where it may. The root of *bahala na* has divine or sacred meaning. *Bathala* is God. *Bahala na* implies God's will. Thus to utter *bahala na* in a prayerful way means "God's will be done" or "Let go, let God be." . . . *Bahala na* is an attitude, a fighting spirit. This is the Filipino resiliency at its best. For victims of sexual abuse, their healing and recovery (indeed, their resurrection!) can begin when they are finally able to say *"Bahala na."*[41]

Pia Sison

As the differences between the oppressor and the oppressed in the cycle of violence are not clear-cut, so examining the healing of the abused as opposed to the abuser is never simple or easy. Nonetheless, muddling through the issue of violence as the path of peace and healing is where we must journey. The Korean concept of 넝한 (*jeonghan*) (情限) may be instructive with regard to this journey. *Jeonghan* means "a release of a long sigh by the person who has experience of *han*," i.e., accumulated suffering from violence.[42] In constructing a Christology based on *jeong*,

40. Nila Bermisa, *That She May Dance Again: Rising from the Pain of Violence Against Women in the Philippine Church* (Philippines: WGC-AMRSP, 2011), 105.

41. Ibid., 9, 103–4.

42. Wonhee Anne Joh, *Heart of the Cross: A Postcolonial Christology* (Louisville, KY: Westminster John Knox, 2006), 22.

Korean-American feminist theologian Wonhee Anne Joh argues that *jeong* "is rooted in relationality," which "creates indeterminacy within the unaccounted-for space between the oppressed and the oppressor, between hate and love, between self and the other, between the semiotic and the symbolic, and between the divine and the world."[43]

As Mary Ann Beavis noted in 1994, the ancient apocalyptic imagery of 2 Thess 2:1-12 "is disturbingly reminiscent of modern warfare, where powerful men vie for ascendancy using terrible weapons, which destroy innocent people (conceived by the 'other side' as evil)."[44] Marlene Crüsemann takes this critique of the apocalyptic rhetoric of the letter to task, observing that merely to write off this imagery as apocalyptic speculation is to overlook its significance for an oppressed minority.[45] She argues, quite rightly, that the letter is a word of comfort to recipients enduring a period of "unrighteousness and bewilderment" and that the authors encourage them with a vision of the imminent parousia, when Christ will "achieve his victory without weapons (2:8)—he will kill the enemy of the Torah by the breath of his mouth" (cf. Isa 11:4).[46] However, this emphasis on "the appearance of Jesus, bringing liberation that all will see and believe"[47] is not enough to excuse the ethical shortcomings of this vision of salvation. The authors are fervent in their insistence that Kyrios Jesus "will destroy" (ἀναλεῖ) and "will annihilate" (καταργήσει) the "lawless one" (2:6-9); the life-giving breath-spirit (πνεῦμα) becomes part of the divine arsenal.

Given the popularity of the "rapture" and "Antichrist" doctrines that have been projected by later generations of interpreters into the Thessalonian correspondence (1 Thess 4:13-18; 2 Thess 2:3-4, 6-10), it is particularly critical that the reader should neither take the text literally nor dismiss it completely as irrelevant to the twenty-first-century context. In fact, contemporary readers should be alarmed by the pervasive influence of fundamentalists who demonize others (other religious groups, minorities) with the rhetoric of "Antichrist" drawn from this text. Robert Fuller's work is helpful; he thoroughly researches the history of the

43. Ibid., 121.

44. Mary Ann Beavis, "2 Thessalonians," in *Searching the Scriptures*, vol. 2, *A Feminist Commentary*, ed. Elisabeth Schüssler Fiorenza (New York: Crossroad, 1994), 268; cf. Mary Ann Beavis, "2 Thessalonians," in *Women's Bible Commentary*, ed. Carol A. Newsom, Sharon H. Ringe, and Jacqueline E. Lapsley, 3rd ed. (Louisville, KY: Westminster John Knox, 2012), 593.

45. Crüsemann, "2 Thessalonians," 826.

46. Ibid., 827.

47. Ibid.

phenomenon of accusing others with the term "Antichrist" that is prevalent in Christian churches in the United States. He notes that this demonization of others has changed throughout history; the face of the Antichrist was Native American in the 1800s, Roman Catholic in the early 1900s, Soviet in the middle 1900s, and Muslim in the late 1900s.[48] While the targeted groups have changed, the goal of the Antichrist label, namely, to ostracize others, has not. To counter such negative use of the text we must ask: what motivated the authors of 2 Thessalonians to use veiled and obscure language? Using the work of Charles Wanamaker,[49] Abraham Smith speculates that we may be able to read between the lines of this odd text by considering its ecclesial context. The authors, he suggests, seek to comfort and instruct those who may be frightened and misled by the false and shocking claim of the end of time by using vague and enigmatic expressions. It is indeed tricky to resolve fear through revenge while at the same time holding those who committed violence accountable. To do so without being complicit in the roots of the violence is arguably one aspect of justice. It is a delicate balance.

Superficially, Crüsemann's observation that the form of "peaceful resistance" against unjust power found in 2 Thessalonians is far from being the equivalent of modern warfare is correct: "This is by no means to be equated with modern ideas of waging 'star wars.'"[50] As she notes, this call to resistance amounts to "saying goodbye to the male prerogative of resistance one usually finds in society"[51]—for human, if not for divine males. It is true that the ancient apocalyptic is resistance literature generated by social groups suffering some form of persecution or oppression and that apocalyptists rarely advocate armed retaliation, leaving their vindication to God.[52] Apocalyptic writings were often a response to

48. Robert C. Fuller, *Naming the Antichrist: The History of an American Obsession* (New York: Oxford University Press, 1995), 11–13.

49. Smith, "1 and 2 Thessalonians," 309, using Charles A. Wanamaker, *Commentary on 1 and 2 Thessalonians* (Grand Rapids, MI: Eerdmans, 1990).

50. Crüsemann, "2 Thessalonians," 827. It should be noted that Crüsemann's assertion that "Mary Ann Beavis speaks of 'troops of men'" warring for "control of the universe" (826) seems to be a misreading; the original wording is actually "powerful male forces . . . engage in a war for control of the universe" (Beavis, "2 Thessalonians," in *Searching the Scriptures*, 2:268), and the reference is not to human but to supernatural male figures.

51. Crüsemann, "2 Thessalonians," 828.

52. See Anathea Portier-Young, *Apocalypse Against Empire: Theologies of Resistance in Early Judaism* (Grand Rapids, MI: Eerdmans, 2011).

"terror and trauma."[53] Possibly, like the ancient Jewish apocalypses studied by Anathea Portier-Young, the prophecies transmitted in 2 Thessalonians "portrayed reality in a new light in order to change not only how
their audiences saw, but also what they did. They challenged readers
and hearers not to withdraw, but to engage."[54] From the standpoint of
reception history, however, it is quite feasible to trace a line of transmission from the dualistic and violent apocalyptic rhetoric of 2 Thessalonians
to the fascination with war, destruction, and apocalyptic futures in contemporary culture.[55] Melissa Raphael's comments concerning the model
of God inherent in the apocalyptic tradition are instructive here:

> The excessively patriarchal god called God could have been—as
> numen—very much present at Auschwitz. In that apocalyptical place
> of fire and smoke, of terror and ultimacy, of the *tremendum*, where the
> Bible's most severe prophetic warnings of desolation and abomination
> were realized, the patriarchal God was indeed almost at home. Ausch-
> witz was *his* place in so far as the conditions of numinous horror were
> graphic illustrations of his threats to bring punitive destruction against
> the House of Israel. But this (sometimes, not always) vindictive, savage
> God of Joshua whose conquest drives all before him is but a scarecrow,
> a paper tiger, a Wizard of Oz. This God of smoke and consuming fire
> before whom all but his technicians cower is merely one aspect of an
> idolatrous projection of patriarchal hubris, cast in the likeness of its
> own aspiration.[56]

While the apocalyptic prophecies of 2 Thessalonians must be distinguished from their reception by later generations, the epistle, as canonical
Scripture, contains the seeds of that history of interpretation and its
real-world outcomes. Further, it is highly questionable whether the stance
vis-à-vis "the enemy" envisioned by the authors deserves the name of
"peaceful" (or nonviolent) resistance. Although the recipients are not
exhorted to take up arms against their persecutors, they are assured of
destruction of the "evil" personified in their opponents to the most ex-

---

53. Ibid., 398.

54. Ibid., 217.

55. See, e.g., Catherine Wessinger, "Apocalypse and Violence," in *The Oxford Handbook of Apocalyptic Literature*, ed. John J. Collins (Oxford: Oxford University Press,
2014), 422–40; and, in the same volume, Lorenso DiTomasso, "Apocalypticism and
Popular Culture," 473–510.

56. Melissa Raphael, *The Female Face of God in Auschwitz* (New York: Routledge,
2003), 51.

treme and permanent degree imaginable: "the punishment of eternal destruction, separated from the presence of the Lord and from the glory of his might" (1:9). This is a strategy that relies on the promise of deferred, extreme, and inevitable punishment, not on the kind of nonviolent resistance, inspired by the teachings of Jesus, that eschews anger, aggression, and revenge.[57]

Women and the Antichrist Legend

Second Thessalonians 2:3-15 has loomed large in the history of the Antichrist legend, although the term never appears in the letter. In fact, the term "antichrist" is found only in the Johannine letters (1 John 2:18, 22; 4:3; 2 John 1:7), with reference to anyone who denies "that Jesus is the Christ" (1 John 2:22). Although the term is associated with the end times, it refers not to a single figure but to a spirit of opposition to Christ expressed by many: "even now many antichrists have come. This is how we know it is the last hour" (1 John 2:18). In subsequent centuries "antichrist" was conflated with various figures embodying evil from biblical apocalyptic literature—the "little horn" in Dan 7:8, 11 (see also 8:23-27); the "beast" and the "false prophet" in Rev 13:3-4; 16:13; 19:20; 20:10, the "false christs" in Mark 13:22, and,

notably, the figure called the "man of lawlessness" and the "son of destruction" in 2 Thess 2:3, 8. As Augustine, writing in the early fifth century, remarked of 2 Thess 2:1-12, "No one can doubt that Paul is here speaking of the Antichrist, telling us that the day of judgment (which he calls the day of the Lord) will not come without the prior coming of a figure whom he calls the Apostate, meaning, of course, an apostate from the Lord God" (*City of God* 20.19.2).[58]

John Chrysostom wrote dismissively of women's interest in the events surrounding the advent of the Antichrist:

> The Thessalonians indeed were then perplexed, but their perplexity has been profitable to us. For not to them only, but to us also are these things useful, that we may be delivered from childish fables and from old women's fooleries. And

---

57. See Mahatma Gandhi, *What Jesus Means to Me*, trans. R. K. Prabhu (Ahmedabad: Navajivan Publishing House, 1959).

58. See Peter Gorday, ed., *Ancient Christian Commentary on Scripture, New Testament IX: Colossians, 1–2 Thessalonians, 1–2 Timothy, Titus, Philemon* (Downers Grove, IL: InterVarsity, 2000), 111.

have you not often heard, when you were children, persons talking much even about the name of Antichrist, and about his bending the knee? For the devil scatters these things in our minds, while yet tender, that the doctrine may grow up with us, and that he may be able to deceive us. Paul therefore, in speaking of Antichrist, would not have passed over these things if they had been profitable. Let us not therefore enquire into these things. For he will not come so bending his knees, but exalting himself against all that is called God, or that is worshiped; so that he sits in the temple of God, setting himself forth as God. . . . For as the devil fell by pride, so he who is wrought upon by him is anointed unto pride. (*Homily on 2 Thessalonians* 1)[59]

Two women have figured significantly in the "malestream" history of the Antichrist legend. The first was Algasia, a Latin laywoman who wrote a letter to St. Jerome (ca. 406 CE), containing a list of twelve questions, one of which asks "What does it mean when the Apostle writes to the Thessalonians, 'Unless the desertion . . . will have first come, and the man of sin will have been revealed,' and so on?"[60] Jerome complimented Algasia on her quest to understand such matters, comparing her to the Queen of Sheba in search of the wisdom of Solomon (with Jerome assuming the place of the all-wise king!).[61] Kevin Hughes describes Jerome's reply as "a compendium of teachings on Antichrist, with little of anything actually original to him."[62] By Jerome's time, the notion that the Antichrist would be an inversion of Christ was commonplace: "Just as in Christ the fullness of divinity existed corporally, so all the powers, signs and prodigies will be in Antichrist, but all of them will be false."[63] The other woman who sparked an influential discussion of the Antichrist was the Frankish

59. *Nicene and Post-Nicene Fathers*, 1st ser., vol. 13, ed. Philip Schaff, trans. John A. Broadus (Buffalo, NY: Christian Literature Publishing Co., 1889). Revised and edited for New Advent by Kevin Knight, http://www.newadvent.org/fathers/23051.htm.

60. Quoted in Kevin L. Hughes, *Constructing Antichrist: Paul, Biblical Commentary, and the Development of Doctrine in the Early Middle Ages* (Washington, DC: The Catholic University of America Press, 2005), 75–76.

61. Ibid., 75.

62. Ibid., 76.

63. *Letter to Algasia* 121.11, 59, cited in Hughes, *Constructing Antichrist*, 77.

Queen Gerberga (ca. 950), whose concern over the impending millennium motivated Adso de Montier-en-Der to write the treatise "On the Origin and Time of the Antichrist." Adso's work is "in essence, a letter of consolation to the Queen Gerberga, promising that Antichrist's coming is forestalled until the Roman Empire, in a later Frankish incarnation, has finally passed away."[64] Neither work shows the originality and incisiveness of Hildegard's account of the birth of the Antichrist discussed above in the introduction, which recalls the submerged imagery of the eschatological birth pangs in 2 Thess 2:6 (see also 1 Thess 5:3). Unfortunately, Hildegard's vision is not discussed, even in passing, by either of the recent books tracing the reception history of 2 Thess 2:1-12.[65]

Mary Ann Beavis

The next identifiable section of the letter is 2 Thess 2:13–3:5, made up of "thanksgiving (2:13-14) and a command to hold to received tradition (2:14); a prayer for the Thessalonians (2:16-17); and a prayer request for deliverance from 'wicked and evil people' (3:1-13), concluding with an expression of confidence in the recipients (3:4) and a final prayer that they will look to God and Christ (3:5), who, it is implied, are on the side of the missionaries."[66] Rhetorically these verses may be classified as a *peroratio*, summing up and amplifying previous arguments, appealing to the emotions of the audience for the authors and against their opponents.[67] Like other ancient perorations, this section recapitulates important elements of the discourse (see 1:13 and 1:3; 2:14 and 1:11-12; 2:15 and 2:2) (*enumeratio*), expresses indignation against the enemy (3:2-3) (*indignatio*), and arouses pity and sympathy for the senders (3:1-2) (*conquestio*).[68]

The second thanksgiving in 2 Thess 2:13-15 mirrors that of 1 Thess 2:13—a feature of the two Thessalonian letters not shared by other letters in the Pauline tradition. Here the additional thanksgiving illustrates the

---

64. Hughes, *Constructing Antichrist*, 168.

65. Ibid.; Anthony C. Thiselton, *1 & 2 Thessalonians through the Centuries* (Oxford: John Wiley & Sons, 2011), 211–30.

66. Beavis, "2 Thessalonians," in Schüssler Fiorenza, *Searching the Scriptures*, 2:269.

67. Frank Witt Hughes, *Early Christian Rhetoric and 2 Thessalonians*, JSNTSup 30 (Sheffield: Sheffield Academic Press, 1989), 42.

68. Beavis, "2 Thessalonians," in Schüssler Fiorenza, *Searching the Scriptures*, 2:269; see Hughes, *Early Christian Rhetoric*, 41–43.

authors' wish to maintain—or reinforce—their influence over the recipients ("beloved by the *Kyrios*") and to emphasize the importance of holding fast to the "tradition" referred to in the *probatio*: "Do you not remember that I told you these things when I was still with you?" (2:5). By echoing the reference to "spirit," "word," or "letter" at the beginning of the section (2:2) the authors signal that it is only the "word of mouth" or "our letter" that stands as authentic sources of authoritative teaching (2:15). The members of the ἐκκλησία are flatteringly described as the "first fruits for salvation [or from the beginning]" (2:13). As noted earlier, this expression may relate back to the motif of the eschatological birth pangs; although the primary reference of the term "first fruits" is to agricultural offerings,[69] it refers also to the dedication of firstborn sons to God, as a remembrance of Israel's liberation from bondage in Egypt (Exod 13:11-16). In Genesis, Jacob refers to his eldest son as the "first fruits of my vigor" (49:3); Jas 1:18 describes God as the Mother who "gave us birth by the word of truth, so that we would become a kind of first fruits of his creatures." However, this firstborn status can be lost, "because God chose you . . . for salvation through sanctification by the Spirit and through belief in the truth" (2 Thess 2:13). It is by heeding "*our* proclamation of the good news" (2:14)— not those of the "deceivers" (2:3)—that the ἐκκλησία will maintain its chosen status and thus "obtain the glory of our Kyrios Jesus Christ" (2:14). Here the authors' adversarial outlook on "those who do not obey the gospel of our Kyrios Jesus" (1:8) shifts inward to the members of the Thessalonian assembly, who must be loyal to the missionaries' preaching ("the truth") lest they lose their chosen, beloved, familial status. Second Thessalonians 2 ends with a prayer for encouragement that the love, grace, eternal comfort, and good hope granted *us* (the authors) by Kyrios Jesus Christ and Father-Mother God may comfort *your* hearts and strengthen them in "every good work and word" (2:16-17), preparing for the somewhat more peaceable tone of chapter 3.

69. E.g., Exod 23:19; 34:26; Lev 2:14; 23:10, 17.

2 Thessalonians 3

Idle No More

Beverly Roberts Gaventa speaks of the anger that permeates the first two chapters of 2 Thessalonians: "Chapter 1 rages against those who afflict believers, anticipating the judgment that will fall on them. Chapter 2 interprets that rage in the larger context of rebellion against God: those who afflict believers are acting not merely out of their own enmity, but out of the wrath of their superiors, evil and lawlessness themselves."[1] She notes further that although these elements are not absent from the third chapter, the authors' fury fades into the background, so that "the rage is not all that speaks, even in the midst of crisis."[2] The somewhat milder tone corresponds with the change in theme. As is the case in other letters in the Pauline tradition, doctrinal teachings (2:2-12) are followed by paraenesis, that is, ethical exhortation and encouragement (3:6-14). Rather than being an afterthought or postscript, the teachings on christian life and conduct flow from the eschatological instruction that precedes it.

The *peroratio* continues ("finally") with a prayer request "for us" that the gospel message will spread "everywhere," citing the Thessalonian

---

1. Beverly Roberts Gaventa, *First and Second Thessalonians*, Interpretation (Louisville, KY: Westminster John Knox, 1998), 124.
2. Ibid., 125.

3:1Finally, brothers and sisters, pray for us, so that the word of the Lord may spread rapidly and be glorified everywhere, just as it is among you, 2and that we may be rescued from wicked and evil people; for not all have faith. 3But the Lord is faithful; he will strengthen you and guard you from the evil one. 4And we have confidence in the Lord concerning you, that you are doing and will go on doing the things that we command. 5May the Lord direct your hearts to the love of God and to the steadfastness of Christ.

6Now we command you, beloved, in the name of our Lord Jesus Christ, to keep away from believers who are living in idleness and not according to the tradition that they received from us. 7For you yourselves know how you ought to imitate us; we were not idle when we were with you, 8and we did not eat anyone's bread without paying for it; but with toil and labor we worked night and day, so that we might not burden any of you. 9This was not because we do not have that right, but in order to give you an example to imitate. 10For

ἐκκλησία ("just as it is among you") as an example of a place where the "word of the Lord" is "glorified" (3:1). The ecclesiology of 2 Thessalonians points to the work of human and divine intertwined. It envisions the assembly of people on whom the grace of God is poured out. Karl Barth, whose ecclesiology focuses solely on God (and not people), describes this outpouring grace of God as explosive: "The Church is constituted by the Word of God," he writes in commenting on the epistle to the Romans. "The Word is nigh unto us. Wherever we cast our eye, the dynamite is prepared and ready to explode."[3] As long as the glimpse of faith is ignited in the hearts of the assembly, the grace of God will spark an event, clearing the way forward despite a gloomy reality due to the delay of the coming Day of the Lord. The faith of the assembly is crucial to the effectiveness of grace, as a match to a fire. Perhaps this is why the authors sound so harshly dualistic, separating those with faith from those without faith for the purpose of emphasizing the importance of faithfulness.

As noted earlier, the most plausible identification of the eschatological restraint mentioned in 2 Thess 2:6 is that the parousia will not occur until the world has been evangelized (see Mark 13:10; Matt 28:8). By emphasizing that the recipients are a prototype of the worldwide mission that

3. Karl Barth, *Epistle to the Romans*, trans. Edwyn C. Hoskyns (London: Oxford University Press, 1933), 380.

even when we were with you, we gave you this command: Anyone unwilling to work should not eat. ¹¹For we hear that some of you are living in idleness, mere busybodies, not doing any work. ¹²Now such persons we command and exhort in the Lord Jesus Christ to do their work quietly and to earn their own living. ¹³Brothers and sisters, do not be weary in doing what is right.

¹⁴Take note of those who do not obey what we say in this letter; have nothing to do with them, so that they may be ashamed. ¹⁵Do not regard them as enemies, but warn them as believers.

¹⁶Now may the Lord of peace himself give you peace at all times in all ways. The Lord be with all of you.

¹⁷I, Paul, write this greeting with my own hand. This is the mark in every letter of mine; it is the way I write. ¹⁸The grace of our Lord Jesus Christ be with all of you.

must be accomplished, the authors both underline the importance of the Thessalonian ἐκκλησία and buttress their argument that the Day of the Lord is still to come (2 Thess 2:2). Furthermore, prayers for the missionaries are needed so that they may be rescued from "wicked and evil people" whose lack of faith is the source of their perversity, "for not all have faith" (3:2). While the authors refer to "evil people" (ἀτόπων καὶ πονηρῶν ἀνθρώπων) as the source of the danger they face, they assure the ἐκκλησία of the faithfulness of "the Lord" to protect them against "the evil one" (τοῦ πονηροῦ) (3:3), probably a reference to Satan, the Adversary (2:9).[4] Implicit in the prayer request is the notion that the authors and recipients are engaged in the cosmic struggle against human and supernatural evil: "The language is dualistic, dividing insiders from outsiders (including dissenting followers of Jesus). The author criticizes those without faith or understanding (3:2, 14), and welcomes God's destruction of opponents (1:8-9). The counterpart to denunciation is the insistence that God protects believers."[5] The authors' expression of confidence in the ἐκκλησία's ongoing adherence to their gospel, "that you are doing and will go on doing the things that we commanded" (3:4; see 1:11-12), contains the veiled warning that to disregard the missionaries' exhortations (ἃ παραγγέλλομεν) is to choose to be aligned with the

4. See also Matt 13:19; 6:13; 1 John 2:13-14; 5:18; Eph 6:16.
5. Adam Gregerman, "2 Thessalonians," in *The Jewish Annotated New Testament: New Revised Standard Version*, ed. Amy-Jill Levine and Marc Zvi Brettler (Oxford: Oxford University Press, 2011), 378.

powers of evil. The prayer ends with the hope that "the Lord" will direct the hearts of the recipients "to the love of God and to the steadfastness of Christ" (3:5).

The reference to the "hearts" of believers is, as Gregerman notes, Jewish language denoting spiritual intentionality (Ps 10:17; 1 Chr 29:18).[6] From a contemporary Christian theological perspective, Shannon Craigo-Snell speaks of the "hearts of believers" as performing "passional knowing." In imagining church as performance she speaks of "performative epistemology," a knowledge that is intellectual, emotional, volitional, and bodily. This kind of knowledge is embodied as communities learn multiple patterns with the whole body, mind, and heart that are particular to Christianity.[7] In order for real learning to occur one must be moved; one should be able to express anger in the face of violence and injustice as much as one should be able to show compassion in the face of danger. Here, learning is not so much about acquiring or transmitting information as about living it out. The work of the "hearts" of believers is thus both spiritual (grounded in physical emotions) and intentional (cultivated by discipline through habitual practices).

Throughout this section the title Kyrios usually refers not, as is usual in this letter, to Jesus but to God. The authors portray Jesus, the Messiah, as an imposing and "lordly" (kyriarchal) figure, but, like the majority of NT writings, the epistle is theocentric: "what is desired is that believers concentrate on God's love for them."[8] Overall, the *peroratio* in 2 Thess 2:13–3:5 is dense with kyriarchal language; the title κύριος appears six times in ten verses, underlining the divine source of the missionaries' authoritative teaching, a rhetorical feature that prepares the audience for the topic of the next main section of the letter, the moral exhortation in 3:6-15—framed as a "command" (παραγγέλλομεν) in the name of Kyrios Jesus Christ (3:6).

The *exhortatio* that makes up the bulk of 2 Thessalonians 3 warns not against outside forces, supernatural and human, that influence believers to deviate from the "traditions received from us" but against threats within the community presented by "believers who are living in idleness and not according to the tradition" modeled by the missionaries (3:6). The word translated as "idle/idleness" throughout the passage (3:6, 7, 11) is ἀτάκτως,

---

6. See ibid., 637.

7. Shannon Craigo-Snell, *The Empty Church: Theatre, Theology and Bodily Hope* (Oxford: Oxford University Press, 2014), 63.

8. Gaventa, *First and Second Thessalonians*, 127.

which has connotations of being "undisciplined" and "disorderly" and is specifically related to the necessity of working to pay one's own way within the community; the audience is reminded of the "toil and labor" the missionaries performed "night and day," not only in the service of the gospel but so that they would be able to "pay for our own bread" and "so that we might not be a burden to any of you" (3:7-8).[9] In Greco-Roman terms, the reference to "how you ought to imitate us" (3:6) reflects the value of mimetic leadership, in which teachers modeled behavior their pupils were expected to emulate;[10] the authors remind the ἐκκλησία that, while they themselves had had the right to demand support from the community while they were with them, they had worked to support themselves "in order to give you an example to imitate" (3:9).

Mimetic Leadership in Pedagogy

Canadian religious educator Greer Anne Wenh-In Ng discusses the role of "modeling" in teaching as she examines the pedagogy of Konzi, the Chinese scholar and teacher known in the west as Confucius. She demonstrates how, for Confucianism, "imitating" is pivotal in learning and teaching. The goal of human life, according to Confucius, is self-cultivation and sagehood, cornerstones of harmony and peace in a society.

The well-being of society cannot be established without the cultivation of moral, responsible personhood. This cultivation occurs in the socialization of young children imitating parents and elders who guide them "in the rituals of daily living." The primary pedagogy of Confucius was teaching "by example and by questioning. He taught in community for service to the community," Ng notes.[11]

HyeRan Kim-Cragg

9. See the woman of valor of Prov 31: "She looks well to the ways of her household, and does not eat her bread in idleness" (31:27).

10. See, e.g., John Chrysostom, *Homilies on First Thessalonians* 5: "A teacher demonstrates great confidence if he uses his own good actions to reprove his disciples. And so Paul writes, 'For you yourselves know how you ought to imitate us.' And he ought to be a teacher more of life than of the word." Quoted in Peter Gorday, ed., *Ancient Christian Commentary on Scripture, New Testament IX: Colossians, 1–2 Thessalonians, 1–2 Timothy, Titus, Philemon* (Downers Grove, IL: InterVarsity, 2000), 121.

11. Greer Anne Wenh-In Ng, "From Confucian Master Teacher to Freirian Mutual Learner: Challenges in Pedagogical Practice and Religious Education," *RelEd* 95 (2000): 308–19, at 312.

In feminist terms, the missionaries' example of carrying a double workload of paid and unpaid work (the latter within the "domestic" setting of the house-church) is reminiscent of the double burden of work within and outside of the home borne by many women throughout history.[12] However, unlike the missionaries, women, like slaves, have not had the "right" to demand pay for their domestic and reproductive work apart from the room, board, and financial "allowances" offered at their husbands'/masters' discretion.

Women's Work according to John Chrysostom

In his homily on 2 Thess 3:3-5, Chrysostom reminds the upper-class men in his audience—in very androcentric terms—of the many kinds of work their wives contribute to their households: "For see how great a service the wife contributes. She keeps the house, and takes care of all things in the house, she presides over her handmaids, she clothes them with her own hands, she causes you to be called the father of children, she delivers you from brothels, she aids you to live chastely, she puts a stop to the strong desire of nature" (*Homily* 5).[13] The men's duty, according to Chrysostom, is to educate their wives, so that their children will gain the benefit of their example: "And do thou also benefit her. How? In spiritual things stretch forth your hand. Whatever useful things you have heard, these, like the swallows, bearing off in your mouth, carry away and place them in the mouth of the mother and the young ones."

Mary Ann Beavis

The question of the identity of the "idlers" and the nature of their unruliness has been answered several ways. The dominant interpretation has been that they were simply members of the community who, perhaps in the light of their conviction that the end times had arrived, felt that working to support themselves was unnecessary: "for we hear that some of you are living in idleness, mere busybodies, not doing any work" (2 Thess 3:11). As E. Elizabeth Johnson observes: "Although there is no

12. On women's work in antiquity see, e.g., the essays in Mary Ann Beavis, ed., *The Lost Coin: Parables of Women, Work and Wisdom* (Sheffield: Sheffield Academic Press, 2002).

13. *Nicene and Post-Nicene Fathers*, 1st ser., vol. 13, ed. Philip Schaff, trans. John A. Broadus (Buffalo, NY: Christian Literature Publishing Co., 1889). Revised and edited for New Advent by Kevin Knight, http://www.newadvent.org/fathers/23055.htm.

evidence of this in 2 Thessalonians, it is conceivable that the exhortation that members 'do their own work quietly and . . . earn their own living' (3:12) is an attempt to hold back revolutionary social forces within the church that were unleashed by apocalyptic speculation, in which case women and slaves—for whom those changes were often greatest—might have felt the impact more keenly than freemen."[14]

Another possibility is that the idle/disorderly were people who had attached themselves to the ἐκκλησία because, like the charlatan Peregrinus satirized by Lucian of Samosata (early second century CE), they thought they could profit from the generosity and gullibility of believers in the disreputable creed of their founder, a crucified man (Lucian, *Death of Peregrinus* 11–13). The *Didachē*, an early christian book of church order, stipulates that visiting believers should be welcomed by the community but should only be allowed to stay two or three days at the expense of the church; if "he wants to settle in with you, and he is a craftsman, let him work and eat . . . no Christian should live with you in idleness. If he is unwilling to do what that calls for, he is using Christ to make a living. Be on your guard against people like this" (12.1-5).[15] A third explanation that has been offered by several recent studies is that the "disorderly" were members of the community who continued prior relationships with wealthy, unbelieving patrons instead of giving up the income and social status the patron-client relationship could provide.[16]

A final proposal that has received little attention but that deserves consideration in a feminist commentary is that the "idlers" were members of the community who had taken on leadership or teaching roles and were claiming the right to be supported by the ἐκκλησία—a prerogative, the missionaries admit, that they themselves had the "authority" (ἐξουσίαν) to expect, but that they had deliberately eschewed (3:8), perhaps following the example of self-supporting rabbis.[17] Although these

---

14. E. Elizabeth Johnson, "2 Thessalonians," in *The Women's Bible Commentary*, ed. Carol A. Newsom and Sharon H. Ringe (Louisville, KY: Westminster John Knox, 1992), 352.

15. Gorday, ed., *Ancient Christian Commentary*, 122.

16. E.g., Sheila E. McGinn and Megan Wilson-Reitz, "2 Thessalonians vs. the *Ataktoi*: A Pauline Critique of White-Collar Welfare," in *By Bread Alone: The Bible Through the Eyes of the Hungry*, ed. Sheila E. McGinn, Lai Ling Ngan, and Ahida Pilarski (Minneapolis: Fortress Press, 2014); Ben Witherington III, *1 and 2 Thessalonians* (Grand Rapids, MI: Eerdmans, 2006), 247–50.

17. See Mary Ann Beavis, "2 Thessalonians," in *Searching the Scriptures*, vol. 2: *A Feminist Commentary*, ed. Elisabeth Schüssler Fiorenza (New York: Crossroad, 1994); and Mary Ann Beavis, "2 Thessalonians," in *Women's Bible Commentary*, ed.

"idle" persons are often called ἄτακτοι ("disorderly/idle persons") by commentators, the masculine plural form does not actually occur in the passage; the words used are the adverb ἀτάκτως and the verbal ἠτακτήσαμεν ("living in idleness").[18] Elsewhere in the Pauline letters the question of material support for believers arises only with reference to compensation for missionaries and leaders. In 1 Thess 2:9 the authors recall that when they were with the ἐκκλησία they had worked "night and day" so as not to burden the brothers and sisters financially while they were preaching to them. Similarly, in 2 Cor 11:7-11, Paul reminds the audience that he had ministered to them "free of charge" (δωρεάν) so as not to impose on them and that he would do so again on his next visit: "I will not be a burden, because I do not want what is yours but you; for children do not lay up for their parents, but parents for their children" (2 Cor 12:14-15). He admits, however, that he had taken support from other communities, including "friends from Macedonia," so that he would not have to rely on the Corinthian ἐκκλησία for his upkeep (11:8-9) as had, he aggrievedly implies, the "super-apostles," whose authoritative claims and miraculous deeds they preferred to Paul's. He contrasts himself with them: "How have you been worse off than the other churches, except that I myself did not burden you? Forgive me this wrong!" (12:11-13). Paul also insists on his apostolic right to demand payment for his services, although he has always preached to the Corinthians without compensation (2 Cor 9:3-18).

First Timothy specifically (and at length) considers, with reference to the women's ministry of the widows (χήρας), which functionaries within the ἐκκλησία should receive support from the community (5:3-16). The widows were an early christian order for which there is substantial evi-

---

Carol A. Newsom, Sharon H. Ringe, and Jacqueline E. Lapsley, 3rd ed. (Louisville, KY: Westminster John Knox, 2012); and Mary Ann Beavis, "If Anyone Will Not Work," in *A Feminist Companion to the Deutero-Pauline Epistles*, ed. Amy-Jill Levine (London and New York: T & T Clark, 2003). Rabbis said to have supported themselves by practicing various trades are the elder Hillel (woodcutter), Shammai (builder), Joshua (blacksmith), Jose (tanner); for references see Mary Ann Beavis, *Mark*, Paideia Commentaries on the New Testament (Grand Rapids, MI: Baker Academic, 2011), 99. According to Acts 18:1-3, Paul practiced his trade of tentmaking along with Priscilla and Aquila while he was in Corinth, although his letters do not specify his profession.

18. The masculine plural could, in fact, like the masculine plural *adelphoi*, include women.

dence.[19] Acts 9:36-43 describes the consternation that ensues after the death of the "woman disciple" (μαθήτρια) Tabitha of Joppa (also called Dorcas), presumably a widow herself, who "was devoted to good works and acts of charity." A community of widows, members of a house-church, had been benefiting from her skills at clothing manufacture (9:39b), as Peter discovered when he arrived, having been summoned by "the disciples" from nearby Lydda. The widows' grief at the loss of their sister— and possibly the loss of material support occasioned by her death—causes such alarm that Peter raises her from the dead (9:40). A hermeneutically suspicious mind might surmise that part of the reason for the extreme reaction to Tabitha's death is the fear that the widows will become a financial burden to the male disciples without her support.

Within a larger discussion of the responsibilities and prerogatives of church leaders,[20] the Deutero-Pauline 1 Tim 5:3-16 also portrays the status of widows as a problem within the community and relegates their maintenance to family members (especially female relatives), rather than recommending that they receive support in payment for their ministry of continuous prayer "night and day" (5:5). The only women who are "true widows" worthy of receiving compensation must be over the age of sixty, only married once, and "she must be well attested for her good works, as one who has brought up children, shown hospitality, washed the saints' feet, helped the afflicted, and devoted herself to doing good in every way" (5:10). Drawing on misogynistic stereotypes of widows as lustful and prone to gossip,[21] 1 Timothy warns the Pastor, as Timothy is addressed in the letter, against recognizing or supporting younger widows, "for when their sensual desires alienate them from Christ, they want to marry. . . . Besides that, they learn to be idle, gadding about from house to house, and they are not merely idle, but also gossips and busybodies" (5:11, 13). As Linda Maloney notes, "They were evidently engaged in the ministry of teaching, though the material they were conveying was not at all what the author would have preferred. They must

19. See, e.g., Bonnie Bowman Thurston, *The Widows: A Women's Ministry in the Early Church* (Minneapolis: Augsburg Fortress, 1989).

20. "Bishops" (3:1-7), "deacons/deaconesses" (3:8-12), and "elders" (5:17-22).

21. For the lustful widow stereotype, see Petronius, *Satyricon* 110.6–113.3, where a disconsolate and virtuous young widow is easily persuaded by a soldier to have sex with him in her husband's own tomb and allows her husband's corpse to be substituted for the missing body of a crucified criminal in order to save her lover from prosecution. On the motif of women, especially elder women, as prone to gossip and loose behavior, see 1 Tim 4:7; 2 Tim 3:6; Titus 2:3; and John Chrysostom, *Homilies on 2 Thessalonians* 1, 2.

have received a regular stipend for their ministerial work (see 1 Tim 5:3 with 1 Tim 5:17)."[22] First Timothy's stipulations as to the qualifications of "official" widows "restrict the widow's order by disqualifying as many women as possible."[23] The contrast between the stinginess toward widows and the generosity and leniency extended to male elders (πρεσβύτεροι) is jarring: elders who "rule well" deserve "double honor"; those who "labor in preaching and teaching" are worthy of payment; two witnesses must attest to any accusation made against an elder (5:17-19).

The language used to exclude the younger widows from the ranks of "true widows" is strikingly similar to that used with reference to the "unruly" members of the Thessalonian ἐκκλησία: they are "idle" (ἀργαὶ); "busybodies" (περιεργαζόμενοι in 2 Thess 3:11; περίεργοι in 1 Tim 5:13), and "gadabouts" (περιπατοῦντος in 2 Thess 3:6; περιερχόμεναι in 1 Tim 5:13). Possibly, like the widows at issue in 1 Timothy, the "unruly" persons criticized by the authors were claiming support not simply because they were indolent but because they were engaging in work in the service of the community, perhaps spreading radical eschatological teachings—as Chrysostom put it, "childish fables and old women's fooleries"[24]—that were opposed by the missionaries.[25] Thus the authors stress that *they* had worked for their own sustenance while ministering to the Thessalonians, unlike the "busybodies, not doing any work" (2 Thess 3:11) who expected to be maintained at the community's expense (3:9). It is impossible to know whether the "idle" members of the Thessalonian ἐκκλησία included women, or whether the authors simply wished to belittle them by accusing them of womanish behavior. In this context the exhortation to the "brothers and sisters" not to weary of doing good deeds (3:13) "may be an admonition to the idle/disorderly among them to bear a double workload of Christian service *and* paid work . . . or, more likely, simply to abandon their disapproved ministerial role"[26]—in other words, "to do their work quietly and to earn their own living" (3:12).

22. Linda Maloney, "The Pastoral Epistles," in Schüssler Fiorenza, *Searching the Scriptures*, 2:361–80, at 373.

23. Ibid., 372.

24. *Homilies on 2 Thessalonians* 1.

25. See also Titus 1:5-12, where a discussion of the qualifications for elders is followed by a warning against "many rebellious people (ἀνυπότακτοι; *anypotaktoi*), idle talkers and deceivers, especially those of the circumcision; they must be silenced, since they are upsetting whole families by teaching for sordid gain what is not right to teach" (1:10-11). These are Jewish-Christian teachers demanding payment for teaching something unacceptable to the Deutero-Pauline authors.

26. Beavis, "If Anyone Will Not Work," 35.

Viewed somewhat more positively, the teaching of moral living and ethical earning embedded in 2 Thessalonians has influenced Protestantism, especially the so-called Calvinist work ethic and worldview. According to Charles Taylor, "Calvin held that we have to control the vices of the whole society, lest the vicious infect the others."[27] His word "vices" would probably include the faults of the "idle" and "busybodies." It is not solely the work of humans to control the vices of society, according to Calvin, but that work depends on the power of God also. As the authors of 2 Thessalonians claim with the admonition to "never tire of doing what is right" (3:13), the inner motive is important, as disciplined personal life and faith can lead to a well-ordered society. Taylor picks up on this issue again when he talks about ordered life, the opposite of "unruly" or "idle" life as "a site for the highest forms of Christian life."[28] This view of life, according to Taylor, was informed by Protestant Puritanism. Arguing against the notion held by some Catholics that there are some higher vocations, Taylor sides with Max Weber, who contends that ordinary life can be the sanctified one. Here he asserts that the positive affirmation of the ordinary life has "a tremendous formative effect on our civilization" as it puts "tremendous importance on family life, or 'relationship.'" He further states that the focus on the ordinary life of the ordinary people "underlines the fundamental importance of equality in our social and political lives."[29]

The centerpiece of the argument in 2 Thess 3:6-15 is the reminder of the missionaries' command that "if any would not work, neither should he eat" (3:10, KJV). As Abraham Malherbe notes, this was "a sentiment that was widespread in Jewish and Greek sources"[30] and very much at home in the biblical Wisdom tradition.[31] This teaching has become proverbial as an expression of a Christian work ethic—"a Golden Rule of work . . . 'a bit of good old workshop mentality.'"[32] The adage was a favorite sermon

27. Charles Taylor, *A Secular Age* (Cambridge, MA: Harvard University Press, 2007), 82.

28. Ibid., 179.

29. Ibid.

30. Abraham J. Malherbe, *The Letters to the Thessalonians: A New Translation with Introduction and Commentary* (New York: Doubleday, 2000), 452.

31. Earl J. Richard, *First and Second Thessalonians*, SP 11 (Collegeville, MN: Liturgical Press, 2007), 381. Also see, e.g., Prov 6:6-9; 12:27; 18:9; 21:25; Sir 7:15; Gen 3:19; see also Gen. Rab. 2:2: "If I do not work, I do not eat."

32. Malherbe, *Letters*, 452, citing Ernst von Dobschütz, *Die Thessalonicherbriefe*, 7th ed. (Göttingen: Vandenhoeck & Ruprecht, 1909), 314; Adolf Deissmann, *Light from the Ancient East: The New Testament Illustrated by Recently Discovered Texts of the Graeco-Roman World* (Grand Rapids, MI: Baker, 1965), 314.

topic in the early church[33] and has received endorsement from such disparate quarters as *laissez-faire* capitalism and Marxism: "Vladimir Lenin claimed the injunction as an essential socialist principle—so that no one would live off the labor of others. The Soviet Constitutions of 1918 and 1936 both employ the phrase."[34] Most famously, the sociologist Max Weber credited the Protestant work ethic epitomized by 2 Thess 3:10 as necessary to the rise of American capitalism.[35] The principle that one is not entitled to eat if one does not work, then, is promoted in capitalism, Marxism, and Protestantism, but it is interpreted in different, yet interlocking ways. For example, the Soviet Union under the Lenin regime expanded its socialist economy by using the slogan "No food for those who do not work."

The concept that the right to eat is only for those who work is complicated by the intersectionality of race and gender. In the nineteenth century, the United States, for example, was busy recruiting Asian immigrants to bring cheap labor into the still-developing capitalist economy. As social critic Lisa Lowe observes:

> Throughout the period from 1850 to World War II . . . Chinese, Japanese, and Filipino laborers were fundamental to the building of the railroads, the agricultural economy, and the textile and service industries. . . . Capital in the 1880s utilized racialized divisions among laborers to maximize its profits. . . . Capital could increase profit and benefit from the presence of a racialized and tractable labor force up until the point at which the Chinese labor force grew large enough that it threatened capital accumulation by whites. . . . The state's attempts to "resolve" the economic contradictions of capital and the political contradictions of the nation-state resulted in the successive exclusions of the Chinese in 1882, Asian Indians in 1917, Japanese in 1924, and Filipinos in 1934 and the barring of all these immigrant groups from citizenship and ownership of property.[36]

The simple message was: "You can work here but you do not belong here." One may paraphrase 2 Thess 3:8 positively as a critique of this kind of economic exploitation system: those in power in the making of the nation ate the food that was produced by foreign workers without properly paying for it. Here economic class is mediated and substantiated by race and national origin.

---

33. See, e.g., Gorday, *Ancient Christian Commentary*, 122–24.
34. McGinn and Wilson-Reitz, "2 Thessalonians," 186.
35. Ibid.
36. Lisa Lowe, *Immigrant Acts: On Asian American Cultural Politics* (Durham, NC: Duke University Press, 2007), 12–13.

Gender is also clearly a dynamic that is mixed with race in the injustices of the capitalist economy. In her book *Also a Mother*, Bonnie Miller-McLemore lifts up the unrecognized labor that women and nonwhite people provide so that Western societies run smoothly. Their labor is like oil for the societal machine. "As unpaid reproductive labor is redistributed and given a minimal wage," she writes, "it simply lands on the backs of poorer women and women of color."[37] Hilda Scott, who has been writing about interlocking issues around socialism, women, and feminism, especially in European contexts, agrees with Miller-McLemore when she argues that woman's unpaid work has been masked by the rhetoric of "labors of love." That labor, she points out, underpins the world's economy even as it is peripheral to that economy as men define it, and therefore it is counted as of little value. "It is this that makes women a category of persons who are economically invisible," she says, "whose work is non-work."[38] If we switch the geographical sphere from Europe to the Americas (especially South and Central America), the reality is not much different. In the neoliberal phenomenon of globalization, "people have become disposable, a situation endured by women, minor ethnics, and immigrants in general," Maricel Mena López observes. Citing the words of Mareia de Los Angeles Lopez Plaza, she continues, "To speak about the feminization of poverty is to speak about one of the most serious consequences of economic globalization."[39] Here globalization is sustained in the hierarchical structure of society where women and children in the global south remain at the bottom along with the natural world, carrying the burden of wealth and profit for those few elites in the global north.

37. Bonnie J. Miller-McLemore, *Also a Mother: Work and Family as Theological Dilemma* (Nashville, TN: Abingdon, 1994), 34.

38. Hilda Scott, *Working Your Way to the Bottom: The Feminization of Poverty* (London: Pandora, 1984), x.

39. Maricel Mena López, "Globalization and Gender Inequality: A Contribution from a Latino Afro-Feminist Perspective," in *The Oxford Handbook of Feminist Theology*, ed. Mary McClintock Fulkerson and Sheila Briggs (Oxford: Oxford University Press, 2012), 158, 163. She is quoting María de Los Angeles Lopez Plaza, "Efectos de las políticas de ajuste estructural en la situación de las mujeres magrebíes," in Virginia Maquieira D'Angelo and Maria Jesús Vara, eds., *Género, clase y etnia en los nuevos procesos de globalización: XI Jornadas de investigacieon interdisciplinaria sobre la mujer* (Madrid: Instituto Universitario de Estudios de la Mujer: Ediciones de la Universidad Autónoma de Madrid, 1997).

Bahala Na *and* Binah

Approximately sixteen miles from Tacloban City is the coastal town of Basey, located in the province of Samar. In that town a small group of women who survived the devastation of typhoon Haiyan gather together in a cave to weave *tikog* (a reed plant) into mats for export. The damp, cool temperature of the cave helps keep the reeds fresh. By weaving the reed plant they are literally weaving back their lives in the hope of eventually attaining *ginhawa*. They are Basey's women weavers. Working with their hands is their livelihood. Reuters reports: "Amongst the despair and devastation wrought by Haiyan . . . hundreds of women weavers have emerged as the main breadwinners in their families. . . . Samar's women weavers stand out as being among the most resilient and industrious workers."[40] One who is familiar with the stories in the Torah cannot help but associate the word *tikog* (reed plant) with the biblical *suph* (סוף) or "reeds" found in a narrative in which the female characters "conspire"[41] to save their boys' lives. This occurs in a crisis situation when the abusive Pharaoh commands the murder of male Hebrew infants, further aggravating the suffering he has already inflicted on the Hebrew people. To recall that particular episode, Jochebed hides her infant son Moshe for three months to protect him from being killed.

> When she could hide him no longer she got a papyrus basket for him, and plastered it with bitumen and pitch; she put the child in it and placed it among the *reeds* on the bank of the river. His sister stood at a distance, to see what would happen to him. The daughter of Pharaoh came down to bathe at the river, while her attendants walked beside the river. She saw the basket among the *reeds* and sent her maid to bring it. (Exod 2:3-5)

This pericope is preceded by the chapter that pays homage to Shiphrah and Puah, the Hebrew midwives who fearlessly disobeyed the orders of the Pharaoh by saving the lives of the Hebrew baby boys. Their fearlessness emanates from יהוה יראת, "the fear of the Lord" (Exod 1:17-21). The midwives' response is comparable to the Filipino attitude *bahala na*, that "fighting spirit" Nila Bermisa describes as

---

40. Roli Ng and Rosemarie Francisco, "After Typhoon, Philippine Women Weave Their Magic," *Reuters*, November 6, 2014, http://www.reuters.com/article/2014/11/06/philippines-typhoon-idUSL4N0SM2FJ20141106.

41. Tikva Frymer-Kensky calls it "a conspiracy of women" in *Reading the Women of the Bible: A New Interpretation of Their Stories* (New York: Schocken Books, 2002), 27.

"Filipino resiliency at its best," deeply rooted in a strong faith in God (*Bathala*).[42] It is the same attitude displayed by Jochebed and Miriam in Exod 2. Biblical women, like the women weavers of Basey and the survivors of sexual abuse, seem to exhibit a special kind of wisdom that drives them to do what needs to be done amid "afflictions" (θλίψεσιν) and "suffering" (πάσχετε)—most especially when these directly affect family and community. Remarkably, the Hebrew term for this sounds like a truncated version of *bahala na*. The word is *binah* (בינה). In kabbalah it is one of The Ten Sefirot (emanations) and is a feminine *sefirah* (ספירה) that complements the masculine *ḥokhmah* (חכמה). Gershom Scholem describes בינה as "the intelligence of God" or "the divine intelligence."[43] Judith Romney Wegner clarifies: "The sages' perceptions of intrinsic differences between men and women include the conviction that women's mental grasp of the world rests not on

knowledge acquired through formal study and intellectual ratiocination (*ḥokhmah*), but rather on an intuitive understanding or common sense (*binah*), closer to instinct than to reason."[44]

In addition, בינה may be defined as "wisdom of the heart" (חכמת לב) as Lazer Gurkow[45] points out, referring to Exod 35:25-26:

> Every *wise-hearted* woman spun with her hands; and they brought the spun yarn of turquoise, purple, and scarlet wool, and the linen. All the women *whose hearts inspired them with wisdom* spun the goat hair.[46]

The NRSV translates בינה as "insight" and, as eloquently stated in Proverbs, it is the first step to understanding יראת יהוה, "the fear of the Lord":

> If you indeed cry out for
> *insight* (בינה)
> and raise your voice for
> *understanding* (תבונה);
> if you seek it like silver,

42. Nila Bermisa, *She May Dance Again: Rising from the Pain of Violence Against Women in the Philippine Church* (Philippines: WGC-AMRSP, 2011), 9, 103–4.

43. Gershom Scholem, *Major Trends in Jewish Mysticism* (New York: Schocken Books, 1995), 213, 220.

44. Judith Romney Wegner, "The Image and Status of Women in Classical Rabbinic Judaism," in *Jewish Women in Historical Perspective*, 2nd ed., ed. Judith R. Baskin (Detroit, MI: Wayne State University Press, 1998), 73–100, at 83.

45. Lazer Gurkow, "Wisdom of the Heart: The Jewish Mother," Chabad.org, http:// www.chabad.org/theJewishWoman/article_cdo/aid/478232/jewish/Wisdom-of -the-Heart.htm.

46. Rabbi Nosson Scherman, *The Stone Edition Tanach: Hebrew and English Edition* (Brooklyn, NY: Mesorah, 2001).

and search for it as for
hidden treasures—
then you will understand
the fear of the Lord (יראת יהוה)

and find *the knowledge of*
God (דעת אלהים). (Prov 2:3-5)

Pia Sison

As Sheila McGinn and Megan T. Wilson-Reitz have noted, 2 Thess 3:10 has been used in contemporary US political debates in the service of an agenda of cuts to social services and other supports to persons marginalized in the globalized market economy, on the assumption that the text provides a simple solution to a straightforward problem: "The problem, they claim, is that certain lazy Thessalonians are exhibiting 'escapist, antisocial behavior' by refusing to work, leading to their poverty and subsequent need to depend upon generous, wealthy members of the community for their sustenance."[47]

This kind of idea was transposed simplistically to the American conservative fundamentalist context by the Reverend Jerry Falwell (d. 2007), a millionaire whose fortune was derived from contributions solicited through televangelism from impressionable donors both rich and poor. Falwell is typical when he describes the text as a "fundamental Judeo-Christian principle at the foundation of American Democracy" in the service of ideologically legitimating cuts in federal welfare services.[48] McGinn and Wilson-Reitz argue that, far from being an indictment of poor and indolent members of the Thessalonian ἐκκλησία intent on sponging off their wealthier brothers and sisters, the "unruly" persons rebuked by Paul, Silvanus, and Timothy were in fact "upwardly mobile social climbers" who were unwilling to cut their ties with wealthy patrons to engage in the indignity of manual labor; thus the *ataktoi* are reproached "for their *obedience* to the cultural norms of their city and the Empire, rather than their *disobedience* to those cultural norms."[49] That is, the "unruly/idle" Thessalonians were reluctant to accept downward economic and social mobility, not opportunists attempting to take advantage of the generosity of their ecclesial community.

---

47. McGinn and Wilson-Reitz, "2 Thessalonians," 187, citing Robert K. Jewett, "1 and 2 Thessalonians," in *Eerdmans Commentary on the Bible*, ed. James D. G. Dunn and John William Rogerson (Grand Rapids, MI: Eerdmans, 2003), 1413–27, at 1417.

48. McGinn and Wilson-Reitz, "2 Thessalonians," 186–87, citing Neil Elliott, *Liberating Paul: The Justice of God and the Politics of the Apostle* (Maryknoll, NY: Orbis Books, 1994), 13.

49. McGinn and Wilson-Reitz, "2 Thessalonians," 188.

On the alternative hypothesis argued above that the *exhortatio* relates not to persons who do not want to work but very specifically to members of the ἐκκλησία who regarded their work of preaching, teaching, and service within the community as worthy of recompense, the perspective of the "unruly" becomes more sympathetic. Rather than being unwilling to work, they were merely claiming their due wages for their ministerial services. Nor did they wish to maintain the status and advantages of established relationships with wealthy, non-christian patrons; rather, they expected to be paid by the ἐκκλησία for services rendered—to pay for their bread through their labor on behalf of the community. The stingy and dismissive attitude of the Deutero-Pauline authors toward unrecognized (by them) religious workers is analogous (although not identical) to a situation replicated in many contemporary churches, where volunteer and low-paid work, much of it done by both ordained and non-ordained women working long hours for "part-time wages," is a staple of the church economy, at variance with the ideals of equality and social justice preached from the pulpit.

Further social and theological reflections on the issue of idleness arise from a reading of 2 Thess 3:6-12. While being idle might benignly suggest lack of motion and busyness, the meaning of v. 11 suggests a negative

On Payment for Religious Work

The Jewish and Christian Scriptures offer some precedent for the attitude that religious work deserves compensation and community support, with particular regard to approved, male teachers (scribes, elders, and missionaries).

The wisdom of the scribe depends on the opportunity of leisure; only the one who has little business can become wise. How can one become wise who handles the plow, and who glories in the shaft of a goad, who drives oxen and is occupied with their work, and whose talk is about bulls? He sets his heart on plowing furrows, and he is careful about fodder for the heifers. (Sir 38:24-26)

Let the elders who rule well be considered worthy of double honor/compensation, especially those who labor in preaching and teaching; for the scripture says, "You shall not muzzle an ox while it is treading out the grain," and, "the laborer deserves to be paid." (1 Tim 5:17-18; see also Deut 25:4; Matt 10:10)

Carry no purse, no bag, no sandals; and greet no one on the road. Whatever house you enter, first say, "Peace to this house!" And if anyone is there who shares in peace, your peace will rest on that person; but if not, it will return to you. Remain in the same house, eating and drinking whatever they provide, for the laborer deserves to be paid. Do not move about from house to house. (Luke 10:4-7)

Cure the sick, raise the dead, cleanse the lepers, cast out demons. You received without payment; give without payment. Take no gold, or silver, or copper in your belts, no bag for your journey, or two tunics, or sandals, or a staff; for laborers deserve their food. Whatever town or village you enter, find out who in it is worthy, and stay there until you leave. (Matt 10:8-11)

Mary Ann Beavis

judgment along the lines of the following "commonsense" definition of "idle": "habitually doing nothing or avoiding work, lazy or of no real worth, importance, or significance."[50] Then as now, those who are labeled "idlers" are often victims of the socially constructed category of otherness. The idle, for example, are often identified with those living in poverty, pushed to the edge of society. Rather than an innate disposition to laziness, however, we know that certain circumstances (illness, abuse, and violence) can often force people into a situation of idleness, unable to support themselves or their families.

There is a perplexing story in the gospels that touches on the connection between poverty, idleness, and women's work. When an unnamed woman broke the costly alabaster jar and anointed Jesus with perfume, he reminded his followers that "you will always have the poor with you, and you show kindness to them whenever you wish; but you will not always have me" (Mark 14:7-8). Linda Maloney points out that this luxurious oil was worth about one year's wages for a male laborer and two years' for a female laborer.[51] Was this act of wasting valuable labor an idle, senseless act? Why did Jesus value and validate it? "Mark's account focuses on the value of the woman's act," as Beavis argues.[52] Unlike most

50. Dictionary.com, s.v. "idle," dictionary.reference.com/browse/idle.

51. Linda Maloney, " 'Swept Under the Rug': Feminist Homiletical Reflections on the Parable of the Lost Coin (Luke 15:8-9)," in *The Lost Coin: Parables of Women, Work and Wisdom*, ed. Mary Ann Beavis (Sheffield: Sheffield Academic Press, 2002), 34–38, at 35. According to her, one drachma (denarius) was about one day's wage for a male person and two days' wages for a female person.

52. Beavis, *Mark*, 209.

work done by women that is treated as nonwork, having no value, this woman's work is viewed as thought-provoking and prophetic, thus "of worth, important, and significant."

A recent Canadian social movement called "Idle No More" further advances reflection about idleness and work. This movement began with four courageous women from Saskatoon, Jessica Gordon, Sylvia Mc-Adam, Nina Wilson, and Sheelah McLean, who raised concern over the privatization of the waterways that may have devastating implications for indigenous communities.[53] Their leadership has inspired thousands of people to action, committing themselves to ongoing resistance against neocolonialism across the globe.[54] It has spread the work in solidarity with many different groups against current and pending governmental policies that impact collective rights, social safety nets, and environmental protection. According to their website,

> Idle No More seeks to assert Indigenous inherent rights to sovereignty and reinstitute traditional laws and Nation to Nation Treaties by protecting the lands and waters from corporate destruction. Each day that Indigenous rights are not honored or fulfilled, inequality between Indigenous peoples and the settler society grows. This website seeks to provide ongoing information on the historical and contemporary context of colonialism, and provide an analysis of the interconnections of race, gender, sexuality, class and other identity constructions in ongoing oppression. This website also seeks to make visible what has often been untold—some of the powerful personal stories of those who have been moved by the spirit of Idle No More. Idle No More has provided hope and love at a time when global corporate profits rule. We invite everyone to join in this movement.[55]

This movement led by many, but not limited to, First Nations people occurs against a backdrop of a racist society in which Aboriginal people are often stereotyped as idle, lazy, and averse to work. The movement challenges that notion and stands together with the kind of prophetic work exemplified by the unnamed woman who anointed Jesus in lifting up and valuing what the world is in the process of destroying and throwing away. Perhaps the Thessalonian wo/men engaged in prophetic

---

53. Febna Caven, "Being Idle No More: The Women Behind the Movement," *Cultural Survival*, February 20, 2013, https://www.culturalsurvival.org/publications/cultural-survival-quarterly/being-idle-no-more-women-behind-movement.

54. Idle No More, "Events," http://www.idlenomore.ca/events.

55. Idle No More, "The Story," http://www.idlenomore.ca/story.

work on behalf of the ἐκκλησία expected that their work would be acknowledged as similarly worthy, sacred, and significant.

John Chrysostom on 2 Thessalonians 3:10 and the Poor

Although John Chrysostom is much criticized by feminist interpreters for his condescending attitudes toward women, his renowned sensitivity to the situation of the poor in his churches is reflected in these comments on 2 Thess 3:10:

> I do not say these things haphazardly now, but rather because many are overly intrusive in their investigation of the needy. They examine their lineage, life, habits, and the vigor of the body. They make complaints and demand immense public scrutiny for their health. For this precise reason, many of the poor simulate physical disabilities, so that by dramatizing their misfortunes they may deflect our cruelty and inhumanity. . . . "Therefore, what did Paul ordain by law," they say, "when he said in the Thessalonians, 'If any one does not wish to work, neither let him eat?'" . . . We criticize them for their laziness, something which is worthy of forgiveness for the most part. However, we often do things which are even more grievous than any laziness. . . . Read not only the threat of punishment but also Paul's admonition to forgiveness, for the one who said "If anyone does not wish to work, neither let him eat" added, "And you, brothers, do not lose heart in doing good." (*On Repentance and Almsgiving* 10.6.23-24)[56]

Mary Ann Beavis

The conclusion to the *exhortatio* (2 Thess 3:14-15) is relatively pastoral after the warnings against the "unruly/idle" that are the topic of the section. The members criticized by the authors are not to be expelled from the community, but they should be taken note of and avoided, "so that they may be ashamed" (3:14); they should not be regarded as enemies but warned as believers (3:15). Although, as Malherbe observes, the exact nature of this procedure of "noting" and avoidance is unclear,[57] the implication is that the wayward believers should be publicly identified in the

---

56. Gorday, *Ancient Christian Commentary*, 124–25.
57. Malherbe, *Letters*, 384.

assembly and that members of the ἐκκλησία should be warned not to associate with them until they amend their behavior: "The purpose of the process, 'putting to shame' (see Titus 2:8 for a similar usage), is that of winning back a fellow believer" where "a fundamental change is sought for the wayward individual, the regaining of family honor by employing its opposite: the loss of honor."[58] The authors' use of the Greco-Roman cultural framework of honor and shame, in which the prestige ("honor") of male family members is upheld by men's reputation in society and by women's modest and sexually circumspect behavior in the domestic sphere, is a risky and manipulative strategy: "Shaming in an honor and shame culture could be a very effective behavior modification technique, but it would also arouse deep emotions and usually controversy."[59] Although, as Gaventa suggests, the shaming procedure can be understood sociologically as a strategy of group boundary maintenance[60] and the instruction not to regard other believers as enemies "sounds a particularly poignant note in these times of ecclesiastical wars,"[61] the procedure reflects not only coercive rhetoric but controlling practice within the ἐκκλησία: the "unruly" must be noted, shamed, and avoided.

The Quarreling of Doves

Augustine of Hippo, like several other early christian authors, softens the impact of 2 Thess 3:15 with the engaging metaphor of an argument among doves:

Here it is as if doves are quarrelling together. The apostle said: "If anyone fails to obey our word by this letter, mark that person and do not mix with him."

There's the quarrel. But notice how it is a quarrel of doves, not of wolves. He immediately added, "And do not regard him as an enemy, but rebuke him as a brother." A dove is loving even when it is beating; a wolf hates even when it is being charming. (*Sermons* 6.4-3)[62]

Mary Ann Beavis

58. Ibid. See 1 Cor 5:1-5, 12-13; 2 Cor 2:6-11; Gal 6:1; 1 Tim 1:20; 2 Tim 2:16-18; Titus 3:10; Matt 18:15-17; Heb 6:4-8.
59. Witherington, *1 and 2 Thessalonians*, 254.
60. Gaventa, *Thessalonians*, 130.
61. Ibid., 132.
62. Gorday, *Ancient Christian Commentary*, 126; for other examples, see ibid., 126–27.

The epistolary closing in 2 Thess 3:16-18 is framed by a conciliatory wish for peace "at all times in all ways" from the Kyrios of peace and a final benediction of divine "grace" or "favor" upon the recipients (see also 1 Thess 5:28). The claim of authenticity is sandwiched between the peace wish and the benediction: "I, Paul, write this greeting with my own hand. This is the mark in every letter of mine; it is the way I write" (2 Thess 3:17). This claim is echoed in several other letters of Paul (Phlm 19; Gal 6:11; 1 Cor 16:21), as well as the Deutero-Pauline Col 4:18. This reference reflects the ancient practice of dictating a letter to a scribe (see Rom 16:22), and the change in handwriting would only be an effective guarantee of authenticity if the recipients were familiar with the author's script in the first place. Significantly for the question of the authenticity of the letter, the ending of 1 Thessalonians contains no such reference. If, as many scholars think, 2 Thessalonians is a pious forgery written in order to address issues of unauthorized apocalyptic teaching and its consequences within the ἐκκλησία, it belongs to the category of letters "as though from us" referred to earlier (2:2, 15), whose contents should be read, interpreted, and preached with sympathy, discretion, and care.

Afterword

Finding Hope in 2 Thessalonians

A lthough it is very brief and of questionable authenticity, 2 Thessalonians has been disproportionately influential in Christian history and interpretation, and it has left its mark beyond the boundaries of Christendom. The multifaceted figure of the Antichrist and the many apocalyptic speculations and anxieties associated with it are drawn heavily from the vision of the "lawless one" in 2 Thess 2:3-4. The work ethic expressed in 2 Thess 3:10 has influenced religious, social, and economic movements as diverse as Calvinism, Marxism, and American Fundamentalism. As such, the letter is ripe for feminist critique but seems to offer little in the way of positive material for feminist theological reflection.

However, despite its relentless androcentrism, manipulative rhetoric, and violent apocalypticism, the feminist theological, antiracist, ecological, postcolonial, pastoral, liturgical, linguistic, and multicultural lenses applied to the letter in this commentary have exposed both positive and negative facets of the text. For example, Raphael's work on the divine presence manifested in the care offered by the women of Auschwitz lends a fresh dimension to the theological consideration of suffering. The Korean rendering of the "lawless one" as a "son" and, even more, the *Inclusive Bible*'s interpretation of the figure as "the lost one" call forth intertextual resonances with the parable of the lost son (Luke 15:11-32) and hold out hope for forgiveness and reconciliation. The medieval abbess Hildegard's vision transforms the received tradition of the Antichrist as the demonic "other" into a critique of corruption within the church that lifts up the possibility of reform. The so-called Protestant work ethic has certainly led to the unfair blaming of the poor for their poverty and the unthinking exploitation of the labor of the marginalized to provide "bread" for the rich, but it also recognizes the sanctity of ordinary work and life.

Although this is the first book-length feminist commentary on 2 Thessalonians, at least four chapter-length such commentaries have been published in the past two decades,[1] as well as several essays on topics related to the epistle.[2] We have been fortunate to be in a position to benefit from the insights of these scholars and, in the case of Mary Ann Beavis, to reconsider and reassess her own work in the light of the work of others. We hope that this volume will not only inform future feminist commentaries, but that scholars, preachers, and teachers will find it useful for continued feminist engagement with this difficult text.

1. E. Elizabeth Johnson, "2 Thessalonians," in *The Women's Bible Commentary*, ed. Carol A. Newsom and Sharon H. Ringe (Louisville, KY: Westminster John Knox, 1992); Mary Ann Beavis, "2 Thessalonians," in *Searching the Scriptures*, vol. 2, *A Feminist Commentary*, ed. Elisabeth Schüssler Fiorenza (New York: Crossroad, 1994), 263–73; Mary Ann Beavis, "2 Thessalonians," in *Women's Bible Commentary*, ed. Carol A. Newsom, Sharon H. Ringe, and Jacqueline E. Lapsley, 3rd ed. (Louisville, KY: Westminster John Knox, 2012), 592–94; Marlene Crüsemann, "2 Thessalonians: Hope in God's Last Judgment," in *Feminist Biblical Interpretation: A Compendium of Critical Commentary on the Books of the Bible and Related Literature*, ed. Luise Schottroff and Marie-Theres Wacker (Grand Rapids, MI, and Cambridge: Eerdmans, 2012).

2. Mary Ann Beavis, " 'If Anyone Will Not Work, Let Them Not Eat': 2 Thessalonians 3:10 and the Social Support of Women," in *A Feminist Companion to the Deutero-Pauline Epistles*, ed. Amy-Jill Levine (London and New York: T & T Clark, 2003), 29–36; Sheila E. McGinn and Megan Wilson-Reitz, "2 Thessalonians vs. the *Ataktoi*: A Pauline Critique of White-Collar Welfare," in *By Bread Alone: The Bible Through the Eyes of the Hungry*, ed. Sheila E. McGinn, Lai Ling Ngan, and Ahida Pilarski (Minneapolis: Fortress Press, 2014).

1 Thessalonians Works Cited

Agosto, Efrain. "Patronage and Commendation, Imperial and Anti-Imperial." In *Paul and the Roman Imperial Order*, edited by Richard A. Horsley, 103–23. Harrisburg, PA: Trinity Press International, 2004.

Ascough, Richard S. *Paul's Macedonian Associations: The Social Context of Philippians and 1 Thessalonians*. WUNT 2, 161. Tübingen: Mohr Siebeck, 2003.

Bain, Katherine. *Women's Socioeconomic Status and Religious Leadership in Asia Minor in the First Two Centuries C.E.* Minneapolis: Fortress Press, 2014.

Balty, Jean Charles, et al, eds. *Lexicon Iconographicum Mythologiae Classicae (LIMC)*. Vol. 6.2. Zürich: Artemis, 1981–.

Benko, Stephen. *The Virgin Goddess: Studies in the Pagan and Christian Roots of Mariology*. Numen Book Series. Studies in the History of Religions. Vol. 59. Leiden: Brill, 2004.

Bickman, Jutta. "1 Thessalonians: Opposing Death by Building Community." In *Feminist Biblical Interpretation: A Compendium of Critical Commentary on the Books of the Bible and Related Literature*, edited by Luise Schottroff, Marie-Theres Wacker, and Martin Rumscheidt, 810–20. Grand Rapids, MI: Eerdmans, 2012.

Bøgh, Birgitte. "The Greco-Roman Cult of Isis." In *The Handbook of Religions in Ancient Europe*, edited by Lisbeth Bredholt Christensen, Olav Hammer, and David Warburton, 228–41. Durham, NC, and Bristol, CT: Acumen Pub. Ltd, 2013.

Boland, Eavan. *In a Time of Violence*. New York: Norton, 1994.

Burke, Trevor J. *Family Matters: A Socio-Historical Study of Fictive Kinship Metaphors in 1 Thessalonians*. JSNTSup 247. London: T & T Clark, 2003.

Castelli, Elizabeth A. *Imitating Paul: A Discourse of Power*. Literary Currents in Biblical Interpretation. Louisville, KY: Westminster/John Knox Press, 1991.

Clines, David J. A. "Paul, the Invisible Man." In *New Testament Masculinities*, edited by Stephen D. Moore and Janice Capel Anderson, 181–92. Atlanta, GA: Society of Biblical Literature, 2003.

Collins, Raymond F. *Accompanied by a Believing Wife: Ministry and Celibacy in the Earliest Christian Communities*. Collegeville, MN: Liturgical Press, 2013.

———. *The Birth of the New Testament: The Origin and Development of the First Christian Generation*. New York: Crossroad, 1993.

Cooper, Kate. *Band of Angels: The Forgotten World of Early Christian Women*. New York: The Overlook Press, 2013.

Delobel, Joel. "One Letter Too Many in Paul's First Letter? A Study of (N)Epioi in 1 Thess 2:7." *LS* 20 (1995): 126–33.

Demand, Nancy H. *Birth, Death, and Motherhood in Classical Greece*. Baltimore, MD: Johns Hopkins University Press, 1994.

Denzey, Nicola. *The Bone Gatherers: The Lost Worlds of Early Christian Women*. Boston: Beacon Press, 2007.

Donfried, K. P. *Paul, Thessalonica, and Early Christianity*. Grand Rapids, MI: Eerdmans, 2002.

Douglass, Laurie. "A New Look at the *Itinerarium Burdigalense*." *JECS* 4 (1996): 313–33.

Drake, H. A. "Models of Christian Expansion." In *Spread of Christianity in the First Four Centuries: Essays in Explanation*, edited by William V. Harris, 1–13. Leiden: Brill, 2005.

Edson, Charles. "Cults of Thessalonica (Macedonia III)." *HTR* 41 (1948): 153–204.

Fatum, Lone. "1 Thessalonians." In *Searching the Scriptures: A Feminist Commentary*, edited by Elisabeth Schüssler Fiorenza, vol. 2, 250–62. New York: Crossroad, 1993.

Fee, Gordon D. *The First and Second Letters to the Thessalonians*. NICNT. Grand Rapids, MI: Eerdmans, 2009.

Gaca, Kathy L. "Early Christian Antipathy toward the Greek 'Women Gods.'" In *Finding Persephone: Women's Rituals in the Ancient Mediterranean*, edited by Maryline G. Parca and Angeliki Tzanetou, 277–89. Bloomington: Indiana University Press, 2007.

Gaventa, Beverly Roberts. *First and Second Thessalonians*. IBC. Louisville, KY: John Knox Press, 1998.

———. *Our Mother Saint Paul*. Louisville, KY: Westminster John Knox Press, 2007.

Gillman, Florence Morgan. *Herodias: At Home in That Fox's Den*. Collegeville, MN: Liturgical Press, 2003.

———. "Jason of Thessalonica (Acts 17, 5-9)." In *The Thessalonian Correspondence*, BETL 87, edited by Raymond F. Collins, 39–49. Louvain: Leuven University Press, 1990.

———. *Women Who Knew Paul*. Collegeville, MN: Liturgical Press, 1992.

Gillman, John. "Signals of Transformation in 1 Thessalonians 4:13-18." *CBQ* 47 (1985): 263–81.

———. "Silas." *ABD* 6 (1992): 22–23.

Glancy, Jennifer A. *Slavery in Early Christianity*. Oxford and New York: Oxford University Press, 2002.

Haines-Eitzen, Kim. "Engendering Palimpsests: Reading the Textual Tradition of the Acts of Paul and Thecla." In *The Early Christian Book*, edited by William E. Klingshirn and Linda Safran, 177–93. Washington, DC: The Catholic University of America Press, 2007.

———. " 'Girls Trained in Beautiful Writing': Female Scribes in Roman Antiquity and Early Christianity." *JECS* 6 (1998): 629–46.

———. *Guardians of Letters: Literacy, Power, and the Transmitters of Early Christian Literature*. Oxford: Oxford University Press, 2000.

Harries, Jill. *Law and Crime in the Roman World*. New York: Cambridge University Press, 2007.

Harrison, James R. *Paul and the Imperial Authorities at Thessalonica and Rome: A Study in the Conflict of Ideology*. WUNT 273. Tübingen: Mohr Siebeck, 2011.

Heyob, Sharon Kelly. *The Cult of Isis among Women in the Graeco-Roman World*. Études Préliminaires Aux Religions Orientales Dans L'empire Romain. Leiden: Brill, 1975.

Horn, Cornelia B., and John W. Martens. *"Let the Little Children Come to Me": Childhood and Children in Early Christianity*. Washington, DC: The Catholic University of America Press, 2009.

Hornblower, Simon, and Antony Spawforth. *The Oxford Companion to Classical Civilization*. Oxford and New York: Oxford University Press, 1998.

Jewett, Robert. *Romans: A Commentary*. Hermeneia. Minneapolis: Fortress Press, 2007.

Johnson-DeBaufre, Melanie. " 'Gazing Upon the Invisible': Archaeology, Historiography, and the Elusive Wo/men of 1 Thessalonians." In *From Roman to Early Christian Thessalonikē*, edited by Laura S. Nasrallah, Charalambos Bakirtzēs, and Steven J. Friesen, HTS 64, 73–108. Cambridge, MA: Harvard University Press, 2010.

Knust, Jennifer Wright. "Paul and the Politics of Virtue and Vice." In *Paul and the Roman Imperial Order*, edited by Richard A. Horsley, 155–73. Harrisburg, PA: Trinity Press International, 2004.

Koester, Helmut. "Egyptian Religion in Thessalonikē: Regulation for the Cult." In *From Roman to Early Christian Thessalonikē*, edited by Laura S. Nasrallah, Charalambos Bakirtzēs, and Steven J. Friesen, HTS 64, 133–50. Cambridge, MA: Harvard University Press, 2010.

Kristof, Nicholas D. "Terror of Childbirth." *New York Times*. March 20, 2004. http://www.nytimes.com/2004/03/20/opinion/20KRIS.html.

Kristof, Nicholas D., and Sheryl WuDunn. *Half the Sky: Turning Oppression into Opportunity for Women Worldwide*. New York: Alfred A. Knopf, 2009.

Lambrecht, Jan. "A Structural Analysis of 1 Thessalonians 4–5." In *Collected Studies on Pauline Literature and on the Book of Revelation*, edited by Jan Lambrecht, AnBib 147, 279–93. Rome: Editrice Pontificio Istituto Biblico, 2001.

———. "Thanksgivings in 1 Thessalonians 1–3." In *Thessalonian Correspondence*, BETL 87, edited by Raymond F. Collins, 183–205. Louvain: Leuven University Press, 1990.

Lamoreaux, Jason T. *Ritual, Women, and Philippi: Reimagining the Early Philippian Community*. Matrix: The Bible in Mediterranean Context Series. Eugene, OR: Cascade Books, 2013.

Lightman, Marjorie, and Benjamin Lightman. *Biographical Dictionary of Ancient Greek and Roman Women: Notable Women from Sappho to Helena*. New York: Checkmark Books, 2000.

MacDonald, Margaret Y. "Early Christian Women Married to Unbelievers." *SR* 19 (1990): 221–34.

MacDonald, Margaret Y., Carolyn Osiek, and Janet Tulloch. *A Woman's Place: House Churches in Earliest Christianity*. Minneapolis: Fortress Press, 2006.

Malherbe, Abraham J. " 'Gentle as a Nurse': The Cynic Background to I Thess 2." *NovT* 12 (1970): 203–17.

———. *The Letters to the Thessalonians: A New Translation with Introduction and Commentary*. AB 32B. New York: Doubleday, 2000.

Mallios, Georgios K. "A Hellenistic Sanctuary at Ano Poli, Thessalonica: The Terra Cotta Figurines." *Egnatia* 8 (2004): 239–66.

Marchal, Joseph A. *The Politics of Heaven: Women, Gender, and Empire in the Study of Paul*. Minneappolis: Fortress Press, 2008.

McNeel, Jennifer Houston. *Paul as Infant and Nursing Mother: Metaphor, Rhetoric, and Identity in 1 Thessalonians 2:5-8*. ECL 12. Atlanta, GA: Society of Biblical Literature, 2014.

Míguez, Néstor Oscar. *The Practice of Hope: Ideology and Intention in First Thessalonians*. Paul in Critical Contexts. Minneapolis: Fortress Press, 2012.

Mitchell, Margaret M. "Concerning περί δέ in 1 Corinthians." *NovT* 31 (1989): 229–56.

Nasrallah, Laura S. "Empire and Apocalypse in Thessaloniki: Interpreting the Early Christian Rotunda." *JECS* 13 (2005): 465–508.

Nasrallah, Laura S., Charalambos Bakirtzēs, and Steven J. Friesen, eds. *From Roman to Early Christian Thessalonikē: Studies in Religion and Archaeology*, HTS 64. Cambridge, MA: Harvard University Press, 2010.

Nava, John. "John Nava Studio: The Cathedral of Our Lady of the Angels," *John Nava*. http://www.johnnava.com/JNS%20Archive/COS/cos.htm.

Palagia, Olga. "The Grave Relief of Adea, Daughter of Cassander and Cynnana." In *Macedonian Legacies: Studies in Ancient Macedonian History and Culture in Honor of Eugene N. Borza*, edited by Timothy Howe and Jeanne Reames, 195–214. Claremont, CA: Regina Press, 2008.

Pascuzzi, Maria. *Paul: Windows on His Thought and His World*. Winona, MN: Anselm Academic, 2014.

Perkins, Pheme. "1 Thessalonians." In *The Women's Bible Commentary*, edited by Carol A. Newsom and Sharon H. Ringe, 349–50. Louisville, KY: Westminster John Knox Press, 1992.

Price, Theodora Hadzisteliou. *Kourotrophos: Cults and Representations of the Greek Nursing Deities*. Studies of the Dutch Archaeological and Historical Society. Leiden: Brill, 1978.

Rawson, Beryl. *Children and Childhood in Roman Italy*. Oxford and New York: Oxford University Press, 2003.

Rebillard, Éric. *The Care of the Dead in Late Antiquity*. Ithaca, NY: Cornell University Press, 2009.

Richard, Earl J. *First and Second Thessalonians*. SP 11. Collegeville, MN: Liturgical Press, 1995.

Rowe, Christopher Kavin. *World Upside Down: Reading Acts in the Graeco-Roman Age*. New York and Oxford: Oxford University Press, 2011.

Šašel Kos, Marjeta. *Pre-Roman Divinities of the Eastern Alps and Adriatic*. Dissertationes Musei Nationalis Sloveniae. Ljubljana: Narodni Muzej Slovenije, 1999.

Schüssler Fiorenza, Elisabeth. *In Memory of Her: A Feminist Theological Reconstruction of Christian Origins*. New York: Crossroad, 1983.

Shogren, Gary Steven. *1 and 2 Thessalonians*. ZECNT. Grand Rapids, MI: Zondervan, 2012.

Smith, Abraham. "Unmasking the Powers: Toward a Post-Colonial Analysis of 1 Thessalonians." In *Paul and the Roman Imperial Order*, edited by Richard A. Horsley, 47–66. Harrisburg, PA: Trinity Press International, 2004.

Smith, Murray J. "The Thessalonian Correspondence." In *All Things to All Cultures: Paul among Jews, Greeks, and Romans*, edited by Mark Harding and Alanna Nobbs, 269–301. Grand Rapids, MI: Eerdmans, 2013.

Soranus. *Soranus' Gynecology*. Translated by Owsei Temkin. Baltimore, MD: Johns Hopkins University Press, 1956. Reprint, 1991.

Šterbenc Erker, Darja. "Gender and Roman Funeral Ritual." In *Memory and Mourning: Studies on Roman Death*, edited by Valerie M. Hope and Janet Huskinson, 40–60. Oxford: Oxbow Books, 2011.

Stubbs, Monya A. "1 Thessalonians." In *Women's Bible Commentary*, edited by Carol A. Newsom, Sharon H. Ringe, and Jacqueline E. Lapsley, 588–91. Louisville, KY: Westminster John Knox Press, 2012.

Suetonius, Gaius Tranquillus. *The Twelve Caesars*. Translated by Robert Graves. Hammondsworth, UK: Penguin Books Ltd., 1957. Reprint, 1972.

Tacitus, Cornelius. *The Complete Works of Tacitus*. Edited by Moses Hadas. Translated by Alfred John Church and William Jackson Brodribb. New York: Modern Library, 1942.

Thomas, Christine M. "Locating Purity: Temples, Sexual Prohibitions, and 'Making a Difference' in Thessalonikē." In *From Roman to Early Christian Thessalonikē*, edited by Laura Nasrallah, Charalambos Bakirtzis, and Steven J. Friesen, HTS 64, 109–32. Cambridge, MA: Harvard University Press, 2010.

Treggiari, Susan. *Terentia, Tullia and Publilia: The Women of Cicero's Family*. London: Routledge, 2007.

Trozzo, Lindsey M. "Thessalonian Women: The Key to the 4:4 Conundrum." *PRSt* 39 (2012): 39–52.

Tsalampouni, Ekaterini G. "The Cult of Theos Hypsistos in Roman Thessalonica and the First Christian Community of the City" (2011). https://www.academia.edu/1462334/The_Cult_of_Theos_Hypsistos_in_Roman_Thessalonica_in_English_.

————. "The Jews and the Agoraioi of Thessaloniki (Acts 17:5)." *The Bible and Interpretation* (2012): 1–9. http://www.bibleinterp.com/articles/tsa368022.shtml.

Tzanavari, Katerina. "The Worship of Gods and Heroes in Thessaloniki." In *Roman Thessaloniki*, edited by D. V. Grammenos, 177–262. Thessaloniki: Thessaloniki Archaeological Museum, 2003.

Tzanetou, Angeliki. "Ritual and Gender: Critical Perspectives." In *Finding Persephone: Women's Rituals in the Ancient Mediterranean*, edited by Maryline G. Parca and Angeliki Tzanetou, 3–26. Bloomington: Indiana University Press, 2007.

Weima, Jeffrey A. D. *1–2 Thessalonians*. BECNT. Grand Rapids, MI: Baker Academic, 2014.

Weingarten, Susan. "Was the Pilgrim from Bordeaux a Woman? A Reply to Laurie Douglass." *JECS* 7 (1999): 291–97.

Werner, Louis. "Via Egnatia: To Rome and Byzantium." *Aramco World* 66 (2015): 20–31.

Witt, R. E. *Isis in the Graeco-Roman World*. Ithaca, NY: Cornell University Press, 1971.

2 Thessalonians Works Cited

Adams, Sean A. "Paul's Letter Opening and Greek Epistolography: A Matter of Relationship." In *Paul and the Ancient Letter Form*, edited by Stanley E. Porter and Sean A. Adams, 33–35. Leiden: Brill, 2012.

Althaus-Reid, Marcella. *The Queer God*. New York: Routledge, 2003.

Althaus-Reid, Marcella, and Lisa Isherwood. *Controversies in Feminist Theology*. London: SCM Press, 2007.

Anderson, Kathryn. *Weaving the Relationships: Canada-Guatemala Solidarity*. Waterloo, ON: Wilfred Laurier University Press, 2003.

Ascough, Richard. "The Thessalonian Christian Community as a Professional Voluntary Association." *JBL* 119 (2000): 325–27.

———. *Paul's Macedonian Association: The Social Context of Philippians and 1 Thessalonians*. Tübingen: Mohr Siebeck, 2003.

Ashcroft, Bill, Gareth Griffiths, and Helen Tiffin. *The Empire Writes Back: Theory and Practice in Post-colonial Literatures*. London: Routledge, 1989.

Aune, David E. *The New Testament in Its Literary Environment*. Philadelphia: Westminster, 1987.

Aus, Roger. "God's Plan and God's Power: Isaiah 66 and the Restraining Factors of 2 Thess 2:6-7." *JBL* 96 (1977): 537–53.

Bailey, Randall C. "In Danger of Ignoring One's Own Cultural Bias in Interpreting the Text." In *The Postcolonial Bible*, edited by R. S. Sugirtharajah, 66–90. The Bible and Postcolonialism 1. Sheffield: Sheffield Academic Press, 1998.

Baird, Joseph L., and Radd K. Ehrman, eds. *The Letters of Hildegard of Bingen*. Vol. 1. Oxford: Oxford University Press, 1994.

Barth, Karl. *The Epistle to the Romans*. Translated by C. Edwyn Hoskyns. London: Oxford University Press, 1933.

Bassler, Jouette M. "The Enigmatic Sign: 2 Thessalonians 1:5." *CBQ* 46 (1984): 496–510.

Beavis, Mary Ann. "2 Thessalonians." In *Searching the Scriptures: A Feminist Commentary*, edited by Elisabeth Schüssler Fiorenza, vol. 2, 263–73. New York: Crossroad, 1994.

———. "2 Thessalonians." In *Women's Bible Commentary*, edited by Carol A. Newsom, Sharon H. Ringe, and Jacqueline E. Lapsley, 3rd ed., 592–94. Louisville, KY: Westminster John Knox, 2012.

———. "Women and the 'City of Tomorrow': Feminist Transformations of the City in the New Millennium." In *Reclaiming the Future: Women's Strategies for the 21st Century*, edited by Somer Brodribb, 23–47. Charlottetown, PEI: Gynergy, 1999.

———. " 'If Anyone Will Not Work, Let Them Not Eat': 2 Thessalonians 3:10 and the Social Support of Women." In *A Feminist Companion to the Deutero-Pauline Epistles*, edited by Amy-Jill Levine, 29–36. London and New York: T & T Clark, 2003.

———. *Mark*. Paideia Commentaries on the New Testament. Grand Rapids, MI: Baker Academic, 2011.

———, ed. *The Lost Coin: Parables of Women, Work and Wisdom*. Sheffield: Sheffield Academic Press, 2002.

Belenky, Mary Field, et al. *Women's Ways of Knowing: The Development of Self, Voice and Mind*. New York: Basic Books, 1986.

Bellis, Alice Ogden. *Helpmates, Harlots and Heroes*. Louisville, KY: Westminster John Knox, 2007.

Benny Liew, Tat-Siong. "Lost in Translation? Tracing Linguistic and Economic Transactions in Three Texts." In *Planetary Loves: Spivak, Postcoloniality, and Theology*, edited by Stephen D. Moore and Mayra Rivera, 102–17. New York: Fordham University Press, 2011.

Bermisa, Nila. *That She May Dance Again: Rising from the Pain of Violence Against Women in the Philippine Church*. Philippines: WGC-AMRSP, 2011.

Biale, Rachel. *Women and Jewish Law: The Essential Texts, Their History, and Their Relevance for Today*. New York: Schocken Books, 1984.

Bialik, Hayim Naman, and Yehoshua Hana Ravnitzky, eds., *The Book of Legends (Sefer Ha-Aggadah): Legends from the Talmud and Midrash*. New York: Schocken Books, 1992.

Collins, Raymond F. *Letters That Paul Did Not Write: The Epistle to the Hebrews and Pauline Pseudepigrapha*. Wilmington, DE: Michael Glazier, 1988.

Craigo-Snell, Sharon. *The Empty Church: Theatre Theology and Bodily Hope*. Oxford: Oxford University Press, 2014.

Craigo-Snell, Sharon, and Shawnthea Monroe. *Living Christianity: A Pastoral Theology for Today*. Minneapolis: Fortress Press, 2009.

Crüsemann, Marlene. "2 Thessalonians: Hope in God's Last Judgment." In *Feminist Biblical Interpretation: A Compendium of Critical Commentary on the Books of the Bible and Related Literature*, edited by Luise Schottroff and Marie-Theres Wacker, 821–29. Grand Rapids, MI: Eerdmans, 2012.

Deissmann, Adolf. *Light from the Ancient East: The New Testament Illustrated by Recently Discovered Texts of the Graeco-Roman World*. Grand Rapids, MI: Baker, 1995.

DiTomasso, Lorenso. "Apocalypticism and Popular Culture." In *The Oxford Handbook of Apocalyptic Literature*, edited by John J. Collins, 473–510. Oxford: Oxford University Press, 2014.

Dobschhutz, Ernst von. *Die Thessalonicherbriefe*. 7th ed. Göttingen: Vandenhoeck & Ruprecht, 1909.

Dodd, C. H. *The Interpretation of the Fourth Gospel*. London and New York: Cambridge University Press, 1953.

Donaldson, Laura E. "The Sign of Orpah: Reading Ruth through Native Eyes." In *Ruth and Esther*, FCB, 2nd series, edited by Athalya Brenner, 130–44. Sheffield: Sheffield Academic Press, 1999.

Donfried, Karl Paul. *Paul, Thessalonica, and Early Christianity*. London: T & T Clark, 2002.

———. "The Cults of Thessalonica and the Thessalonian Correspondence," *NTS* 31 (1985): 336–56.

Dube, Musa. *Postcolonial Feminist Interpretation of the Bible*. St. Louis, MO: Chalice Press, 2000.

———. "The Unpublished Letters of Orpah to Ruth." In *Ruth and Esther*, FCB, 2nd series, edited by Althalya Brenner, 145–50. Sheffield: Sheffield Academic Press, 1999.

Duck, Ruth C. "Expansive Language in the Baptized Community." In *Primary Sources of Liturgical Theology: A Reader*, edited by Dwight W. Vogel, 286–94. Collegeville, MN: Liturgical Press, 2000.

Dunn, J. D. G. *The Theology of Paul the Apostle*. Grand Rapids, MI: Eerdmans, 2006.

Edson, Charles. "Cults of Thessalonica." *HTR* 41 (1948): 153–204.

Elledge, Allison Jaines. "Contextualizing Hildegard of Bingen's Violent and Apocalyptic Imagery." *Academia* (May 3, 2010): https://www.academia.edu/494645/Contextualizing_Hildegard_of_Bingens_Violent_and_Apocalyptic_Imagery.

Elliott, Neil. *Liberating Paul: The Justice of God and the Politics of the Apostle*. Maryknoll, NY: Orbis Books, 1994.

Elm, Susanna. "Montanist Oracles." In *Searching the Scriptures: A Feminist Commentary*, edited by Elisabeth Schüssler Fiorenza, vol. 2, 131–38. New York: Crossroad, 1994.

Emmerson, Richard K. "The Representation of Antichrist in Hildegard of Bingen's *Scivias*: Image, Word, Commentary, and Visionary Experience." *Gesta* 41 (2002): 95–100.

Fatum, Lone. "1 Thessalonians." *In Searching the Scriptures: A Feminist Commentary*, edited by Elisabeth Schüssler Fiorenza, vol. 2, 250–62. New York: Crossroad, 1994.

Flanagan, Sabina. *Hildegard of Bingen, 1098–1179: A Visionary Life*. New York and London: Routledge, 1988.

Friesen, Steven J. "Second Thessalonians, the Ideology of the Epistle, and the Construction of Authority: Our Debt to the Forger." In *From Rome to Early Christian Thessalonike: Studies in Religion and Archaeology*, ed. Laura Nasrallah, Charalambos Bakirtzis, and Steven J. Friesen, HTS 64, 207–8. Cambridge, MA: Harvard University Press, 2010.

Frymer-Kensky, Tikva. *Reading the Women of the Bible: A New Interpretation of Their Stories*. New York: Schocken Books, 2002.

Fuller, Robert C. *Naming the Antichrist: The History of an American Obsession*. New York: Oxford University Press, 1995.

Gandhi, Mohandas K. *What Jesus Means to Me*. Translated by R. K. Prabhu. Ahmedabad: Navajivan Publishing House, 1959.

Gaventa, Beverly Roberts. *First and Second Thessalonians*. Interpretation. Louisville, KY: Westminster John Knox, 1998.

Gilligan, Carol. *In a Different Voice: Psychological Theory and Women's Development*. Cambridge, MA: Harvard University Press, 1982.

Gorday, Peter, ed. *Ancient Christian Commentary On Scripture, New Testament IX: Colossians, 1–2 Thessalonians, 1–2 Timothy, Titus, Philemon*. Downers Grove, IL: InterVarsity, 2000.

Gregerman, Adam. "2 Thessalonians." In *The Jewish Annotated New Testament: New Revised Standard Version*, edited by Amy-Jill Levine and Mark Zvi Brettler, 378–82. Oxford: Oxford University Press, 2011.

Gurkow, Lazer. "Wisdom of the Heart: The Jewish Mother." *Chabad.org*. http://www.chabad.org/theJewishWoman/article_cdo/aid/478232/jewish/Wisdom-of-the-Heart.htm.

Harris, Stephen L. *The New Testament: A Student's Introduction*. Boston: McGraw-Hill, 2002.

Hendrix, Holland. "Thessalonicans Honor Romans." ThD diss., Harvard Divinity School, 1984.

Horsley, Richard A. "Submerged Biblical Histories and Imperial Biblical Studies." In *The Postcolonial Bible*, edited by R. S. Sugirtharajah, 152–73. The Bible and Postcolonialism 1. Sheffield: Sheffield Academic Press, 1998.

Hughes, Frank Witt. *Early Christian Rhetoric and 2 Thessalonians*. JSNTSup 30. Sheffield: Sheffield Academic Press, 1989.

Hughes, Kevin L. *Constructing Antichrist: Paul, Biblical Commentary, and the Development of Doctrine in the Early Middle Ages*. Washington, DC: The Catholic University of America Press, 2005.

Isasi-Diaz, Ada Maria. "Solidarity: Love of the Neighbor in the 1980s." In *Lift Every Voice: Constructing Christian Theologies from the Underside*, edited by Susan Brooks Thistlethwaite and Mary Potter Engel, 31–40. San Francisco: Harper and Row, 1990.

Jewett, Robert. *The Thessalonian Correspondence: Pauline Rhetoric and Millenarian Piety*. Philadelphia: Fortress Press, 1986.

————. "1 and 2 Thessalonians." In *Eerdmans Commentary on the Bible*, edited by James D. Dunn and John William Rogerson, 1413–27. Grand Rapids, MI: Eerdmans, 2003.

Joh, Wonhee Anne. *Heart of the Cross: A Postcolonial Christology.* Louisville, KY: Westminster John Knox, 2006.

Johnson, E. Elizabeth. "2 Thessalonians," In *The Women's Bible Commentary*, edited by Carol A. Newsom and Sharon H. Ringe, 351–52. Louisville, KY: Westminster John Knox, 1992.

Johnson, Elizabeth A. *Quest for the Living God: Mapping Frontiers in the Theology of God.* New York and London: Continuum, 2008.

Johnson-Debaufre, Melanie. " 'Gazing Upon the Invisible': Archaeology, Historiography, and the Elusive Wo/men of 1 Thessalonians." In *From Roman to Early Christian Thessalonike: Studies in Religion and Archaeology*, edited by Laura Nasrallah, Charalambos Bakirtzis, and Steven J. Friesen, HTS 64, 73–108. Cambridge, MA: Harvard University Press, 2010.

Keller, Catherine. *Apocalypse Now and Then: A Feminist Guide to the End of the World.* Minneapolis: Fortress Press, 1996.

Keller, Catherine, and Laurel Schneider. "Introduction." In *Polydoxy: Theology of Multiplicity and Relation*, edited by Catherine Keller and Laurel Schneider, 3–4. New York: Routledge, 2011.

Kim-Cragg, HyeRan. *Story and Song: A Postcolonial Interplay between Christian Education and Worship.* New York: Peter Lang, 2012.

————. "A Theology of Resistance in Conversation with Religious Education in Unmasking and Unmaking Violence." *RelEd* 110 (August 2015): 420–34.

Klassen, William. "Vengeance in the Apocalypse of John." *CBQ* 28 (1966): 300–311.

Levenson, Jon D. "The Jerusalem Temple in Devotional and Visionary Experience." In *Jewish Spirituality: From the Bible through the Middle Ages*, edited by Arthur R. Green, vol. 1, 32–62. New York: Crossroad, 1994.

Lopez Plaza, María de Los Angeles. "Efectos de las políticas de ajuste estructural en la situación de las mujeres magrebíes." In *Género, clase y etnia en los nuevos procesos de globalización: XI Jornadas de investigación interdisciplinaria sobre la mujer*, edited by Virginia Maquieira D'Angelo and Maria Jesús Vara. Madrid: Instituto Universitario de Estudios de la Mujer: Ediciones de la Universidad Autónoma de Madrid, 1997.

Lowe, Lisa. *Immigrant Acts: On Asian American Cultural Politics.* Durham, NC: Duke University Press, 1994.

Malherbe, Abraham J. *The Letter to the Thessalonians: A New Translation with Introduction and Commentary.* New York: Doubleday, 2000.

Maloney, Linda. "The Pastoral Epistles." In *Searching the Scriptures: A Feminist Commentary*, edited by Elisabeth Schüssler Fiorenza, vol. 2, 361–80. New York: Crossroad, 1994.

————. " 'Swept under the Rug': Feminist Homiletical Reflections on the Parable of the Lost Coin (Luke 15:8-9)." In *The Lost Coin: Parables of Women, Work and Wisdom*, edited by Mary Ann Beavis, 34–38. Sheffield: Sheffield Academic Press, 2002.

Manson, T. W. "St. Paul in Greece: The Letters to the Thessalonians." *BJRL* 35 (1952–53): 428–47.

McGinn, Sheila E. "The Acts of Thecla." In *Searching the Scriptures: A Feminist Commentary*, edited by Elisabeth Schüssler Fiorenza, vol. 2, 800–28. New York: Crossroad, 1994.

McGinn, Sheila E., and Megan Wilson-Reitz. "2 Thessalonians vs. the *Ataktoi*: A Pauline Critique of White-Collar Welfare." In *By Bread Alone: The Bible through the Eyes of the Hungry*, edited by Sheila E. McGinn, Lai Ling Ngan, and Ahida Pilarski, 185–208. Minneapolis: Fortress Press, 2014.

McKibben, Bill. *The End of Nature*. New York: Random House, 1989.

McKinlay, Judith E. *Reframing Her: Biblical Women in Postcolonial Focus*. Sheffield: Sheffield Phoenix Press, 2004.

Mena López, Maricel. "Globalization and Gender Inequality: A Contribution From a Latino Afro-Feminist Perspective." In *The Oxford Handbook of Feminist Theology*, edited by Mary McClintock Fulkerson and Sheila Briggs, 157–79. Oxford: Oxford University Press, 2012.

Mercer, Joyce Ann. "Call Forwarding: Putting Vocation in the Present Tense with Youth." In *Compass Points: Navigating Vocation*, 29–43. Princeton, NJ: Princeton Theological Seminary, 2002.

Meyers, Carol, Toni Craven, and Ross S. Kraemer, eds. *Women in Scripture: A Dictionary of Named and Unnamed Women in the Hebrew Bible, The Apocryphal/ Deuterocanonical Books, and the New Testament*. Boston: Houghton Mifflin, 2000.

Miller-McLemore, Bonnie J. *Also a Mother: Work and Family as Theological Dilemma*. Nashville, TN: Abingdon, 1994.

Mollenkott, Virginia Ramey. *The Divine Feminine: The Biblical Imagery of God as Female*. New York: Crossroad, 1987.

Newman, Barbara. *Hildegard of Bingen: The Woman of Her Age*. New York: Doubleday, 2001.

———, ed. *Hildegard of Bingen: Voice of the Living Light*. Berkeley: University of California Press, 1988.

———. *Sister of Wisdom: St. Hildegard's Theology of the Feminine*. Berkeley: University of California Press, 1987.

Pippin, Tina. "The Revelation to John." In *Searching the Scriptures: A Feminist Commentary*, edited by Elisabeth Schüssler Fiorenza, vol. 2, 109–30. New York: Crossroad, 1994.

Portier-Young, Anathea. *Apocalypse Against Empire: Theologies of Resistance in Early Judaism*. Grand Rapids, MI: Eerdmans, 2011.

Priests for Equality. *The Inclusive Bible: The First Egalitarian Translation*. Lanham, MD: Rowman & Littlefield, 2009.

Raphael, Melissa. *The Female Face of God in Auschwitz*. New York: Routledge, 2003.

Richard, Earl J. *First and Second Thessalonians*. SP 11. Collegeville, MN: Liturgical Press, 2007.

Ruether, Rosemary Radford. "Is Christ White? Racism and Christology." In *Christology and Whiteness: What Would Jesus Do*, edited by George Yancy, 101–13. New York: Routledge, 2012.

Ryken, Leland, James C. Wilhoit, and Tremper Longman III, eds. *Dictionary of Biblical Imagery*. Downers Grove, IL: InterVarsity Press, 1998.

Saliers, Don E. "Human Pathos and Divine Ethos." In *Primary Sources of Liturgical Theology: A Reader*, edited by Dwight W. Vogel, 276–83. Collegeville, MN: Liturgical Press, 2006.

Schaff, Philip, ed. *Nicene and Post-Nicene Fathers*, 1st series, vol. 13. Translated by John A. Broadus. Buffalo, NY: Christian Literature Publishing Co., 1889.

Schmidt, Daryl D. "The Syntatical Style of 2 Thessalonians: How Pauline Is It?" In *The Thessalonian Correspondence*, edited by Raymond F. Collins, 382–93. Louvain: Leuven University Press, 1990.

Scholem, Gershom. *Major Trends in Jewish Mysticism*. New York: Schocken Books, 1995.

Schüssler Fiorenza, Elisabeth. "Paul and the Politics of Interpretation." In *Paul and Politics: Ekklesia, Israel, Imperium, Interpretation*, edited by Richard A. Horsley, 40–57. Harrisburg, PA: Trinity Press International, 2000.

———. *Changing Horizons: Explorations in Feminist Biblical Interpretation*. Minneapolis: Fortress Press, 2013.

Scott, Hilda. *Working Your Way to the Bottom: The Feminization of Poverty*. London: Pandora, 1984.

Simon, Roger. *The Touch of the Past: Remembrance, Learning and Ethics*. New York: Palgrave MacMillan, 2005.

Smith, Abraham. "The First and Second Letters to the Thessalonians." In *A Postcolonial Commentary on the New Testament Writings*, edited by Fernando F. Segovia and R. S. Sugirtharajah, 304–22. The Bible and Postcolonialism 13. New York: T & T Clark, 2007.

Sölle, Dorothee. *Revolutionary Patience*. Translated by Rita and Robert Kimber. Maryknoll, NY: Orbis Books, 1997.

Spivak, Gayatri Chakravorty. "Bonding in Difference: Interview with Alfred Arteaga." In *The Spivak Reader*, edited by Donna Landry and Gerald MacLean, 15–28. New York: Routledge, 1996.

Sugirtharajah, R. S. "Postcolonial and Biblical Interpretation: The Next Phase." In *A Postcolonial Commentary on the New Testament Writings*, edited by Fernando F. Segovia and R. S. Sugirtharajah, 455–65. The Bible and Postcolonialism 13. New York: T & T Clark, 2007.

Sung Park, Andrew. "Church and Theology: My Theological Journey." In *Journeys at the Margin: Toward an Autobiographical Theology in American-Asian Perspective*, edited by Peter C. Phan and Jung Young Lee, 161–72. Collegeville, MN: Liturgical Press, 1999.

Taylor, Charles. *A Secular Age*. Cambridge, MA: Harvard University Press, 2007.

Taylor, Mark Lewis. *The Executed God: The Way of the Cross in Lockdown America*. Minneapolis: Fortress Press, 2001.

Thiselton, Anthony C. *1 & 2 Thessalonians through the Centuries*. Chichester, UK: Wiley, 2011.

Thurston, Bonnie Bowman. *The Widows: A Woman's Ministry in the Early Church*. Minneapolis: Augsburg Fortress Press, 1989.

Tsalampouni, Ekaterini G. "The Cult of *Theos Hypsistos* in Roman Thessalonica and the First Christian Community of the City." Paper presented at the SBL International Meeting, July 5, 2011.

Wanamaker, Charles A. *Commentary on 1 and 2 Thessalonians*. Grand Rapids, MI: Eerdmans, 1990.

Watkins, Susan. "Future Shock: Rewriting the Apocalypse in Contemporary Women's Fiction." *Literature Interpretation Theory* 23 (2012): 119–37.

Wegner, Judith Romney. "The Image and Status of Women in Classical Rabbinic Judaism." In *Jewish Women in Historical Perspective*, 2nd ed., edited by Judith R. Baskin, 73–100. Detroit, MI: Wayne State University Press, 1998.

Wenh-In Ng, Greer Anne. "From Confucian Master Teacher to Freirian Mutual Learner: Challenges in Pedagogical Practice and Religious Education." *RelEd* 95 (2000): 308–19.

Wessinger, Catherine. "Apocalypse and Violence." In *The Oxford Handbook of Apocalyptic Literature*, edited by John J. Collins, 422–40. Oxford: Oxford University Press, 2014.

Westerink, Herman. "The Great Man from Tarsus: Freud on the Apostle Paul." *PsychoanalQ* 76 (2007): 217–35.

Whiston, William, trans. *The Works of Josephus*. Peabody, MA: Hendrickson, 1987.

White, James F. *Sacraments as God's Self-Giving*. Nashville, TN: Abingdon, 1983.

Williams, Patrick, and Laura Chrisman. "Colonial Discourse and Post-Colonial Theory: An Introduction." In *Colonial Discourse and Postcolonial Theory: A Reader*, edited by Patrick Williams and Laura Chrisman, 1–20. New York: Columbia University Press, 1994.

Witherington, Ben III. *1 and 2 Thessalonians*. Grand Rapids, MI: Eerdmans, 2006.

Wittgenstein, Ludwig. *Lectures and Conversations on Aesthetics, Psychology, and Religious Belief*, edited by Cyril Barrett. Berkeley: University of California Press, 1967.

Woolf, Virginia. *A Room of One's Own*. 2nd ed. New York: Harcourt, Brace & World, 1957.

Wrede, William. *Die Echtheit des zweiten Thessalonicherbriefs*. Leipzig: Hinrichs, 1903.

Index of Scripture References
and Other Ancient Writings

Index of Subjects

Adams, Sean A., 119
Agosto, Efrain, 92–93
Akiba, 132
Alexander III (the Great), 12–14
Algasia, 160
Althaus-Reid, Marcella, 112, 115
Amphipolis Tomb, 41
Anderson, Janice Capel, 24
Anderson, Kathryn, 124–25
Antichrist, 110, 112–16, 131, 156–57, 159–61, 185–86
anti-imperial perspective, 26, 50, 55–56, 86–88
Antiochus IV Epiphanes, 146
apocalyptic 106, 108, 109, 110, 111, 112, 113, 115, 116, 117, 127, 128, 131, 133, 134, 143, 156–59, 169, 184, 185
Aquila, 28–29, 134, 170; *see also* Priscilla
Argead Dynasty, 12–15
Aristarchus, 102
Ascough Richard S., 31–32, 102, 125
Ashcroft, Bill, 136
Augustine, 149, 159, 183
Aune, David E., 127
Aus, Roger, 150

Auschwitz, 128–29, 135, 158, 185

Bailey, Randall C., 115
Bain, Katherine, 18
Baird, Joseph L., 113
Bakirtzēs, Charalambos, 31, 38, 64, 76
baptism, 112, 121
Barnabas, 23–24
Barth, Karl, 149, 164
Bassler, Jouette M., 127–28
Beavis, Mary Ann, 3, 6, 103, 104, 110, 117, 118, 124–25, 126, 127, 128–30, 135, 138, 142, 156–57, 159–61, 168, 169–70, 172, 179–80, 182, 183, 186
Belenky, Mary Field, et al., 152
Bellis, Alice Ogden, 103
Benko, Stephen, 66–67
Bermisa, Nila, 133, 154–55, 176–77
Biale, Rachel, 154
Bialik, Hayim Naman, and Yehoshua Hana Ravnitzky, 154
Bickman, Jutta, 7
Bøgh, Birgitte, 64, 79
Boisclair, Regina, 10, 54–55
Boland, Eavan, 62
Bordeaux Pilgrim, 11–12
Burke, Trevor J., 8, 33, 44

General Editor

Barbara E. Reid, OP, is a Dominican Sister of Grand Rapids, Michigan. She holds a PhD in biblical studies from The Catholic University of America and is vice president and academic dean and professor of New Testament studies at Catholic Theological Union, Chicago. Her most recent publications are *Wisdom's Feast: An Invitation to Feminist Interpretation of the Scriptures* (2016) and *Abiding Word: Sunday Reflections on Year A, B, C* (3 vols.; 2011, 2012, 2013). She served as president of the Catholic Biblical Association in 2014–2015.

Volume Editors

Dr. Mary Ann Beavis is professor in the Department of Religion and Culture, St. Thomas More College, University of Saskatchewan. She is the author of many articles and several books in the subject areas of biblical studies and religious studies.

Linda M. Maloney, PhD, ThD, is a native of Houston, Texas. She studied at St. Louis University (BA, MA, PhD), the University of South Carolina (MIBS), and Eberhard-Karls-Universität Tübingen, where she earned her ThD in New Testament in 1990 under the direction of Prof. Gerhard Lohfink. She has taught at public and private colleges, universities, and seminaries in the United States and was academic editor at Liturgical Press from 1995 to 2005. She is a priest of the Episcopal Church (USA) and lives in Vermont and California.

Authors

Florence Morgan Gillman is professor of biblical studies, former coordinator of the Classical Studies Program, and former chair of the Department of Theology and Religious Studies at the University of San Diego. Following completion of the BA and MA at the Catholic University of America, she received her STL, PhD, and STD from the Katholieke Universiteit te Leuven (Belgium). The author of numerous books and articles, she is especially interested in the Pauline churches, women in early Christianity, and the world behind the text of the New Testament literature.

Dr. Mary Ann Beavis is professor in the Department of Religion and Culture, St. Thomas More College, University of Saskatchewan. She is the author of many articles and several books in the subject areas of biblical studies and religious studies.

Rev. Dr. HyeRan Kim-Cragg is Lydia Gruchy Professor of Pastoral Studies, St. Andrew's College, University of Saskatchewan. She is the author of many articles and several books in the subject areas of religious education and worship.